'A typical boy from Riga. That is what I was like at twelve, and that is the way I have stayed.' (*Memoirs*)

Soviet Cinema

General editors: Richard Taylor and Ian Christie

Eisenstein Rediscovered

Edited by
Ian Christie and Richard Taylor

London and New York

First published 1993
by Routledge
11 New Fetter Lane, London EC4P 4EE

Simultaneously published in the USA and Canada
by Routledge
29 West 35th Street, New York, NY 10001

Typeset in 10/12pt Times by
Florencetype Ltd, Kewstoke, Avon
Printed in Great Britain by
Butler & Tanner, Frome and London

British Library Cataloguing in Publication Data
Eisenstein Rediscovered
   I. Christie, Ian   II. Taylor, Richard
   791.430233092

Library of Congress Cataloging in Publication Data
Eisenstein rediscovered / edited by Ian Christie and Richard Taylor.
   p.   cm. — (Soviet cinema)
   Papers from a conference held at Keble College, Oxford, July 1988.
   Includes bibliographical references and index.
   1.   Eisenstein, Sergei, 1898–1948 – Criticism and interpretation –
Congresses.   I. Christie, Ian.   II. Taylor, Richard.
III. Series.
PN1998.3.E34E33   1993
791.43'0233'092 – dc20   92-26363

ISBN 0 415 04950 4

In memory of D.J. ('Charles') Wenden (1923–92) who inspired the study of cinema as an integral part of history.

Contents

III   The practice of theory

Illustrations

Notes on contributors

François Albera is Professor of the History and Aesthetics of Cinema at the University of Lausanne. He is the author of *Notes sur l'esthétique d'Eisenstein*, *Jean-Luc Godard* and *Eisenstein et le constructivisme russe*. He has also edited two collections of Eisenstein's writings, *Cinématisme: peinture et cinéma* and *Le mouvement de l'art*, and two catalogues for the Locarno Festival: *Boris Barnet: Ecrits, documents, études, filmographie* (with Roland Cosandey) and *Kuléchov et les siens*.

Ian Christie is Head of Special Projects at the British Film Institute, where he has organised many Soviet and Russian retrospectives and events. His books include *FEKS, Formalism, Futurism: 'Eccentrism' and Soviet Cinema 1918–36* (with John Gillett), *Powell, Pressburger and Others* and *Arrows of Desire: The Films of Michael Powell and Emeric Pressburger*. With Richard Taylor he has co-edited *The Film Factory: Russian and Soviet Cinema in Documents 1896–1939* and *Inside the Film Factory: New Approaches to Russian and Soviet Cinema*; and with Julian Graffy, *Iakov Protazanov: The Continuity of Russian Cinema*.

Edoardo G. Grossi is a doctoral candidate at the University of Paris 3. He has published widely on Eisenstein's aesthetics and on twentieth-century Russian theatre, and is the author of *Eisenstein. L'ottava arte*.

Arun Khopkar is a film-maker who trained at the Film and Television Institute of India as a film director and now teaches there regularly. He has made several short films, some of which have won national and international awards, and is the author of a book on the Indian director Guru Dutt.

Naum Kleiman is Director of the Central Film Museum, Moscow, and Curator of the Eisenstein Kabinet Museum. He assisted Pera Attasheva in editing the original Russian six-volume edition of Eisenstein's writings and has helped restore and reconstruct many of the films, as well as guiding scholars from many countries in their study of Eisenstein and Soviet cinema. His expanded version of Eisenstein's memoirs, *YO! Ich Selbst*, appeared in German in 1987 and is forthcoming in English.

N. M. Lary is Associate Professor of Humanities at York University, Toronto. He is the author of *Dostoevsky and Dickens* and *Dostoevsky and Soviet Film*. His current projects include a translation of Medvedkin's scripts and film writings, and books on Viktor Shklovsky and on Eisenstein and the Elizabethans.

Robert Leach is Senior Lecturer in Drama and Theatre Arts at the University of Birmingham. He has experimented practically with Biomechanics and Expressive Acting and staged Tretyakov's *Gas Masks* in Britain, as well as directing the Russian premiere of *I Want a Baby* in Moscow in 1990. He is the author of *Vsevolod Meyerhold* and the forthcoming *Revolutionary Theatre*, and is editing *The Cambridge History of Russian Theatre*.

Håkan Lövgren is a translator and a researcher at Stockholm University. He is co-editor, with Lars Kleberg, of *Eisenstein Revisited* and has published a number of articles on Eisenstein and on Soviet cinema and theatre.

Michael O'Pray is a Course Co-ordinator in the Department of Art and Design of the University of East London. He has edited *Andy Warhol: Film Factory* and, with Jayne Pilling, *Into the Pleasure Dome: The Films of Kenneth Anger*, and has published widely, especially on avant-garde film. He is a Contributing Editor of *Sight and Sound* and is currently working on books about Adrian Stokes and film aesthetics and about Derek Jarman.

Elena Pinto Simon is Associate Dean and Adjunct Assistant Professor of Cultural History at the Tisch School of the Arts of New York University. She is revising her *Guide to the Arts Resources of New York City* and is co-author of *From the Storehouse of Creation: Reconstructing Eisenstein's 'Bezhin Meadow'*. She is executrix of the estate of Jay Leyda, is cataloguing the Leyda papers and co-curated the exhibition *Jay Leyda: A Life's Work*.

David Stirk is Instructor in Photography at the Tisch School of the Arts at New York University. He is co-author of *From the Storehouse of Creation: Reconstructing Eisenstein's 'Bezhin Meadow'* and is completing doctoral work at Yale University in American Studies.

Richard Taylor is Reader in Politics and Russian Studies at the University of Swansea, Wales. He is General Editor of the British Film Institute's edition of Eisenstein's *Selected Writings*. His books include *Film Propaganda: Soviet Russia and Nazi Germany* and *The Politics of the Soviet Cinema, 1917–1929*. He has edited, with Ian Christie, *The Film Factory: Russian and Soviet Cinema in Documents, 1896–1939* and *Inside the Film Factory: New Approaches to Russian and Soviet Cinema*; and, with Derek Spring, *Stalinism and Soviet Cinema*.

Kristin Thompson is an Honorary Fellow in the Communication Arts Department at the University of Wisconsin-Madison. Her most recent books are *Breaking the Glass Armour: Neoformalist Film Analysis* and *Wooster Proposes, Jeeves Disposes: or, The Mot Juste*, a study of P.G. Wodehouse. She is currently collaborating with David Bordwell on an introductory history of international cinema.

Myriam Tsikounas is a Lecturer in Contemporary History at the University of Paris I, Panthéon-Sorbonne, teaching social history and the history of cinema. She has studied the portrayal of the Paris Commune in Kozintsev and Trauberg's *New Babylon* and her book *Les origines du cinéma soviétique: un regard neuf* is based on her doctoral thesis. Current research interests include Tsarist cinema and the representation of social themes in French nineteenth-century literature.

Yuri Tsivian graduated from the Latvian State University and has since been a Senior Research Fellow of the Latvian Academy of Sciences. He held a Visiting Research Fellowship at the British Film Institute in 1990 and has been a Visiting Professor in the School of Cinema and Television at the University of Southern California since 1991. He supervised the restoration of early Russian films at Gosfilmofond and edited (with others) *Silent Witnesses: Russian Films 1908–1919*. His book on the history of film reception in Russia from 1896–1930 is forthcoming from Routledge.

Mikhail Yampolsky graduated from the Moscow Pedagogical Institute and was a Senior Research Fellow at the All-Union Institute for the History of Cinema, during which time he published numerous articles in *Iskusstvo kino* and *Soviet Film*. His work has appeared in translation in *Iris*, *Afterimage* and the *Historical Journal of Film, Radio and Television*, as well as in *Inside the Film Factory*.

General editors' preface

Cinema has been the predominant popular art-form of the first half of the twentieth century, at least in Europe and North America. Nowhere was this more apparent than in the former Soviet Union, where Lenin's remark that 'of all the arts for us cinema is the most important' became a cliché and where cinema attendances were until recently still among the highest in the world. In the age of mass politics Soviet cinema developed from a fragile but effective tool to gain support among the overwhelmingly illiterate peasant masses in the Civil War that followed the October 1917 Revolution, through a welter of experimentation, into a mass weapon of propaganda through entertainment that shaped the public image of the Soviet Union – both at home and abroad and for both elite and mass audiences – and latterly into an instrument to expose the weaknesses of the past and present in the twin processes of *glasnost* and *perestroika*. Now the national cinemas of the successor republics to the old USSR are encountering the same bewildering array of problems, from the trivial to the terminal, as are all the other ex-Soviet institutions.

Cinema's central position in Russian and Soviet cultural history and its unique combination of mass medium, art-form and entertainment industry, have made it a continuing battleground for conflicts of broader ideological and artistic significance, not only for Russia and the Soviet Union but also for the world outside. The debates that raged in the 1920s about the relative revolutionary merits of documentary as opposed to fiction film, of cinema as opposed to theatre or painting, or of the proper role of cinema in the forging of post-revolutionary Soviet culture and the shaping of the new Soviet man, have their echoes in current discussions about the role of cinema *vis-à-vis* other art forms in effecting the cultural and psychological revolution in human consciousness necessitated by the processes of economic and political transformation of the former Soviet Union into modern democratic and industrial societies and states governed by the rule of law. Cinema's central position has also made it a vital instrument for scrutinising the blank pages of Russian and Soviet history and enabling the present generation to come to terms with its own past.

This series of books intends to examine Russian and Soviet films in the context of Russian and Soviet cinema, and Russian and Soviet cinema in the context of the political and cultural history of Russia, the Soviet Union and the world at large. Within that framework the series, drawing its authors from both East and West, aims to cover a wide variety of topics and to employ a broad range of methodological approaches and presentational formats. Inevitably this will involve ploughing once again over old ground in order to re-examine received opinions, but it principally means increasing the breadth and depth of our knowledge, finding new answers to old questions and, above all, raising new questions for further enquiry and new areas for further research. The present volume, *Eisenstein Rediscovered*, is intended to fulfil all these objectives.

The continuing aim of the series is to situate Russian and Soviet cinema in their proper historical and aesthetic context, both as a major cultural force in Russian history and Soviet politics and as a crucible for experimentation that is of central significance to the development of world cinema culture. Books in the series strive to combine the best of scholarship, past, present and future, with a style of writing that is accessible to a broad readership, whether that readership's primary interest lies in cinema or in Russian and Soviet political history.

Richard Taylor and Ian Christie

Acknowledgements

The essays in this volume were first presented as papers at the 'Eisenstein at 90' conference, held at Keble College, Oxford in July 1988, to mark the opening of the touring exhibition *Eisenstein: His Life and Work* at the Museum of Modern Art, Oxford. This exhibition was organised by David Elliott, Director of the Museum of Modern Art, Oxford, and Ian Christie, then Head of Distribution at the British Film Institute, in association with the USSR Union of Cinematographers and with support from Visiting Arts and the Arts Council of Great Britain. Naum Kleiman, curator of the Eisenstein Archive, Moscow, served as consultant and Richard Taylor as historical adviser.

Thanks are due to all who participated in the conference, including those whose contributions have not been included in the present volume, and to the chairs of conference sessions: Bernard Eisenschitz, David Elliott, the late Maria Enzensberger, Geoffrey Nowell-Smith and Peter Wollen. Generous assistance with organising the conference was provided by the late D. J. Wenden, then Bursar of All Souls, and by Anthony Smith, President of Magdalen. Natasha Ward ably interpreted for the Russian-speaking participants.

Ian Christie also wishes to thank Penelope Houston, former editor of *Sight and Sound*, for commissioning the article 'Eisenstein at 90', on which the introduction to this book is based; and Melanie Tebb, for expert help with the complex communications that editing this collection has involved. Robert Christie provided working space when it was needed and help with references. Much more than thanks are due to Patsy Nightingale, who encouraged, supported and kept other commitments going throughout the whole trajectory that led from planning the exhibition and conference to seeing this book completed.

Richard Taylor would like to thank his family and friends for their usual moral support, and the Department of Politics, University of Swansea, for providing financial and secretarial assistance.

ILLUSTRATION ACKNOWLEDGEMENTS

Many Eisenstein photographs and film stills exist in versions of widely differing quality in a number of archives and collections. We have tried to find the best versions, drawing mainly on the resources of BFI Stills, Posters and Designs, but supplementing this with items taken from *S. Eizenshtein. Risunki* (Moscow: 1961); *S. M. Eisenstein. Dibujos Mexicanos Ineditos* (Mexico City: 1978); *Eisenstein at Work* (New York: 1982/ London: 1985) and the GDR edition of the memoirs, *YO! Ich selbst* (Berlin: 1987). Other pictures and frame enlargements are from the collections of the authors and editors. Stills from Eisenstein's films appear by kind permission of Contemporary Films. Drawings and personal memorabilia reproduced by courtesy of the Union of Cinematographers/Central State Archive of Literature and Art (TsGALI).

Note on transliteration and translation

Transliteration from the Cyrillic to the Latin alphabet is a perennial problem for writers on Russian subjects. We have opted for a dual system: in the text we have transliterated in a way that will, we hope, render Russian names and terms more accessible to the non-specialist, while in the notes we have adhered to a more accurate and consistent system for the specialist. Accepted English spellings of Russian names have been used wherever possible and Russian names of German origin have been returned to their roots.

The translation of titles poses a special problem, since Russian has neither the definite nor indefinite article. We find the tradition of certain Soviet films being known by bald titles like *Earth*, *Mother*, *Mirror* misleading and arbitrary, since literary, dramatic and musical works are not normally translated in this way – consider, for instance, *The Brothers Karamazov*, *The Cherry Orchard* and *A Life for the Tsar*. We have therefore continued our practice, begun in *The Film Factory*, of inserting articles where English fluency requires them: hence *The Strike* and *The Battleship Potemkin*.

Figure 1 'You can find the cruelty that I did not inflict on flies or frogs in my work as a film-maker.' (*Memoirs*) Filming the massacre on the Odessa Steps, with Eisenstein at right.

Introduction

Rediscovering Eisenstein

Ian Christie

Sooner murder an infant in its cradle than nurse unacted desires.

William Blake[1]

How does Eisenstein's reputation stand today? Ostensibly it is secure. He ranks among the acknowledged founding fathers of cinema, with at least one title in most lists 'the greatest films ever made', while the Odessa Steps sequence from *The Battleship Potemkin* must be almost as widely quoted and parodied as the 'Mona Lisa'.[2] Whenever film teaching and theory are discussed, his name is invariably invoked – even if only to warn against the dangers of both enterprises. But behind, or perhaps because of, these tokens there is also an undeniable ambivalence. This was well expressed by Richard Roud's editorial note in his *Cinema: A Critical Dictionary*, where every line of praise sounds qualified:

> That Eisenstein is one of the most important figures of world cinema can hardly be questioned; but except for *Strike* and some of those 'rushes' from *Que Viva Mexico!*, his lack of humanity becomes more disturbing with every passing year. A man of science? Yes. A great theorist of film practice? Of course. The first great teacher? Well, given his lack of followers, one has doubts.[3]

Roud and many others, it seems, would *like* to question the whole edifice of Eisenstein's reputation, to argue that – despite undeniable local successes – it was all built upon a series of massive mistakes: Soviet Communism, the doctrine of montage, the notion that science or theory have any place in art. It is as if they have only been prevented from toppling Eisenstein from his pedestal, like the tsar's statue in *October*, by the power of the myth or, to borrow Benjamin's term, 'aura' that surrounds him.[4]

Will that 'aura' survive the collapse of the Soviet state which created and sustained it? Quite apart from Western empiricist mistrust of Eisenstein's intellectualism and systemic aspiration – the director Lindsay Anderson diagnosed him as 'compulsively an intellectual'! – there is a different current of hostility within the Russian dissident tradition.[5] For Solzhenitsyn's Convict X 123, *Ivan the Terrible* amounted to a 'justification of political tyranny. . . . A mockery of the memory of three generations of Russian intelligentsia', while Eisenstein was 'an arse-licker, obeying a vile dog's order'.[6] Nadezhda Mandelstam recalled her husband's distaste for 'the specious glitter of the then fashionable Eisenstein with his mechanical splendours' in her memoir of the inter-war period.[7] And more recently, hostile references to Eisenstein pepper the writings of Andrey Tarkovsky.[8] None of this is surprising. In a culture dedicated to inner resistance, neither Eisenstein's many public humiliations nor his acts of personal bravery were likely to be credited against the canonic status of his films.

Indeed the period of *glasnost* saw a rising tide of impatience and recrimination. Few of the classic Soviet film-makers escaped condemnation at some point as 'Stalinist', and in Naum Kleiman's contribution to this book there is an echo of the defence that he and other scholars had to make against such irresponsible allegations.[9] Despite Eisenstein's steadfast refusal of triumphalism – and it should be recalled that both *Alexander Nevsky* and *Ivan the Terrible* would have been profoundly elegiac had they not suffered censorship – there remains a vague implication of complicity between tyrant and victim.[10]

Even before the terms of a post-Soviet Russian culture have emerged with any clarity, it has long been obvious that Eisenstein's achievement demanded to be seen in a new, more sophisticated totality than his 'Soviet' persona allowed. There is even perhaps a useful reinterpretation to be made here of the identification with Leonardo which Eisenstein himself professed. Just as we have to disentangle the historical Renaissance Leonardo from the 'genius' and technological visionary promoted by Italian Fascism, so the 'little boy from Riga' who grew up in Russia's Silver Age needs to be distinguished from the 'Master of Soviet cinema' who became a vital ambassador for, as well as prisoner of, Stalin's regime.[11] Both artists emerged from highly traditional cultures to face the challenge of new scientific values. Both eagerly embraced the new paradigms, while also retaining much of their heritage: hence no doubt the lack of any simple relationship between the theory that both so passionately professed and their brilliant, fragmentary and essentially intuitive pictorial practice.[12]

Certainly we must now question the familiar verdict attributed to Shklovsky that 'the books Eisenstein wrote were the films he did not make'. Even if planning major studies like *Direction* and *Method* helped ease his desperation after the loss of, first, *Que Viva Mexico!* and then *Bezhin Meadow*, it is clear that Eisenstein had already defined his goal and distinctive method. While still in Mexico, he wrote in a letter to Maxim Strauch:

Although I have deftly adjusted to 'armchair' work in a Pushkin-like *kibitka* – my own kind of thinking gyroscope! – I still feel a terrible need to settle down and finally consolidate the theoretical organism. Yes, and what's more, I'm doing a great deal of drawing!

Actually, the filming, theory and drawing are done in 'relays' so as to keep going at all costs.[13]

Despite the traumas of the following eighteen years, he succeeded as few others of his generation did in 'keeping going'. Teaching, writing and drawing were undoubtedly easier to practise when film production became a high-risk affair of state, but they never simply 'replaced' film-making, as is clear from the stream of concrete film projects which he continued to formulate. The fact remains that Eisenstein's unique enterprise was as difficult to accept for his Soviet contemporaries of 1935 and the late 1940s as it is for many today.[14]

The exhibition *Eisenstein: His Life and Art* was organised as a deliberate challenge to the images of Eisenstein that make him seem remote, dogmatic, naive; a victim of the same familiarity that has bred snobbish contempt for those two great near-contemporaries he was proud to call friends, Chaplin and Disney.[15] Alongside the celebrated films, it laid equal stress on what has previously seemed marginal to his main achievement – private drawing, theatre work, friendships, collecting, travels – and revealed how much, even now, remains unexplored in the legacy of this most famous of film-makers and compulsive autobiographer. For Eisenstein became the first and most persuasive expert on 'Eisenstein'. There is scarcely any aspect of his career and life on which he did not first comment, often with a wit and apparent candour that has inhibited dissent. But to make progress in a world which certainly does not regard Eisensteinian precepts as axiomatic, scholars have to look beyond or behind the erudite self-analysis of 'one's own scholarly self' to gain other vantage points.[16] Hence the origin of this book in a conference commemorating Eisenstein's '90th birthday', with participants from a dozen countries and, thanks to *glasnost*, younger Soviet scholars gaining their first international platform.[17] In addition to the scholars present, Tatyana Gomolitskaya, daughter of Sergei Tretyakov, was a welcome guest who brought vivid first-hand memories of Eisenstein as *enfant terrible* of the early Soviet theatre and avid collector of both detective stories and risqué jokes. The conductor Alan Fearon talked about how his experience of restoring the original music for *Potemkin* and *October* had given him a new respect for this almost forgotten collaborator of Eisenstein's. And finally, the playwright Richard Crane and director Faynia Williams read from their kaleidoscopic play based on Eisenstein's life and work, *Red Magic*, later performed at the Edinburgh Festival and in London.

It was an occasion to assert simultaneously the 'wholeness' of Eisenstein and the striking diversity of approaches, lessons and influences that his legacy embraces, with a particular emphasis on neglected contexts and the importance of texts only now being published. Consideration of what he planned but did *not* achieve, as a number of contributors stress, can be just as revealing as the apparently 'finished' works. In light of this continuing process of rediscovery, what follows here by way of introduction is a condensed stocktaking of work in progress and work still remaining to be done which will eventually re-establish the 'mythic' Eisenstein of the Comintern and Cold War years on firmer historical and analytic ground.

HOW LONG (AND FAST) IS A PIECE OF FILM?

Eisenstein's completed films at least may seem to pose no problem of accessibility. In Britain and the United States, as in most developed countries, all seven features, as well as *Time in the Sun* and the *Bezhin Meadow* reconstruction, are currently in commercial distribution. After early censorship skirmishes, they have remained more or less continuously available since their first appearance, and all are now also on home video. But how complete and authentic are the available versions?

From empirical research such as Kristin Thompson's, reported here, much more is now known about the vanguard role played by Eisenstein's films in creating a world-wide market for the early Soviet cinema.[18] This success also contained the seeds of future problems, since the foreign returns to the Soviet state – in a rare conjunction of the economic with the political – were so great that pragmatic expediency soon governed their international distribution. Before this, Eisenstein's first feature, *The Strike*, had won early recognition at the 1925 Exposition des Arts Décoratifs in Paris, but was little seen at home and not actually distributed abroad until after Eisenstein's death, by which time preservation material had been secured by the Soviet archive, Gosfilmofond.[19] Although the original titling seems to be lost, the fact that it was never submitted for pre-war foreign censors' approval seems to have preserved an essentially complete and common version.[20]

With the subsequent silent films, on which Eisenstein's fame mainly rests, matters are more complex. As Thompson confirms, Germany was by far the most important market for *Potemkin* and, with hard currency and film stock both in acutely short supply, it must have seemed expedient to sell the negative directly to the German distributor, Prometheus.[21] There it was edited to meet the censor's demands, so that the material which was eventually regained from Germany to become Gosfilmofond's main source reflected these changes and the 1925 Soviet 'original' was effectively lost. When Kleiman came to restore the film in the 1960s, using as additional sources an early copy which had survived at the Institute of

Cinematography, VGIK, and one sent by Eisenstein with Leyda as a gift to the Museum of Modern Art in New York, he discovered that Eisenstein had almost certainly used his Berlin trip of 1926 to re-edit the film while complying with the censor's requirements. So, while the MoMA-based restoration remains the most complete, there are still important textual cruxes to be explored (including those which Kleiman could then not broach for political reasons, such as a Trotsky quotation).[22] Also missing from all release versions to this day is the original red stencil tinting of the ship's flag, which Eisenstein considered vital to the film's impact on audiences.[23]

October was to follow a similar pattern, after being caught in the cross-fire of Trotsky's final challenge to Stalin. Montagu, who probably knew Eisenstein better than any foreigner but was constrained by pro-Soviet loyalties, wrote laconically of *October* being 'slashed to ribbons in response to political changes'.[24] The film's co-director Grigori Alexandrov, meanwhile, was quoted in 1963 describing a visit by Stalin to the cutting room 'just before the film's première on the tenth anniversary of the Revolution in 1927', at which he allegedly 'asked for cuts of several important scenes totalling . . . approximately 3000 feet'.[25] Apart from the date given for Stalin's intervention, this is roughly compatible with Eisenstein's published claim in late December 1927 to be working on 'two films: *Before October* and *October*. 13,000 feet in all'.[26] The longest version known today is approximately 9200 feet.

As with *Potemkin*, the original negative appears to have been sold to Germany to earn much-needed hard currency for new production, but does not appear to have returned. In addition to four differing positives held by the Soviet archive, a few cut sequences survived until the 1960s, when Kleiman considered inserting these into a 'research version' for limited circulation. This modest ambition was overtaken by Alexandrov's proposal for a new sound version to mark the 'Jubilee' of the Revolution in 1967. Once again, more complete material was found abroad, this time a 16mm print in Britain.[27] Alexandrov was able to add sequences of the Mensheviks and of Lenin and the Central Committee. But his version, originally furnished with a voice-over commentary as well as extensive sound effects and music, proved little short of disastrous and was modified. Close examination of what was finally released – which became the new international release version – shows that Alexandrov made numerous minor cuts in a vain effort to make the film more like a conventional narrative.

But *October* resists such 'normalisation'. Quite apart from the political reasons for its lacunae, Eisenstein effectively discovered the potential of metaphoric or 'intellectual' montage while working at intense pressure on its editing. He was inspired to contemplate a filmic analogue of Marx's *Capital*, and many sequences such as the 'gods' and Kerensky's entry into the Imperial apartment bear witness to this new formal interest, doubtless at the expense of narrative material already filmed.[28] More than almost any other major film, *October* is essentially uncompleted, as was noted by contemporary Soviet reviewers; and even after the political forces which shaped and constrained it can be openly explored, it remains highly enigmatic.[29] As Tsivian's important study here of a variant script shows, it also permits more readings than Soviet-authorised orthodoxy has so far allowed, including the marked influence of Russian Symbolism as mediated through Blok and Bely and evidence of the erotic complexity of Eisenstein's genius.[30]

The General Line poses an immediate issue of identity with its alternative title, *The Old and the New*, adopted for the film's delayed release in late 1929. Were there in fact two fundamentally different films? And which of these survives today? Again, the evidence so far available is scant and opinions differ. Seton states bluntly that changing agricultural policies required a fresh start and a new scenario,[31] while Barna quotes Eisenstein on the film's 'shattered vertebrae and broken spine', adding without any further source that 'of the original conception there remained only the first three reels, and the agitation scene in the second part'.[32] Leyda, however, casts doubt on whether the film was radically changed when production resumed after *October*: 'Putting together the available evidence, I should say that when the crew returned to *The General Line* in Spring 1928, there was no more than further shooting on the long-before determined story.'[33] But he goes on to indicate the more probable reason for the film as it stood in early 1929 excluding much that had been shot in both periods of filming. Perhaps because of the exceptional demands of *October*, Eisenstein had developed an unusually free approach to 'composition' by editing:

> in the cutting-room, there was, of course, the always painful whittling process that reduced twice too much material to a normal running length of film. Here, as in both *Potemkin* and *October*, Eisenstein had to throw away almost as many ideas as the best ones that the finished films retained.[34]

One instance of what was discarded from the earlier period of shooting is an episode that featured the Constructivist artists Alexander Rodchenko and Varvara Stepanova as 'foreigners', apparently visiting the Soviet countryside by aeroplane.[35] A rather different element also now missing is the image of Leonardo's 'Mona Lisa' which Seton claims was juxtaposed with a sleeping peasant woman in the evocation of the 'old' village – surely a case of post-*October* intellectual montage?[36] At least one copy had hand-coloured fireworks accompanying the bull's 'wedding', in succession to the red flags of the 'Potemkin'.[37] In fact the completion of *The General Line* coincided with an explosion of teaching, theory and polemic on Eisenstein's part, much of which seems to have left some trace on the film.[38]

Figure 2
The artists
Alexander
Rodchenko and
Varvara Stepanova
in a 1926 flying
sequence later
dropped from *The
General Line*.

Thus it may be necessary to reinterpret Shklovsky's account of Eisenstein hastily assembling a 'carnivalesque film on abundance' to divert the bankers who came to see why the production was so far behind schedule.[39] Was this perhaps more than a temporary expedient, marking the point at which an intended simple, didactic film became the riot of fertility symbolism and utopian magic that Stalin saw in February 1929 and that largely survives today? For, although most changes to the film have conventionally been attributed to Stalin's intervention in February 1929, it is not clear that this resulted in more than an elaborate search for 'the correct end' – which eventually replaced the Chaplinesque original and introduced Andrei Burov's Constructivist 'vision' of the new collective farm.[40] Even the emblematic change of title seems to have been a cautious move by the producers Sovkino rather than an order from Stalin and the film was in any case withdrawn from distribution in 1931 (as were many other Soviet films of the previous decade) before being pillaged for a 1932 documentary.[41]

What this account suggests is that probably neither a 1926 *Urtext* nor the actual late 1929 Soviet release version still exist, because the former was never completed and the latter partially dismembered. On balance, it would seem that we have only *The General Line* as it was finalised in the first six months of 1929. But there remain important differences between the versions of *this* currently available, noted here by Myriam Tsikounas, which must stem from the prints originally sent abroad in 1929 or, more recently, from the partial reconstruction undertaken by Kleiman using a Belgian print.[42]

The 'new' history of early cinema points to a radically different understanding of textual stability throughout the silent period.[43] Because individual copies of films could be and were easily altered for many different reasons in the course of their circulation, it makes little sense to search for a unique original or authentic version of each production. Films routinely existed in multiple versions, with opportunities for modification occurring at all stages from the producing studio to the point of exhibition. Synchronised sound drastically reduced, without wholly eliminating, the scope for such changes. Today, it is certainly possible to seek the longest or the earliest version of a silent film, but this may not represent the final wishes of the maker(s) or indeed what any actual audiences saw.[44] To trace the reasons for variation, on the rare occasions when this is possible, is to come closer to understanding the complex workings of a system that was in some ways less akin to mass production than is now widely supposed.

Soviet silent cinema belonged to this general international regime, but has also been subject to some highly specific circulation factors. For Eisenstein's silent films, four distinct processes of textual variation can be identified:

1 politically motivated alterations before and after domestic release;
2 foreign distributors' changes, as demanded by local censorship, but also arising from translation, projection practice and commercial judgement;
3 Eisenstein's own revisions when the opportunity or need presented itself;
4 deliberate 'modernisation', especially when synchronised sound was added (including 'step-printing').[45]

It is the last of these, together with many generations of 'duping' from positive material, that has rendered most of the widely available prints (and consequently the videos made from them) of Eisenstein's silent films so inadequate. Equally damaging is the widespread use of inappropriate projection speeds. While no 'correct' speed can be claimed with confidence – since this was a matter of widespread variation and controversy in the silent period – the 16 or 18 frames per second often regarded as 'silent speed' today is undoubtedly too slow for many of the montage rhythms and tropes to cohere.[46] Eisenstein discovered how damaging this could be when he witnessed *Potemkin* shown more slowly than he at least was used to at its London première in 1929, allegedly in order to synchronise with Meisel's music, and the audience laughed at the rearing stone lions.[47] Recent experience has shown that the impact of restored versions, shown at an appropriate speed under proper cinema conditions, is nothing short of revelatory.[48]

An important step towards realising this goal has been the revival of interest in Edmund Meisel's original music for *Potemkin* and *October*. Whereas Prokofiev's contribution to *Nevsky* and *Ivan* has long been acknowledged, Meisel has remained no more than an obscure footnote to Eisenstein's early career, with only seriously deficient scores surviving. The restoration and performance of his two major scores by Alan Fearon has made a strong case for reassessing the original success of *Potemkin* as a more equal partnership between film and music than might have seemed possible – and for wondering if *October* would have fared better had Meisel's score been properly synchronised and more widely performed.[49]

Meisel, it transpires, broke decisively with the '*pot-pourri*' tradition of film music and launched boldly into a musical architecture that responded to the challenge of Eisenstein's non-narrative montage construction. His *Geräuschmusik*, or 'noise music', deploys often ironic leitmotivs and quotations against a background of rhythmic ostinati (supported by a large percussion section) and massive dynamic contrasts, all couched in the Modernist idiom of the 1920s.[50] Only the young Shostakovich's 1929 score for *New Babylon* rises as completely to the challenge of the late Soviet montage idiom, with its sardonic play on 'Belle époque' operetta to underline the tragedy of the Paris Commune.[51] With authentic performances, it is now possible to appreciate how much the response to Meisel's

Figure 3 The Berlin-based composer Edmund Meisel (1874–1930) responded in a Modernist idiom to the challenge of Eisenstein's non-narrative films.

music must have shaped Eisenstein's idea of sound–image counterpoint. For in performance with the film, if not so obviously on the page, it interacts with Eisenstein's images to make plausible the otherwise utopian concept of a 'single denominator' which would combine the visual and the auditory.[52]

It was inevitably with Meisel that Eisenstein planned to demonstrate how synchronised sound-on-film could be used non-naturalistically. Unfortunately the detailed plans he had prepared to post-synchronise *The Old and the New* in London came to nothing, and indeed probably could not have been realised with the limited sound technology of the period.[53] But Eisenstein's faith in the potential of natural sound and music to become as malleable and meaningful as film images clearly stemmed from what he had already learned through Meisel. And we may wonder if *The Old and the New* can be considered in any way complete without its intended soundtrack that would have combined natural sound, *musique concrète* and musical 'typage'.[54]

The saga of *Que Viva Mexico!* has been extensively researched, but mainly in terms of the politics and personalities involved. Although Eisenstein was never able to edit his cherished Mexican footage, surprisingly little attention has been paid to what can be discerned from the mass of surviving film material. While controversy has continued over Seton's intervention to make *Time in the Sun* – claiming to follow Eisenstein's own editing plan – Leyda patiently assembled all the remaining material into a 'study version' of the Mexican project, based on the assumption that Eisenstein would in fact have created the film in the course of editing it, as he had always done previously.[55] This unique opportunity to examine the raw material for an Eisenstein film seems so far to have prompted no further study of his compositional practice beyond the suggestions offered in Leyda's commentary titles.

After the loss of the Mexican footage and other frustrated projects of the early 1930s, *Bezhin Meadow* was completed in rough-cut by the end of 1936, before being finally banned in March 1937. Its material is believed to have been destroyed during the battle for Moscow in 1941, but the hope of discovering a hidden print still haunts Eisenstein scholars.[56] Meanwhile, the reconstruction that was made from surviving single frames in 1967 by Kleiman and Yutkevich gives at least a partial impression of this most elaborate production. But the intense, hieratic impression conveyed by these frozen images and the music subsequently added needs to be supplemented by other information about the production, most of which we owe to Jay Leyda, as David Stirk and Elena Pinto Simon explain in their contribution here.[57]

The uncertainties about the films of Eisenstein's last decade stem largely from that period's climate of terror and secrecy. In the case of *Alexander Nevsky*, we know from Eisenstein himself that the original scenario continued after Nevsky's defeat of the Germans at Lake Peipus to show him first paying tribute to the Khan in order to buy time for military preparations, then dying before reaching his home. But Eisenstein was told that the scenario should end with the triumph of Lake Peipus and, in a phrase often attributed to Stalin, that 'such a fine prince could not die'.[58] We owe to Shklovsky the further anecdote of the 'missing reel' from *Alexander Nevsky*. The story is that, when a hasty Kremlin preview of the film was arranged while Eisenstein slept at the cutting room, one sequence was accidentally omitted and could not later be inserted for fear of upsetting Stalin.[59] This is supposed to have included a fight on the bridge at Novgorod which resulted from the ordinary people challenging the merchants' decision not to resist the Teutonic invasion – a sequence that would surely have met with Stalin's approval? Shklovsky's anecdote carries 'poetic' conviction, but is not entirely convincing in technical detail, although Leyda and Voynow reproduce stills from such an episode which is not in any known version of the film.[60]

A much larger issue is the web of supposition still surrounding *Ivan the Terrible* and its legendary third part. We know that Eisenstein enlarged his original plan for a two-part film early in the production process, and that a full 'literary script' for three parts was published in advance, as had been the Soviet custom. According to Seton, only Parts I and II were actually shot; but Leyda and Voynow claim, more plausibly, that material for all three parts was shot simultaneously, not least because many of the same sets and props were needed.[61]

Part I appeared in 1945, already differing somewhat from the published scenario, with the childhood prologue detached. When Part II was eventually released in 1957, the prologue had become a subjective flashback, and it was apparent that the film covered considerably less ground than indicated in the Part II scenario. Was this in fact Eisenstein's own conception of Part II? And, if so, was it the first version which he had completed in 1946 before his heart attack? Or was it, as Leyda and Voynow assert, 'a roughly corrected cutting of Part II' also made in 1946, for which Eisenstein 'lacked the strength to make the new sequences that were needed'?[62] They go on to state categorically that by mid-1946, 'there was no talk of or plan for Part III: all materials for it, including four edited reels, had, by then, been destroyed'.

Two further *Ivan* fragments have since come to light: the Knight Staden's interrogation (a fully dubbed and edited sequence) and several shots of Mikhail Romm's screen test to play Queen Elizabeth I in a Windsor Castle scene. Both belong to the original scheme for Part II, which leaves open the possibility that other sequences from this larger conception known to have been filmed – including the great Last Judgement confrontation between Ivan and the 'Tsar of Heaven', familiar from stills – could yet be unearthed.[63] Other recent discoveries in the

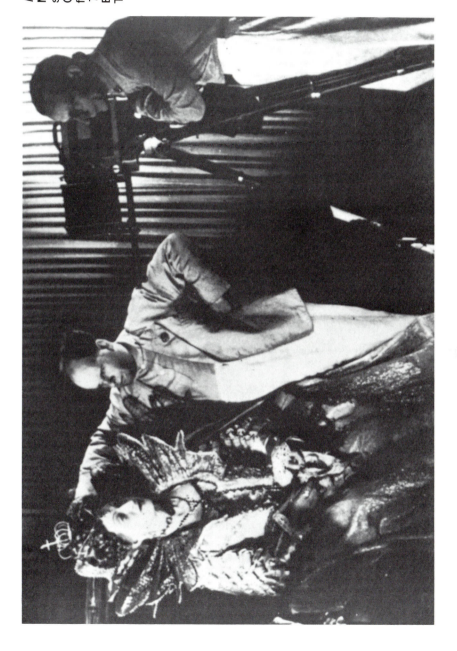

Figure 4
Mikhail Romm
screen-testing as
Queen Elizabeth I
for *Ivan the
Terrible*, with
Eisenstein and
Tisse (*right*).

ex-Soviet archives encourage such hopes, but it must also be admitted that disappointingly little scholarly attention has so far been paid to earlier expansions of the Eisenstein canon, such as the discovery of his filmed insert, *Glumov's Diary*, for the 1923 theatre production *Enough Simplicity for Every Wise Man*.[64] Nor indeed has the rich legacy of well-developed projects been extensively explored; and Håkan Lövgren's valuable study of the Pushkin project here indicates how revealing these can be in the case of a film-maker who managed to realise publicly so few of his ambitions.[65]

Much remains to be done, even with that most familiar part of the Eisenstein legacy. A useful first step would be to identify the published Eisenstein 'scripts' as merely transcriptions from whatever material has been to hand, rather than allowing them the dubious status they still enjoy as works of reference.[66] More valuable would be an international census and 'genealogy' of versions of the films in circulation, which would enable scholars to identify which copies they are using and compare these with others. And with the Russian archives now more able, in theory at least, to co-operate with other archives on restoration, may we not hope to see eventually an Eisenstein film-text 'variorum' collection? The principles that should guide such work were proposed as long ago as 1972 by Ivor Montagu, in an exemplary report he prepared on *Potemkin* copies held by the National Film Archive in Britain: 'as in Shakespearean scholarship, the wisest recension would be to synthesize everything *probable* from all copies, giving due weight to intuition and poetic fitness.'[67]

'THIS MAY ALL BE PRINTED SOME DAY'

Eisenstein knew that his reputation as a writer would be almost entirely posthumous. Although he published numerous articles throughout his career, only two books actually appeared during his lifetime. The first of these was Leyda's collection of his essays in English translation, *The Film Sense* in 1942; the second was the literary scenario of *Ivan the Terrible* in 1944.[68] As Kleiman has reminded us, the official Soviet verdict on Eisenstein remained strongly negative for nearly a decade after his death. None of his films after *Potemkin* could safely be mentioned while Stalin lived, and his theoretical work was dismissed as the meanderings of a 'muddler'.[69]

The first Soviet collection of his essays appeared in 1956, an early harbinger of Khrushchev's 'Thaw'. When the second part of *Ivan* was released in 1957, the way was now clear for a more substantial monument to his extraordinary gifts as an art historian, philosopher, teacher and polemicist. Hence his widow Pera Attasheva's project for a *Selected Works* and, given the unpredictability of official policy, the need to realise this speedily.[70]

Since neither of the major book-length projects, *Direction* and *Method*, was in readily publishable form when Eisenstein died, the strategy of the *Selected Works* was to 'sample' these as an interim measure. And since there was no existing biography, or the scope to write one at that juncture, the remarkably frank memoirs which Eisenstein had started while convalescing in 1946–7 were pressed into service as an impromptu autobiography, to become Volume 1. Therein lay the root of a future problem. For to assemble the free-association pattern of Eisenstein's 'immoral memoirs' into a more or less chronological sequence involved (literally) cutting up the original typescript and discarding material that would not fit this format.[71]

It was only when the Eisenstein Archive materials were taken into the Central State Archive for Literature and the Arts (TsGALI) after Attasheva's death in 1965 that Naum Kleiman began a new collation. Gathering all the material not used in the published version, he discovered that Eisenstein had often indicated where an already published article should be dropped into the expanding structure of the memoirs, sometimes in a revised form. Meanwhile the covers of notebooks had been found, papers and inks compared, and the order of composition could now be used to deduce how Eisenstein planned his 'Portrait of the Author as a Very Old Man', which turned out to be also the portrait of an epoch and its generation.[72]

Unfortunately, just at the point when Kleiman had arrived at a new, expanded structure for the memoirs and succeeded in getting this published under Eisenstein's chosen polyglot title *YO! Ich selbst* in an East German/Austrian edition in 1984, Marshall's English translation of the now-superseded 1964 text appeared.[73] That this should have made no reference to the scholarship of the intervening twenty years was all the more deplorable since a 1978–80 French edition had already made considerable use of the revised ordering and contents.[74] Only now, in 1993, is an English translation of *YO!* imminent, nearly thirty years after the first Russian edition.[75]

Similar delays and omissions have dogged the publication of the writings as a whole. According to Kleiman's estimate, the Russian *Selected Works* contains no more than about a quarter of Eisenstein's known writing. A further twelve volumes have long been contemplated to replace the published six and even these would still not include the VGIK lectures and director's working notes. Nor would they deal with the extensive diaries or Eisenstein's letters, selections from which could greatly expand the current range of Eisenstein studies and confirm much that has remained speculative and rumoured, judging from the wit and candour of what little is so far available.[76] Ultimately, Kleiman estimates, twenty volumes would be needed, but the likelihood of this being achieved in the foreseeable future after the collapse of the Soviet system must be low.

Meanwhile, a steady stream of articles, notes and correspondence has appeared in Soviet journals since the early 1950s and many scholars have benefited from access to hitherto unpublished manuscripts under the guidance of Kleiman ('Imitation as Mastery' and 'A Few Personal Reflections on Taboo', making their first appearances in English here, are good examples of this process at work).[77] Publication of this material abroad in translation has not kept pace and the overall picture is complicated by significant national differences of approach. Two major 'selected works' series, in France and West Germany, set new standards of selection and annotation and included previously unavailable material before both came to a premature end.[78] Now the Italian and British series, still in progress, have built on this example and are actively helping to redraw the map of Eisenstein's writings, while each following different organisational principles.[79] Alongside these, the lively variety of Leyda's Calcutta series and Albera's two volumes in French have filled important gaps in our knowledge of, especially, Eisenstein's later views on visual art, cinema and psychology.[80]

These developments make a reassessment of Eisenstein's intellectual and critical work pressing and, with some difficulty, possible. From the response to the first volume of the new British edition, it seems clear that many non-specialists still have real difficulty distinguishing stages and contexts in his writing and recognising how its chronology vitally governs what *could* be said as well as the external prompting and inner development of his thinking. Thus it is still not uncommon to find polemical statements of the late 1920s and obligatory ones of the 1930s, quoted as triumphant proof that ultimately he 'was wrong about everything'.[81] Leyda, who did so much to create the first Western image of Eisenstein as a theorist, remarked ruefully, but perhaps also rather naïvely, on how

> his vision of film as a synthesis of all the arts and sciences, instead of convincing his colleagues of his determination and devotion to his art, had the effect of dividing them from him; and it is from the other side of this barrier that the Eisenstein portrait formed and hardened.[82]

How, it may be wondered, could Eisenstein's colleagues and later filmmakers *not* be daunted by such a prospectus? And for as long as his theoretical work was disguised or justified as practical 'teaching', how could it fail to be misconstrued?[83]

With all the political inhibitions that Leyda faced in editing the first and most influential of his essay collections, *The Film Sense* (1942) and *Film Form* (1949), it is scarcely surprising that he stressed the more conservative aspects of Eisenstein's immense range. In 1964, when he compiled *Film Essays* and there was reason to believe the major works would soon appear in translation, Leyda's concern was still with filling gaps in the biography of Eisenstein the director-teacher. Thus we have Eisenstein as the admirer of Griffith, Chaplin and Ford (although few would realise the peril even these innocuous enthusiasms caused when they were expressed). But consider another essay, written between 1946–8, in which he mentions *inter alia* Welles's *Citizen Kane*, Wilder's *The Lost Weekend*, Leisen's *Lady in the Dark*, Montgomery's *Lady in the Lake*, Hitchcock's *Spellbound* and Powell and Pressburger's *A Matter of Life and Death*, in addition to Surrealism and Sartre.[84] Such a range of references was no doubt made possible by the wartime Allied presence in Moscow which brought films, magazines and conversation from abroad, but it also confirms that Eisenstein's isolation from cinema beyond the USSR was far from voluntary. As Albera observes, this essay also develops some ideas similar to those which appeared contemporaneously in France when the backlog of American wartime films began to arrive.[85]

If the constraints on Eisenstein the film-maker and viewer are still underestimated, there is even greater unwillingness to recognise that from a very early stage his intellectual and speculative interests had a momentum of their own, increasingly independent of his film projects. The fact that his studies undoubtedly provided some consolation amid the aborted projects and productions of the 1930s did not necessarily mean they embodied the same ideas or impulses. Instead it is necessary to trace how the 'theoretical organism' born of Eisenstein's kaleidoscopic interests and influences of the late 1920s progressed to become the 'building to be built' of his last decade – a unique work of research, synthesis and introspection on the fundamental sources of human expression.

As Grossi shows here, the direction of this study was not unprecedented: in many ways it followed directly from the Russian literary–scientific tradition which was to have a belated yet profound effect on social sciences and cultural studies in the West.[86] Eisenstein was a near contemporary of Shklovsky, Vygotsky, Tynyanov and Bakhtin; he had close intellectual relations with the first three of these, and twice he planned lecture courses on the psychology of art at the request of the neuro-psychologist Luria.[87] As other contributors to this book make clear, Eisenstein's actual achievements in cultural semiotics and the theory of art demand to be taken seriously.[88]

His studies, however, were never merely academic and, as I have suggested elsewhere, there is a demonstrable convergence between Eisenstein's scientific work and his personal quest.[89] Two linked themes which recur frequently in his writings over twenty years are the semantic potential of 'montage' and the non-narrative or 'musical' import of film. These are most obviously brought together in the concept of counterpoint which serves as a bridge between silent and synchronised-sound cinema. Indeed Eisensteinian montage, when it is not caricatured as a kind of conjuring trick, is often understood as an elaborate counterpoint of signification. Music, meanwhile, comes to stand for what lies beyond verbal signification, for what is perceptible, though ineffable. In *Non-Indifferent Nature*, he writes of 'the musical line of landscape begun by *Potemkin*'; and he analyses the 'Odessa mist' sequence in that film in terms of 'a type of "postpainting" passing into a distinctive type of "premusic (proto-music)" '.[90] As Eisenstein pursues these themes in his later writings, where they stand for the 'specificity' of film, it seems that he may in fact be seeking to locate the place of the film-maker in the machinery of cinema, to identify the scene of creation, and thus confirm his own identity as an artist on the cusp of the era of Constructivism – engineer or magus?[91] In effect, he shared Leonardo's belief that science was necessary, but by no means sufficient 'to transform the mind of the painter into the likeness of the divine mind'.[92]

'I NEVER LEARNED TO DRAW'[93]

Eisenstein's drawings have long been prized by initiates, but the rarity of exhibitions and lack of any representative anthology of reproductions have held back recognition of their crucial importance. There has also been the same unwillingness, as with the writings, to grant them due autonomy. On the evidence of the 1988 exhibition, graphic expression provided the most intimate and uncensored record of Eisenstein's emotional life – it is tempting to say on both a conscious and an unconscious level. And in the later writings, it is the motif of drawing that gives greatest insight into his complex processes of self-analysis.[94]

Eisenstein drew constantly for all but about six years of his life. The directors Josef von Sternberg and Grigori Roshal were among many later witnesses of this compulsive, almost automatic, activity.[95] Sternberg recalled how Eisenstein 'always had paper and pencil in front of him', while Roshal described how work colleagues gathered up the drawings so prodigally abandoned.[96] As a child, Eisenstein filled notebooks with ambitious caricatures, strip cartoons and fantastic compositions. The earliest of these preserved (by his mother) date from 1913 when he was 15 and already publishing his drawings in the school magazine, which he also edited.[97] They contain a fascinating array of imagery, based variously on the animal stories of childhood, topical events and the 'pure pleasure' of metamorphosis and incongruity. There are meticulously drawn animals paying court to the Tsar of the Universe, a chicken wooing a pig in party dress, animals queuing for admission to the circus and performing an opera. Political sophistication appears early. Germany and Britain fence with each other across the Channel in a *Punch*-style cartoon, while a sinister figure surrounded by policemen is captioned 'Not an important criminal, but a British Minister!' And narrative makes its appearance with strip cartoons of a bear's adventures and of traditional summer holidays at Trouville.

By 1917 he was selling his sophisticated political cartoons, now signed with the punning pseudonym 'Sir Gay', to leading Petrograd newspapers.[98]

According to Seton, this was also when he became interested in Leonardo, no doubt encouraged by his own developing graphic skills, which led him to Freud's study and an 'explosive' identification with Leonardo's famous 'childhood memory' of being struck in the mouth by a bird's tail, or at least Freud's controversial diagnosis of this as a sign of the artist's repressed homosexuality.[99] Then the final throes of the war and the revolutions of 1917 rescued him from civil engineering studies (also from the possibility of pursuing his discovery of Freud as far as Vienna), and offered a welcome escape into the theatre.[100] Between 1918 and 1921, it was primarily his design ability that took him from the amateur fringe to the heart of a theatre undergoing its own revolutionary upheaval amid the chaos of the Civil War.[101]

The drawing which had begun as an only child's precocious response to the books and journals around him, and increasingly compensated for the loss of family life after his parents separated (allowing him to fantasise a 'normal' family and attack the father he blamed for the divorce) would not resume until 1930.[102] However the adolescent drawings that have been preserved provide us with important evidence of what would later distinguish Eisenstein as a film-maker, when another unexpected juncture launched him on that career.

In the memoirs he makes a telling connection between childhood delight in the vitality of line drawing, the linear contour as 'the trace of movement', and *mise-en-scène* considered as the 'lines of an actor's movement in time', which points to an essential continuity between childhood caricature and the markedly graphic dynamism of the silent films.[103] There is also ample evidence of an apprenticeship in observation, condensation and 'pars pro toto' caricature which would become the basis of his later 'typage'.[104] Although this drew on theories of expression which had wide currency in the Russia of Eisenstein's youth, and would later acquire an ideological dimension – opposing the fiction of the actor's disguise with the physiological reality of the 'ordinary person' – its successful use depended upon the cultivated ability to recognise and isolate 'social and personal biography condensed into physical form'.[105] We see this on a truly social scale in the great panoramic drawing of 150 Petersburg 'types', but also in more personal terms in the drawing of an inordinately fat man with a ludicrously thin servant. These are proto-typage figures, as well as cruel caricatures of his hated father and a family servant.

The adolescent drawings amount to a laboratory in which Eisenstein first perfected his skill with visual metaphor. His exuberant animal drawings initiated a lifelong 'zoomorphism', which delighted in animal–human comparisons and would yield many of the most striking images of his films, from the *agents provocateurs* of *The Strike* to the tsar–eagle metaphor of *Ivan*.[106] Nor was this a facility merely for isolated comparisons. A parody of conventional encyclopedia illustrations showing man's evolutionary descent, done in reverse and titled 'People of the 21st Century', looks forward to the structure of the *agents provocateurs* sequence and perhaps even to more abstract conceptions like the 'gods' sequence in *October*.[107] And was the adolescent drawing of a transparent house a distant source of his later Hollywood project *The Glass House*?[108]

The fact that there are almost no drawings from the period 1924–30 suggests that for Eisenstein film-making and drawing fulfilled what was essentially the same desire in different ways, so that one could not easily substitute for the other. True, there were many preparatory drawings for *Alexander Nevsky* – he was fascinated by the image of the Teutonic knights in their sinister heraldic helmets – but only for *Ivan the Terrible* among all his completed films was there any quantity of actual design and *mise-en-scène* sketches (which may be explained by the fact that he acted as his own designer on this production). From his equally intensive involvement in theatre as a designer and director between 1917 and 1923, there are literally hundreds of drawings in as many styles as the kaleidoscopic Soviet theatre of that period embraced – by turns Cubist, Cubo-Futurist, Constructivist, *commedia dell'arte*, pantomime, American 'dime novel' style and Gogolian grotesque.[109] But although these gave full rein to his love of allusion and caricature, they constituted graphic design, with the distractions of colour, texture and implied volume, rather than the 'pure' line drawing, or 'ascetic search for form', that continued to fascinate him.

It was during his fourteen months in Mexico, recalled in the memoirs as 'paradise regained', that Eisenstein experienced some kind of epiphany which started him drawing again with an intensity which would continue for the rest of his life. Mexico's montage of the primitive, the sensual and the religious seems to have reconnected him with whatever was lost during the emotional traumas of his childhood, or repressed during adolescence and youth.

He responded to the Mexican primitivism that Diego Rivera had synthesised 'from the *bas-reliefs* of Chichen-Itzá, through primitive toys and decorated utensils, to José Guadalupe Posada's inimitable illustrations for street songs'.[110] Direct contact with this raw material and with 'the astonishingly pure linear structure of the Mexican landscape itself' prompted a return to 'the correct linear fashion' of the unbroken, usually closed, line tracing an abstracted calligraphic image. In fact there is a 1931 portrait by Gabriel Ledesma which shows Eisenstein's features and form as a plan of the hacienda of Tetlapayac where, according to Seton, he found 'the place I had been looking for all my life'.[111] Here indeed is a 'map of the heart', a record of his identification of self with place.

Mexico licensed him to revel in religious iconography and ritual *kitsch*, sometimes exaggerating its intrinsic latent sensuality, as in the 'Jesus Polychrome' and 'Gilded Madonna', elsewhere mingling it with the equally erotic imagery of the bullfight to produce such emblematic montage compositions as an 'Adoration of the Matador', 'Crucified Bull' and the

Figure 5 'Paradise regained': Eisenstein posing with Lina Boytler at the Tetlapayac hacienda.

specifically titled 'Synthesis: Eve, Europe, Jesus, Torero'.[112] The suite of variations on a theme became established as Eisenstein's basic drawing strategy in Mexico, and among those preserved are a Judas and Gethsemane group, a Samson and Delilah, and two scandalously, though hilariously, blasphemous series: one offering suggestions for commercialising the Christian sacraments, the other starring Veronica as the patron saint of photographers and printers.[113]

Central to this period were the many drawings based on the motif of Duncan's murder, which is portrayed as a joint undertaking by Macbeth and Lady Macbeth, as if following Leskov's 'Lady Macbeth of Mtsensk' rather than Shakespeare.[114] Eisenstein had actually designed a 'Cubo-

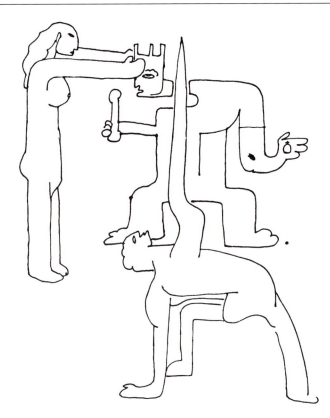

Figure 6 Castration, represented as decapitation, recurs in many of Eisenstein's variations on 'The Death of King Duncan', May–June 1931.

Futurist' *Macbeth* for the Moscow Proletkult Theatre in 1921–2, but his prodigious variations on the murder theme in (mainly) 1931 represent at once the most 'purified' and the most disturbing of all his closed-line drawings. The dramatic kernel of the Macbeth/Duncan series is the Macbeths' simultaneous guilt and exultation at the murder and their lust for power. Some sequences emphasise the savagery of the killing, its gruesome absurdity and Lady Macbeth's active participation, even Duncan's acquiescence, in it. Others concentrate on the erotic satisfaction of the Macbeths; and yet other grotesque and ironic suites explore anachronistic (a post-coital cigarette!) and stylistically allusive variations.[115]

These remarkable drawings shed considerable light on the peculiar relationship between the analytic and the affective in Eisenstein's sensibility. They reveal a passionate intellect restlessly, obsessively trying to solve the equations of sexual difference. The king/father is shown as passive or complicit in his assassination; while the ensuing accession to power is portrayed in frankly erotic (albeit ironic) terms. Here Eisenstein's well-attested interest in the Christian mystics' pursuit of religious ecstasy takes profane form as he seeks the link between pathos and ecstasy.[116]

Did Mexico also make possible Eisenstein's fullest exploration of his hitherto repressed sexuality? This would not be surprising, if only because Tetlapayac provided more personal and social freedom than he enjoyed at any other time in his life (bearing in mind that he lived mostly with his mother and old nanny in Moscow). Apart from the story Seton recounts about his deliberate attempt to embarrass Upton Sinclair by sending a trunk packed with scandalous drawings to be found by United States customs, it is from this period that most of the known erotic drawings date.[117] One at least of these creates an extensive tableau of male coupling around a central figure identifiable as a self-portrait. It is pornographically explicit, yet also playful and clearly referential in a variety of ways – the vulture biting a penis could be a mocking allusion to Freud's notorious analysis of Leonardo's dream.[118]

Yet the catalogue-like 'showing of acts' cannot simply be treated as evidence of Eisenstein's sexual activity in Mexico or anywhere else. The dominant motif of the drawing in question is castration, which links it directly with the recurrence of decapitation in such contemporaneous suites as 'Salome' and 'Ten Aspects of the Death of Werther', not to mention 'Samson and Delilah'. Whether or not Eisenstein went beyond graphic fantasy and play-acting in Mexico to explore the 'unacted desires' of the homosexuality he had previously mistrusted ('a retrogression . . . a dead-end', according to Seton's report) cannot yet be established with any certainty.[119] If he did, it is unlikely that any evidence would have been revealed by Russian scholars, however liberal, in view of the Russian homophobic tradition which the Soviet era crudely reinforced and criminalised. While evidence is appearing of early liaisons with women, there is now a growing consensus among gay commentators that Eisenstein was indeed homosexual and may even have become the victim of blackmail after Mexico.[120] We may never know how his experiences there affected what was certainly an ambiguous sexuality, but the 'unresolved' Oedipal conflict running through most of his subsequent projects is apparent: most obviously in *Bezhin Meadow* and *Ivan the Terrible*, but also the Pushkin project (discussed here by Lövgren) and, in different ways, both *Alexander Nevsky* and the Tamerlane episode of *Ferghana Canal*.[121]

The artist Jean Charlot, who watched him drawing in Mexico 'very quickly so as not to disturb the subconscious elements', recalled that he planned to analyse the drawings to discover 'what had happened in this release of "stream of consciousness"'.[122] His discussion of drawing in the memoirs comes in a chapter titled ironically 'How I Learned to Draw – A Chapter about Dancing Lessons', in which he recalls failing as dismally to learn formal dancing as he did academic still-life drawing.[123] But he later

discovered that he could embroider the foxtrot as fluently as his impro-
vised line danced on paper. Instinctively rejecting what could be taught,
his method in all creative work was to let loose a 'capricious flood' of
images, words or drawing, then seek ways of shaping or analysing the
torrent.[124]

The analysis of his own drawings took several forms. One strand has
only come to light recently, with the publication of 'A Few Personal
Reflections on Taboo', in which Eisenstein starts by noting the injunction
against creating images shared by many religions.[125] From the presumed
identity of naming and being, he passes to the idea of depiction as a
magical act: the ability to 'capture' a likeness depends upon the subject's
consent – and there are coded references here which imply specific
(sexual?) relationships: 'I remember that it was the same on at least three
other occasions (L., V. and E.). The moment the image was captured on
paper, the subject submitted psychologically.'[126] He then sketches a distinction between women's 'objectivisation' of their (male) loved ones'
thoughts and words, compared with men's 'externalisation' or projection
on to, for instance, the heroine of a novel or film – or into a drawing. This
leads to a complex reflection on the psychic transaction involved in
drawing:

> We do however remember what it means to 'know' one's wife in the
> biblical sense. It does not just mean to fuse with her. But, from the position
> of an admirer – to possess her.
>
> You can only imagine another person at the second stage. After the
> first stage in which you mimic the model. You reproduce her subjec-
> tively in yourself in order to return her once again to objectivity, as an
> image on paper.
>
> It is only when this process of mutual penetration – getting inside the
> model and accepting her within you – is achieved that the image will
> come on paper.[127]

If this text clarifies the 'talismanic' aspect of Eisenstein's drawing, we
find the theme of 'mutually penetrating objects in painting and drawing' as
early as 1932 in a notebook entry which also introduces the metaphoric
concept of 'protoplasm' in relation to both his own and Disney's drawing.
Just as protoplasm is the basis of all biological life, so 'non-anatomical'
drawing offers the 'truly appealing theme [of] *the coming into being* of the
human form from plasma'.[128] The 1941 drafts for an unfinished essay on
Disney continue this exploration of the appeal of the 'plasmatic' in
Disney's early animation: the infinite flexibility of figures, their inter-
changeability with natural objects, and ability to collapse and reanimate at
will. 'The very idea . . . of the animated cartoon is like a direct embodiment of the method of animism. . . . And thus, what Disney does is
connected with one of the deepest traits of man's early psyche.'[129] For

Eisenstein, Disney's mastery and depth of appeal are little short of overwhelming:

> I'm sometimes frightened when I watch his films. Frightened by the absolute perfection in what he does. This man seems to know not only the magic of all technical means, but also the most secret strands of human thought, images, feelings, ideas. Such was probably the effect of Saint Francis of Assisi's sermons.[130]

Disney, he concluded, represents 'a complete return to a world of complete freedom . . . freed from the necessity of another primal extinction'.[131]

From which it is a short step to Eisenstein's preoccupation with the 'return to the womb', which Lövgren sees as the cornerstone of his psychology of art.[132] It may be significant that Hanns Sachs was among the Freudians particularly interested in the *Mutterleibsversenkung* or 'womb complex', and it was he who first wrote about Eisenstein and met him in Berlin in 1929.[133] In a striking note from 1932, Eisenstein brought together the motifs of ecstasy, drawing as 'creation' and imagined pre-natal experience:

> This is the graphic equivalent to the sensation of 'flight' among ecstatics: an identical uterine sensation of gyroscopicness and the identical phylo-genetic pre-stage – the floating of the amoebic-protoplasmic state in a liquid environment.[134]

'How I Learned to Draw', nearly fifteen years later, ends with an evocation of 'paradise . . . the happiest period of our life, that blessed age when . . . we dream in the warm wombs of our mothers'. By then he had added to the technique of graphic that of autobiographical free-association as a means of reproducing that primal pleasure.[135]

THE BUILDING TO BE BUILT

Drawing preserved a link with childhood, with the paradise from which his parents' divorce expelled the young Eisenstein. It absolved him from the responsibility of language, obedience to the word of the father – was this why he fought so hard against the union of image and speech in sound film; why his books remained unfinished? – and it offered direct access to the pleasure of creation. It could be confessional, therapeutic, experimental and speculative, none of which the public nature of cinema, especially in its increasingly censored, ceremonial Soviet form, could ever permit.

Amid the bitter personal disappointments and political horrors of the late 1930s, he redefined the 'theoretical organism' first mentioned in Mexico in the form of an allegorical drawing, 'The Building to be Built', which was intended to 'picture my whole future opus'.[136] The image is of a classical temple, in which 'the expressiveness of man' rests upon a

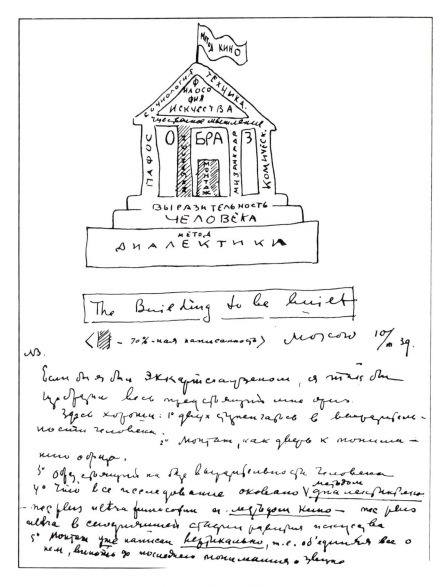

Figure 7 'The Building to be Built', 10 March 1939.

foundation of 'dialectic method' and supports a pediment of 'the philosophy of art', crowned by the pennant of 'film method'. Thus theory and practice are linked as expressions of the same human drive, with film achieving the new synthesis of the arts, as Eisenstein declared in his essay on the production of *Die Walküre* in the same year: 'Men, music, light, landscape, colour and motion brought into one integral whole by the single piercing emotion, by a single theme and idea – this is the aim of modern cinematography.'[137] Despite its Marxist structure, this temple also evokes the architectural symbolism of Freemasonry and the spiritual evolutionary doctrine of Theosophy, recalling the influence of these movements on Russian Symbolism, which was indeed the culture in which Eisenstein grew up, however hard he, like many others, later tried to cast its ideals in 'materialist' terms.[138] Thus, for instance, we find the mystical theme of the search for collective immortality which runs through much Symbolist philosophy expressed by Eisenstein:

> Of all the living beings on earth we are alone privileged to experience and relive, one after the other, the moments of the substantiation of the most important achievements in social development. More. We have the privilege of participating collectively in making a new human history.[139]

In the centre of the temple, 'Montage appears as a door to the understanding of the image'. There is the implication of a secret, or mystery, beyond the door, only to be revealed by an initiation into 'montage'; that linking of the primitive with the transcendental, which Yampolsky explores here in his essay on mimesis, and which Eisenstein traced back to the origins of human society in *Non-Indifferent Nature*.[140] Nor is this the only drawing in which a whole philosophy is compressed: there is 'EX-TASIS' from Mexico; and the very last cycle, 'Les Dons', a *haiku*-like series about the ephemerality of nature and its 'gifts'.[141] The importance of these and other graphic works to any understanding of Eisenstein's distinctive synthesis of traditions and philosophies makes serious study of the drawings a high priority.

NOSTALGIA FOR THE FUTURE

Already in 1988, when the symposium which led to this book took place, the Soviet system that Eisenstein knew had changed beyond recognition. From the perspective of 1993, it has all but disappeared and there is a corresponding danger that the 'official' culture of the Soviet era will now be repudiated *en bloc* amid the massive waves of disillusion sweeping the former Soviet empire. Eisenstein will no doubt incur fresh charges of 'collaboration' with the tyranny which oppressed him and yet made possible his art; and yet it also seems likely that the impetus for a truly

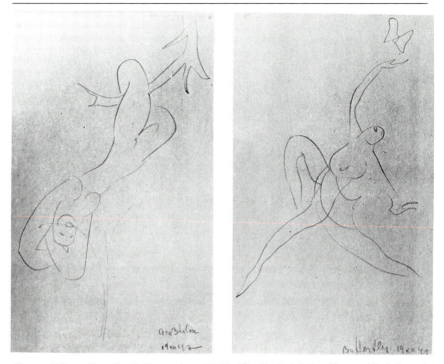

Figure 8 'Les Dons', 19 December 1947: 'Graßhalm' (*sic.*, 'Grass blade') and 'Butterfly'.

international study of his legacy, established during the transitional years of *glasnost*, will continue. The 1990 Venice Biennale conference expanded the range of approaches begun at Oxford and there are encouraging signs that scholarly relationships which cut across boundaries of continent, tradition and language will take Eisenstein studies into a new era of improved access to materials and franker debate about its many themes that have a resonance for both the present and the future.[142]

For the study of Eisenstein's work in all its interrelated forms cannot – *should* not – be a passive affair conducted exclusively within the academy. It offers a continuing challenge to received ideas in history, philosophy, politics and sexuality; and in an era suspicious of two-way traffic across the bridge between 'theory' and 'practice', it offers important models and insights. Not the least important aspect of the 1988 exhibition and conference in Britain was a parallel series of workshops for young people held in Oxford, which took Eisenstein's call to 'have the vision' as their motto. These and educational events held around the exhibition in London and Manchester confirmed Eisenstein's lasting importance as a pedagogic stimulus.[143]

He may also offer a new 'window on Russia', at a time when its cultural history stands in urgent need of reinterpretation.[144] The television images of Soviet statues toppling in August 1991 will have recalled for many most immediately the demolition of the tsar's statue in *October*, which inaugurates that film's elaborate deconstruction of the symbolism of power. Eisenstein was no simple apologist for Lenin or Stalin. Indeed the many accusations of heresy directed against him – first by his colleagues in the LEF group, later by Stalin's apparatchiks and posthumously by Western Marxists – are perhaps the surest proof of his essential originality and independence.

It was the Revolution that first freed him from the conformism of bourgeois culture, set to follow in his father's footsteps as an 'obedient little boy from Riga'. Then the liberated theatre of Proletkult and Meyerhold drew him to the Revolution, until film beckoned as a more efficient medium of propaganda. But although he initially identified cinema with the challenge of building communism – Dreiser found him in 1928 'more communistically convinced' than any other artist he met in the Soviet Union – it was in fact cinema that led him to the philosophy and history of art.[145] For in cinema he found – combined – a stage, a canvas and a laboratory beyond any artist's dreams. Henceforth, for him at least, theory and practice would be indissoluble, while the furtherance of the materialist dialectic would join with his personal vocation in a 'joyful science' suffused with the ecstasy of discovery and creation. Aumont has rightly termed this synthesis a 'theoretical *tour de force*', which also conscripted the Stalinist theme of 'unity' for Eisenstein's quite un-Stalinist purposes.[146] Like Galileo, he found an accommodation with absolutism uniquely appropriate to these times.

Certainly it goes against the grain of most contemporary readings of the Russian Revolution, which routinely trace a uniformly falling graph. As we survey its brightest talents exported, silenced, murdered or reduced to 'internal exile', the continuing commitment of a battered survivor is hard to credit. After the extirpation of the LEF-Constructivist movement which had most closely shared his hopes and values (even while criticising his experimental exuberance and refusal of purism), Eisenstein found himself increasingly isolated. One by one, he lost his mentors, colleagues and friends (they were often all three) – Bely, Mayakovsky, Vygotsky, Tretyakov, Babel, Malevich, Meyerhold. Yet he could write in 1940:

> The future does not need to be predicted.
> It's right here with us. Coming into being. Being born. Being made. It's presently a matter for our hands. But already it's starting to work in reverse. It's breaking into the sphere of relations. Problems of consciousness. Morals. Ethics. Activity. The superstructures are cracking. The new. The unprecedented. Classlessness is entering into them![147]

This could almost be by the 'futurian' poet Khlebnikov.[148] It echoes that moment when modernist revolt combined with revolutionary millenarian-ism to produce the clarion call of the early Soviet era. In doing so it recalls the earlier materialist utopianism of the 'god-builders' who, before Lenin's denunciation, had included Lunacharsky, Eisenstein's protector during the 1920s.[149] Nor is this incompatible with claiming Eisenstein as an heir to the Russian Symbolists who ushered in that uniquely mystical and moral Modernism that we still too often consider distinctively 'Soviet'. For above all Eisenstein's visionary zeal pays tribute to the essential syncretism of Russian culture, orientated towards the common good and the future.

It was this impulse, essentially humane and utopian, that led him along similar paths to those of Bakhtin and Tynyanov. This generation of com-munist scholars, *pace* Solzhenitsyn's scholar-convicts, did not disgrace the Russian intelligentsia.[150] Rather they kept its ideals alive in dark times, adding fresh insights to its already powerful analysis of the Western cultural tradition and, in the case of Eisenstein's *Ivan the Terrible*, creating an expression of the age as complex and resonant in its own terms as Pushkin's *Boris Godunov*.[151]

There can be little doubt that his work, grasped in its totality, will long outlive the collapse of the system that made it possible. Indeed, the continuing study of Eisenstein as an international and inter-disciplinary enterprise, together with his profound influence on succeeding generations of truly experimental film-makers, should serve as a beacon for the future that he could not predict but tirelessly worked to create out of his profound understanding of the past. As Samuel Palmer wrote of Blake, 'the Inter-preter':[152]

In him you saw at once the Maker, the Inventor; one of the few in any age . . .

Part I

Eisenstein studies today: text and context

Chapter 1

Arguments and ancestors

Naum Kleiman

I am quite sure that all Eisenstein enthusiasts could contribute to the subject that I address today. If this introduction is rather *pointilliste* in character, this is because my basic aim is to provoke thought. There has been a new impetus in Eisenstein studies and this is not only due to the anniversary of his 'ninetieth birthday'. There have been many changes in our world, many changes in our cinema and in the relationship between cinema and the other mass media as well.

Paradoxically, our image of Eisenstein is also changing all the time. The most positive aspect of this whole process is that he has not yet been canonised. We can still argue about him. Indeed he does not allow himself to be canonised. I would draw your attention to the ending of one of the chapters in his unfinished book of essays, *People from One Film*, which has as yet been translated into very few other languages.[1] Here he describes the group working on *Ivan the Terrible* and there is a passage about Esfir Tobak, who was helping him with the montage. It is called 'The Ant and the Grasshopper'. At the very end of this chapter Eisenstein makes a very curious remark. He recalls his theories, the declarations which had resounded over the years, and at the end he says that it never occurred to anyone to check whether the author of these statements actually followed his own theories.

Unfortunately we sometimes try to illustrate his theories too directly with examples from his films, or to understand his films as a direct realisation of his theories. But, as I am now beginning to understand, his practical work is on the one hand richer than his theory, while his theory is on the other hand so much richer than his body of work. They do not merely correspond: indeed sometimes they conflict with one another. Some of the ideas that he expressed as hypotheses are substantiated in his work, while others are not substantiated at all.

We should not lose sight of the fact that he worked over a span of twenty-five years and many changes occurred during that time. There were not only political and social changes in the Soviet Union. The first thing we must do is to dispose of the notion that Eisenstein followed closely these political and social changes or reacted to the pressure they put upon him in his working career. Of course they are of enormous significance: indeed we must make more of an effort to understand the context in which his work unfolded, because we just do not know enough about that period.

At the same time, however, there are many immanent processes, both in his development as an artist and as a theoretician which we must understand. Eisenstein referred again and again to the enormous influence upon him of Professor Sukhotsky, his teacher at the Institute of Civil Engineering in Petrograd. But we know very little about Sukhotsky, although he is one of the most interesting figures in Russian culture at the beginning of the twentieth century.[2] Sukhotsky was one of the first to grasp the importance of Eisenstein's theories and one of the first to understand the new study in physics of the infinitesimal and to explain its poetic significance. Eisenstein recalls that it was Sukhotsky who taught him the theory of the limits to which objects aspire. If we take this on trust from Eisenstein then we can see that many of these theoretical statements represent limits towards which his work aspires. But remember that in his *Memoirs* he was always referring to King Gillette and this idea that you have to make a half turn of the screwdriver back from the limit towards which you aspire when talking in terms of your own practice. It is this half turn backwards that gives you the whole range of stylistic and even individual variables. We have not studied this relationship between the limit and the concrete variable adequately. Let me give just a few examples.

One of the most frightening things that Eisenstein ever said in his arguments with Dziga Vertov was, 'It is not a "Cine-Eye" that we need but a "Cine-Fist"'.[3] This statement has given rise to a mass of speculation. When we were celebrating Eisenstein's anniversary, the philosopher Yuri Davydov gave a speech that was very critical of Eisenstein, arguing that he had been a kind of Stalinist who had wanted to take this 'cine-fist' and crush people's skulls with it, as distinct from Brecht who, by contrast, had stimulated independent thought. This image of the 'cine-fist' comes from Gorky's *Reminiscences of Lenin* where he recalls Lenin's remark that when you listen to Beethoven you feel like stroking people's heads when what you ought to be doing is thumping them with your fists. However, Eisenstein would say that he wanted to use this fist 'to plough over the audience's psyche'.[4]

Of course you can interpret that as an attempt to intrude violently on people's thinking but, if you look at it in the context of what he was writing at the time, you will understand what he is really saying. For instance, in his notebooks on Bekhterev, which have unfortunately not yet been published, he remarks that art must change the conditioned reflex that is provoked by the social context and, in particular, the audience must be diverted from reflex reactions of servility and terror.[5] The idea that people have not merely an instinct but also a psychological reflex towards fear and servility and that we must free them from both is a very important one, especially in the context of the situation in the Soviet Union at present. If you look at Eisenstein's work, that is the direction in which it is going, people ridding themselves of their automatic reaction of fear when they are faced with violence and terror.

From *The Strike* right through to *Ivan the Terrible* both the subject and the structure of the films can be seen as a kind of inoculation against this reflex reaction of panic and fear. Of course that raises the question of Eisenstein's so-called sadism: is he really a sadist? Perhaps, on the contrary he is trying to give us a kind of inoculation against sadism. I will come on to Eisenstein's personality later but it is already clear that the kind of brutality that appears in his work had nothing to do with any kind of sadism *per se*. That is one example of where we have to re-examine our established views. Let me give you another: Eisenstein's ideas on acting in cinema.

Eisenstein made many statements criticising the so-called 'academic' acting school and it is known how much he built on 'types' in cinema, in both his films and his theoretical teachings. In actual fact the entire Proletkult collective acted in *The Strike*. In *The Battleship Potemkin* a few Proletkult actors were joined by more from the Odessa actors' union. Almost all the characters in the Odessa Steps sequence are actors. In *October* many of the actors came from the Leningrad union. Even the procession with the cross in *The General Line* was made with actors from *October* because both films were made at the same time. There are far more actual actors than 'types'. So we have to understand how he worked with actors as 'types' and with his 'types' as actors.

Let me give another example to illustrate this relationship between theory and practice. His first article, 'The Eighth Art', written with Yutkevich, is very much a criticism of German Expressionism and he criticised it again later, but once more the situation is also more complex.[6] The impact of Expressionism on *Ivan the Terrible* has already been researched.[7] The word *vyrazitel'nost'* (expressiveness) was one of Eisenstein's favourite words. We have discovered a note which again has unfortunately not yet been published but is certainly worth summarising here. It is the only note that Eisenstein made while editing *The Battleship Potemkin*. The provisional title is 'Acting with Objects and Acting through Objects': it is incomplete but he makes a very interesting observation that, whereas in theatre you have acting *with* an object, in cinema you have acting *through* an object.[8] In *Potemkin* he gives the name 'everyday Expressionism' (*bytovoi ekspressionizm*) to the method in which the external aspect of the object is unaltered but various expressive schemas are deployed to place the object in different contexts. This 'everyday Expressionism' is partly a contrast to, and partly a continuation of the object. It is unusual for Eisenstein but it does make us understand all his statements much more clearly.

The next matter that I want to raise is the context of Eisenstein, which is really much broader than we have ever suspected. Take the theory of influence: *who* influenced *whom*? When we are looking for influences we search for similarities and traces. But I should like to propose a somewhat different model here. There are a number of well-known photographs from La Sarraz of Eisenstein as Don Quixote, sitting on a horse and holding a camera and a pike in his hand. He is comparing himself to Don Quixote. I believe we can make an analogy here with Pushkin who always had the image at the back of his mind of himself as a knight in shining armour at a tournament. This is important because a knight is prepared to take up a challenge and fight in a tournament. So, when we talk about the Byronic influence in Pushkin I think it is more a question of Pushkin being prepared to take up the Byronic challenge, to 'fight it out' with Byron, rather than just passively accepting Byron's influence. The same is true of the relationship between Pushkin and his teacher Zhukovsky or his friend Vyazemsky.

Eisenstein felt as if he were constantly engaged in a tournament, and of course the medieval ideal was that the tournament was not a war but a friendly contest. This started with his 'tournament' with Meyerhold, which led to such battles as the one that raged around the production of *Puss in Boots*.[9] One of Eisenstein's favourite expressions was 'Me too', but it is not just a question of 'Me too' because his other favourite expression was 'That's wrong'.[10] This is dialectics in the classical sense of the word, the possibility of fighting while seeing the other side of the question as well. So when we look at the context of who his teachers were, who his friends were, we can see how much broader it is than we are used to thinking. The exhibition showed his fascination with Constructivism and Cubism, how important these were for him, for instance in his drawings for Picasso's 'Parade'. At the same time, we must remember that he was a child of Symbolism, the Russian Symbolism of Blok, Bely and Ivanov, and the echoes of this can be traced right through to the end of his life. For instance, there was intended to be an epilogue to *Alexander Nevsky*, which was an integral part of the film. Unfortunately Stalin's personal censorship excised the death of Alexander Nevsky from the film but the finale, the victory over the Tartars at Kulikovo Polye, is taken directly from Blok.[11] Throughout Eisenstein's life we can find both conscious and unconscious elements of the epoch that formed him and from which he emerged. This is also true of Nikolai Evreinov, the writer, director and theorist of theatre.[12] We must remember Evreinov's influence when we talk about Joyce and 'inner monologue' and the influence that all that had on Eisenstein.

But there are even more unexpected contexts for Eisenstein: there is, for instance, the so-called commercial cinema. Until now we have underestimated the influence of such hits as *The Exploits of Elaine*, *The Grey*

Figure 9 Eisenstein as Don Quixote defending independent film against commercial cinema at the International Congress of Independent Cinema, La Sarraz, September 1929.

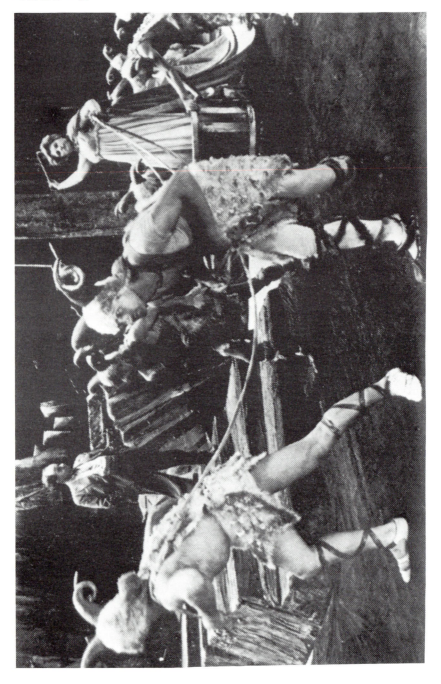

Shadow and *Fantômas*, but they were very important.[13] Alan Upchurch was looking at the cover of the first edition of the *Fantômas* book, recalling the scene in Feuillade's film in which the criminal world is peeping out of a barrel, and he immediately thought of that scene in *The Strike* where the strikers peep out of a barrel![14] These 'tournaments', or tunnels, that link the cultures of different countries are very important for our understanding of Eisenstein. If one remembers the scene in the Valley of Death at the end of *Greed*, Eisenstein's scenario for *Sutter's Gold* begins with that same scene.[15] This is no coincidence: it is just a continuation and a re-examination of the same phenomenon from another country and another historical context. Or take a famous case like that of *Chapayev*.[16] In the 1930s it was the accepted view that the 'psychological attack' of *Chapayev* exceeded that of the Odessa Steps sequence. So then Eisenstein depicted an attack in *Alexander Nevsky* to demonstrate to his students just how a psychological attack *could* be made. But he went further than this in jousting with his students who were beginning to turn away from him. There is a scene in *Chapayev* where potatoes are used to show where the commander should be and a scene in *Ivan the Terrible* where, in response to the tragic Vladimir Staritsky, Ivan says 'The Tsar must always be in front!' I think that this is an answer, not only to *Chapayev*, but also to his own pupils as to where the leader should be. It is also, apart from anything else, a profoundly autobiographical moment.

I have to leave out so many things here but I feel I must say something about what we might call his 'ancestors', rather than his immediate prede-cessors or advisers. We already have very stereotyped views about the importance of Zola, Leonardo da Vinci and so on. But why do we pay so little attention to Ben Jonson whom Eisenstein regarded as his teacher? Jonson's theory of humour and his linear dramaturgical composition were very important to Eisenstein. We also completely ignore the influence of the medieval mystery plays. We in Moscow have just finished reconstructing Eisenstein's article on Gogol and the language of cinema, which is a sort of complement to his Pushkin articles. Eisenstein is saying that Gogol is his parent as well as Pushkin. One thing that he does not mention in that article but which is perfectly clear is that the image that he used in *Bezhin Meadow* when Stepok, who is already mortally wounded, falls from a height, has three stages, three separate shots, and it transpires that this is a direct reference to a scene in Gogol's *Taras Bulba*, because there is a passage in which Eisenstein discusses the moment when the father shoots the son and the son falls like a sheaf of wheat that has been cut. If you think of the biblical imagery in *Bezhin Meadow*, of the image of wheat falling on the ground, you can see how important this is.

Another very important factor is Eisenstein's own personality, which we need to discern more clearly now. There used to be just the legends that surrounded him in the 1930s but now new legends are appearing. I suppose it is natural that any great artist has legends growing up around him. For instance the image now emerging is of Eisenstein the conformist, the faithful student, who only went beyond the bounds of the orders that were issued to him because he was a genius. The evidence cited for this is his decision to produce *Die Walküre*.[17] However it is not the case that he agreed to produce *Die Walküre* because he was afraid. In fact we now know a lot more about the production, as a result of new research on it. I have myself noticed how gingerly we approach a subject which seems to us to be ethically ambiguous! But when we grasped the nettle and opened up the files on *Die Walküre* we found that it was an anti-fascist treatment of a subject that the fascists regarded as fascist in itself. It was compassion and humanity that shone out from Eisenstein's interpretation. You can imagine that the theme of compassion was not exactly the top priority at the end of the 1930s.

There are many prejudices that we have to shed when we approach his work and there are whole fields that we have not even begun to touch. We know very little about Eisenstein's theatre work and I welcome Robert Leach's contribution on this subject.[18] The subject of Eisenstein's ethics has also suddenly emerged. The fact that ethics is a very ambiguous word in itself is important to our work. We must include it alongside our purely cinematic research. His teaching work is also a very important part of our research.

We can see from all this how much more publishing lies ahead. In the first instance that is *our* responsibility. It is our responsibility and our fault in the Soviet Union that so little of Eisenstein's work is being published and so slowly. I think that the most important things we should be preparing for publication now are his diaries and also the definitive text of *Non-Indifferent Nature*[19] and the *Method* which is something that is beginning to take shape. The twelve volumes that we hope to publish in the Soviet Union will not cover everything but at least they will provide us with a basis on which we can hope to build.[20]

The time has now come for us all to work together. Perhaps the time has also come for a dream to come true and for us to set up an International Eisenstein Society. I should like to conclude by mentioning the person who did more than anyone else to promote the understanding of Eisenstein, Jay Leyda. He dreamed of setting up such a Society and he was the first to make a contribution to it. I should like you to mark his memory.[21]

Translated from the Russian by Richard Taylor

Chapter 2

Jay Leyda and *Bezhin Meadow*

David Stirk and Elena Pinto Simon

Jay Leyda's death on 15 February 1988 ended a remarkable career that
managed, over the course of six decades, to encompass an astonishing
range of interests. Bridging East and West in a manner unique for an
American scholar, his life was deeply interwoven with the great historical
changes of this century.[1] Now that Leyda's resolute modesty can no longer
intervene, it is important to reflect upon and re-evaluate one of the most
important aspects of his contribution: his work as a Soviet film historian
and Eisenstein scholar. This chapter might be considered as such an act of
reflection and re-evaluation, informed by an investigation into the biographical, historical and political context of his work.[2] Interest in Leyda's
Eisenstein scholarship is prompted in this case not only by a real sense of
loss felt in his absence, but also by the important juncture scholars now
face in Soviet film historiography, especially in the United States.[3]

We have decided to look at one episode from Leyda's continually
recurring interest in the concept of 'Eisenstein at work': his participation in
the filming of the lost film *Bezhin Meadow* (1935–7), and his subsequent
writing about the experience.[4] As still photographer and production historian on this shoot, Leyda produced a substantial body of images as well as a
production diary. Our intention here, in the light of recent biographical
research, is to contextualise these images and to refer to the historiographical issues raised by the different manifestations of his written documentation. In doing so, we have two purposes in mind: to contribute towards
an increased understanding of Eisenstein and *Bezhin Meadow*, and to
acknowledge Leyda's active role in the construction of this understanding.

I

Jay Leyda grew up in an industrial town in the middle of America. He once
admitted that the only exciting thing about that town he could remember
from his childhood was 'cheering the troops as they went off to the great
War across an ocean'. As a student in a very conventional American high
school, he 'learned to take photographs and daydream about making

films'. 'I heard that Russia had a film school and made films', he once said, 'but these were never shown in Dayton, Ohio.' His life changed forever when he arrived in New York City late in 1929, at the age of 19, to serve as Ralph Steiner's darkroom assistant. Here he received his first exposure to the Soviet cinema, an experience that would determine his life's work.[5]

In those days, before an academy existed to certify experts in film, there were few limits to the range of Leyda's interests. He immersed himself in the extraordinarily rich cultural scene of New York in the early 1930s. He wrote poems and short stories for the 'little magazines', while he assisted Steiner with studio and darkroom work, perfecting his craftsmanship in both photography and film along the way.[6] Leyda eked out an existence during these depression years by holding down a bewildering variety of jobs: he sold projectors on the boardwalk at Atlantic City, selected sound recordings for silent film screenings in the Bronx (where he saw his first Eisenstein), tried his hand at fashion photography and carried out weekly portrait assignments for a short-lived arts journal.[7] All the while he threw himself into the world of New York's dance, music, theatre, museums and galleries, and even visited the grand old man of New York Modernism – Alfred Steiglitz.

Leyda found himself drawn toward two distinct circles of artists and intellectuals. One was the group of fine art photographers, aspiring film-makers and patrons who gathered around Julien Levy's extraordinary salon and gallery on Fifty-Seventh Street. Here he was befriended by Walker Evans, Paul Strand and Lincoln Kirstein, all central figures in the legacy of American Modernism.[8] The second circle reflected Leyda's emerging political consciousness and included several members of the New York Workers' Film and Photo League: Leo Hurwitz, Sam Brody, Leo Seltzer, Irving Lerner and Ben Maddow. These young photographers and film-makers had an explicitly political agenda: the production of agitational newsreels and photographs aligned with working-class concerns, depicting the ravages of the economic class war.[9] Moving back and forth between the two circles, Leyda was clearly interested in radical aesthetics *and* radical politics, and the cultural scene in New York at the time resonated with both.

The convergence of art and politics during Leyda's early years in New York reached its logical culmination in a desire to make films himself. Around this time, the introduction of 16mm film-making as a viable option had changed many of the rules governing production and distribution. The use of 16mm meant not just increased accessibility to equipment, but also a chance to produce independent films with a social message, capable of reaching a wide audience outside the Hollywood system of distribution. Film, more than any other art-form, came to be seen as a potential instrument of social change. In this context, Soviet films of the 1920s provided concrete evidence of the kind of cinema rendered possible by socialist revolution and thus assumed supreme importance for radical film-makers in America. Eisenstein exerted a particularly profound influence, made even more immediate by his trip to America and visit to New York. When he gave a lecture at Columbia University in 1931, Leyda, along with many of New York's left film community, was in attendance.

The story of how Leyda came to make his first film is revealing, in that it prefigures the important role played by chance in his life. As a young boy in Dayton, he had been allowed to spend any extra money earned from after-school jobs on subscriptions to avant-garde magazines and inexpensive art objects. In this way he came to possess an old wooden figure from a downtown Dayton junk shop, purchased for ten or fifteen dollars. It turned out to be a statue of Henry Ward Beecher and an important piece of American folk art. In 1931 he sold it to a representative of Abby Aldrich Rockefeller, who was then setting up her folk museum. With this substantial sum of money he purchased an Eyemo camera and made *A Bronx Morning*, a beautiful 'city symphony' film showing a variety of avant-garde influences. He took this film to Moscow, after his acceptance by G.I.K., then the only film school in the world.[10]

As the only American at the school, Leyda began his studies with trepidation, and only a month of Russian language study. Originally accepted for the cinematographer's course, he very much wanted to enroll instead in Eisenstein's directing course. In his Moscow diary for 8 October 1933 Leyda notes that he had already shown his film to a few people in Moscow. When it was suggested that the film be shown to Eisenstein as a way into the course, Leyda was at first hesitant, but then agreed. 'OK', he writes in the diary, 'let's have it over with.'[11]

His first introduction to Eisenstein had been a shaky one, but on 9 October 1933 he notes in the diary that 'Eisenstein seems to feel better towards this Leyda upstart, and is going to look at my film tomorrow at 3.30. So 3.30 tomorrow will mark a beginning or an end.' Although Eisenstein had been told in advance that the film was not interesting by the only other English-speaking student, Herbert Marshall, the screening was a success, resulting in Leyda's acceptance into the directing course. Both Eisenstein and Dziga Vertov were present, and both claimed the film bore their influence, as indeed it does. Leyda's diary goes on to note, 'so now [Eisenstein] has changed his whole attitude towards me and things are looking up generally'.[12]

It should not be overlooked that Leyda continued to correspond, throughout his three years in the Soviet Union, with both circles of New York artists and intellectuals mentioned above. Today these letters constitute a remarkable record of American responses to Soviet culture, and demonstrate the centrality of Soviet art and politics for the American left during the mid-1930s. The list of Leyda's correspondents includes several of the most important figures in socially committed American art of the period: Harold Clurman, Lee Strasberg, Joseph Losey, Ralph Steiner, Aaron Copland, Alfred Barr, Iris Barry, Lincoln Kirstein and Walker Evans, among others.[13] Leyda was a vital link for this group, disseminating news from the front on a wide variety of cultural topics. He was particularly important in relation to theatre, and edited two special magazine issues on Soviet theatre from Moscow.[14]

Leyda enrolled at the state film school in Moscow just as the Workers' Film and Photo League was attempting to set up its own course of film instruction in New York. The New York school, which never really materialised, was a response to a growing need for institutional support for aspiring film-makers on the American left. Leyda's activities, especially his studies with Eisenstein, were understandably of great importance to those interested in becoming film-makers themselves.[15] Walker Evans summarised the feelings of the New York circle in a letter dated 22 November 1933: 'How I wish there could be a film school here. Could you tell me how the Moscow one works in some detail? Who teaches, and what?'[16]

By the summer of 1934, the rules governing foreign students at G.I.K changed and Leyda found himself scrambling for a summer job. In a letter of application, he expressed some dissatisfaction with his lack of production activity: 'I will be glad for any practical work near a film camera again, as nine months of talk minus practice is too much talk and too little practice.' He eventually received an assignment on Vertov's crew, making a film for Intourist about Leningrad. However, he soon became disenchanted with the work, going so far as to draft a letter to Vertov, who was not with the crew, in which he outlined everything wrong with the shoot. He later assisted Joris Ivens during the same summer on the realisation of a Russian version of Ivens's *Borinage*, a 1932 film about Belgian coal workers, made with Henri Storck. He also helped Ivens shoot additional footage in the recently opened Moscow subway.[17]

Leyda's year of study with Eisenstein and his brief production experience prepared him for what was undoubtedly his most important and formative experience in the Soviet Union: participation in the *Bezhin Meadow* shoot. His indefatigable spirit and persistence in the face of obstacles, qualities characteristic of his later academic career, are revealed in a letter to Eisenstein applying for the position:

Last summer, you and Pera and I considered the possibilities and advantage of my joining the E. group as a photographer. To this day, I am not sure whether an uninterested factory [studio] or the postponement of the expedition was the main obstacle to this plan. Anyway, it was dropped. But as soon as I read the announcement of your work on a new film, I remembered this prospect of last summer, and compared my present parched prospects to the usefulness and excitement of working in your group, particularly working in such a position where I could observe each moment of work from the film's beginning to its completion. THEN I would have something to take back to the Film & Photo League – participation in the practical application of the theories contained in your lectures. I would have Soviet experience to take back with me – real knowledge of Soviet life that I cannot get in our present isolated 'foreign' position.

As for photography, I know that I have taken good photos in the past, and if my job is to take photos, the discipline will jolt me out of this year and a half of frightened modesty, and I will give you photos as good as any still photographer in Potilikha – (or better).

Now the Yes-Or-No rests in your hands. Once the factory gives its OK, I am ready to start straight off to work. Pera says that very soon (in about two weeks) you will look at locations. This will need a photographer, and I hope that I may start work with your group at this point.

Well, what do you say?[18]

Eisenstein accepted the proposal and Leyda was actively involved on the *Bezhin Meadow* production as apprentice director for most of 1935. One of four apprentices selected from Eisenstein's directing class, he assisted in the casting, took still photographs both on location and in the studio, and kept a diary as a means of documenting the progress of the shoot. The experience was to have a profound and decisive impact on the future course of his career.

II

The fact that Eisenstein assigned one of his apprentice directors to keep a visual and written record of the production is an indication of his archival sensibility. The conception of the documentary assignment also demonstrates the extent to which he was fully aware of the historical importance of his film, as well as of its potential impermanence as a completed work of art. Perhaps for the same reasons, Eisenstein saved individual frames of each edited shot, thereby providing the basis for a reconstruction of the film in still images by Kleiman and Yutkevich in 1964. With remarkable historical foresight, the director thus made certain that *Bezhin Meadow* would somehow survive for future generations.[19]

Eisenstein gave Leyda very specific instructions when it came to the actual photography: cover the shoot from as many angles as possible, and avoid duplicating Tisse's frame compositions. He was issued a 35mm Leica by Mosfilm studios, marking the first and only time he worked with this format. The versatility of the Leica accounts for the roving, all-encompassing nature of Leyda's photographs, an indication that he must have been a constantly moving presence around the film camera. This freedom of movement was something entirely new and undoubtedly exciting for Leyda, as he had previously worked only with bulky and static 4×5 and 8×10 view cameras for his portraits.

The photographs provide a remarkable record of most of the shooting of the first version of *Bezhin Meadow*. After covering the filming on location in the Ukraine and in the Moscow studio, Leyda was forced to give up his duties late in 1935, after Eisenstein's illness brought shooting to a halt. Although he missed the controversial church sequence and the subsequent revision and reshooting of the script (production continued until March 1937), the importance of his photographic documentation should not be underestimated. It constitutes the most complete visual account in existence of Eisenstein at work on a single project. More importantly, it provides much-needed insight into Eisenstein's intentions for *Bezhin Meadow*, intentions that unfortunately remain shrouded in mystery, myth and controversy.

Some of the most illuminating images of the documentation are those of Eisenstein working with actors. They hint at the difficult directorial task he faced on this film, namely that of synthesising a number of acting methods, covering a spectrum of his stylistic influences and allegiances. They hint as well at the ways in which Eisenstein was moving to encompass the doctrines of Socialist Realism within his own aesthetic system.

The mix of seemingly contradictory performance styles would eventually prove to be one of the principal causes of the film's political problems. It was charged that the acting was too individualised and psychologised (resulting in an atypical father–son relationship) and at the same time too mythic and iconographic (resulting in an interpretation of the father as Pan and the son as the Christ child).[20] Both of these tendencies posed problems for the socialist realist aesthetic, and both were 'corrected' in the second version of the script.

Three different traditions are legible in the studio production stills. We see Eisenstein at work on his own typage system, which he had employed with great success in the silent films of the 1920s. A number of the actors for *Bezhin Meadow* were without previous training or experience, selected (after exhaustive searches) precisely for their look. These included the protagonist, Viktor Kartashov (Stepok), as well as the grandmother, who was found at an institute for aged working women. Elisaveta Teleshova (the head of the collective), on the other hand, was an accomplished stage actress and a director with the Moscow Art Theatre, while Boris Zakhava (the father) was trained in the Meyerhold school. Both were well-known figures in the world of Moscow theatre, although they represented what in the 1920s constituted radically opposed methods: the naturalism of Stanislavsky and the experimental biomechanics of Meyerhold.[21]

Eisenstein's attempt to wed these latter two styles in this, his first sound film, is embodied in a quite literal manner by his choice of Nikolai Garin, an actor from the Meyerhold school, to play the role of Teleshova's

Figures 11 and 12 Eisenstein directing two of his 'typage' discoveries for *Bezhin Meadow*: Vitya Kartashov as Stepok (*top*) and a recruit from the institute for aged working women as his grandmother.

Figure 13 Tisse changing lenses during the filming of *Bezhin Meadow*.

husband. While it is interesting to note this evidence of creative synthesis, it should not be overlooked that the Stanislavsky school would eventually triumph. As noted above, Zakhava's performance was roundly condemned and excised from the film, while Teleshova went on to work with Eisenstein on *Alexander Nevsky*.

And how did Eisenstein plan to use the actor's voice in his first sound film? Leyda gives us one of the most practical answers to this crucial but unanswerable question in his account of the importance of the *monologue* in the acted scenes. He explains how emotion was to be conveyed by the *silence* of Stepok in the face of his father's increasingly threatening speech.[22]

Leyda's stills, understandably, provide some of the best documentation available on the nature of the Eisenstein–Tisse working relationship. In an unpublished essay written after observing this collaboration, Leyda notes that they were both 'inventors and problem solvers, who approached difficulties with relish'. Several of the photographs show Tisse choosing the appropriate lens and Eisenstein and Tisse together framing the shot. Leyda notes Tisse's careful precision in the choice of lenses and the relation of particular focal lengths to the emotional and psychological weight of a scene. He noted: 'It was Tisse's great gift to build climaxes without drawing the spectator's attention to the camera equipment. This absence of showy photography is one of the clearest indications of integrated photography and direction.'[23]

Besides their historical value, however, Leyda's stills are also of great interest in a purely formal sense. In his very first production photographs, taken in a sun-dappled apple orchard outside Moscow in May 1935, he successfully captured the quality of light Eisenstein himself sought to record in the prologue to the film, meant as a lyrical evocation of Turgenev's prose.[24] The conscious reference to nineteenth-century Romanticism and Impressionism in these photographs reveals the extent to which Leyda was consciously attempting to infuse his own images with Eisenstein's directorial intentions. Furthermore, the marked tendency to frame compositions from oblique and overhead angles is a reminder of the important influence of the Constructivists, and specifically Rodchenko's photography, on Leyda's work.[25] Finally, in several instances Leyda shot frames in quick succession, searching for his own version of 'the decisive moment'. One might recall here the importance of Cartier-Bresson's early Leica photography to the Workers' Film and Photo League, and that he, along with Leyda, exhibited work at the Julien Levy Gallery in 1932–3.[26]

Looking at Leyda's *Bezhin Meadow* photographs today one detects a real tension between the formal aspects of the composition of elements within the frame and the more utilitarian function of the photograph as a piece of history, as a record or document of an important event. The tension results, perhaps, from Leyda's simultaneous absorption of two distinct yet related currents in the early 1930s: the aesthetics of the art photography movement and the radical politics of the Workers' Film and Photo League. The photographs, therefore, are more than illuminations of Eisenstein and *Bezhin Meadow*: they refer back to Leyda's brief career as a New York photographer and they refer forward to his future success as a film historian and Eisenstein scholar. In this sense, the experience of working on the film for eight months of 1935 marks a fundamental transition in his work and in his life.

III

In addition to his job as still photographer on *Bezhin Meadow*, Leyda kept a production diary between May and October of 1935, documenting and commenting upon the progress of the shoot. Although the diary manuscript appears lost (apparently having been misplaced by a publisher), a partial reconstruction from various appearances in print is possible. Excerpts from the diary and essays based upon it have appeared in many different contexts over the subsequent fifty years.

The reconstruction raises a number of interesting historiographical questions, for it is clear that Leyda's editing of the diary changed significantly over time. Some sections first appeared in print in 1936, in an article written from the Soviet Union, prior to the halt in the film's production. A second, longer essay, which remained unpublished, was written at around the same time, prior to Leyda's departure from Moscow in July of 1936. Extended excerpts from this were used by Marie Seton in her 1952 Eisenstein biography and Leyda used edited selections himself from 1959 onwards in books and articles. When 'the diary' is viewed historically patterns begin to emerge: it becomes clear that the different ends to which Leyda employed the text over a fifty-year period corresponded with different rehabilitations of Eisenstein and *Bezhin Meadow*, which in turn corresponded with alternations in Western, and specifically US, attitude towards the Soviet Union since the mid-1930s.[27]

In an historiographical sense, Leyda's written record and commentary on the *Bezhin Meadow* affair becomes an opening through which it is possible to re-evaluate the larger question of the nature of his contribution to Eisenstein scholarship. The politics embedded within this publishing history point toward the need to historicise our understanding of Leyda, not only in relation to Eisenstein, but also in relation to Soviet film scholarship in general.

To begin with, we must locate his position within the bitter and divisive conflicts taking place on the American left in the late 1930s. News of Stalin's purges and the Moscow show trials had accelerated an already deepening split between Trotskyists on one side and members of the American Communist Party and intellectual fellow-travellers on the other.[28]

Against this background, changes in the form and content of Soviet film became a focal point for an ideologically charged debate over the aesthetics of Socialist Realism and the politics of popular culture. The wider implication of this debate in relation to modernist art and literature brought into prominence a group of anti-Stalinist intellectuals at the *Partisan Review*.[29] Here, in 1938, the critic Dwight Macdonald published his 'History of the Soviet Cinema', which concluded with a polemical denunciation of production in the 1930s.[30]

Leyda, meanwhile, had returned to New York in 1936 to assume a position as assistant film curator at the Museum of Modern Art. He began his own history of the Russian and Soviet film, eventually published in 1960 as *Kino*, during his years at the museum. At the same time, he continued his political film-making activity, working as an editor on several Frontier Films productions.[31] He also corresponded regularly with Eisenstein and late in the decade had already started the task of translating and editing what would become Eisenstein's first volume of essays to appear anywhere, *Film Sense*, published in 1942.

As might be expected, Leyda's response to Macdonald's articles provides a fascinating glimpse of the politics and personalities involved in the debate. When Macdonald was preparing his article, he sent the manuscript to both Leyda and Seymour Stern, an anti-Stalinist critic to Macdonald's right, for 'possible criticism and correction'. Leyda's answer was printed in the same issue of *Partisan Review* as the article itself and reads, in part:

> My only criticism that you may care to hear is that your article exhibits its motives too clearly. I would prefer to think that the errors, in premise and detail, are unconscious, but the distortion of fact and quotation are too obviously channeled towards some childishly destructive purpose.
>
> Forgive me if I have been too general in my comments, but I did not feel that you either needed or wanted them.

Macdonald printed this response along with a lengthy and highly favourable letter from Stern. Furthermore, under the text of Leyda's succinct reply, he added the following note:

> On receiving this extraordinary letter, I at once called up Mr Leyda to make it clear that I both needed and wanted his specific comments. As a result, we ate a most friendly lunch together, in the course of which it became clear that we disagreed profoundly as to both the aesthetic and political nature of the recent Soviet cinema, and that this disagreement was the basis for Mr Leyda's letter.[32]

The exchange calls attention to the fact that tracking the trajectory of American response to Soviet film is a crucial element in understanding Leyda's work. Although Macdonald later qualified the monolithic conception of the Soviet film industry expressed in his original *Partisan Review* articles, his viewpoint remained the dominant model, especially after the revolutionary socialism of the anti-Stalinist left evolved into reactionary anti-Communism after 1945.

In the ideology responsible for this conception it is possible to locate the reasons why Leyda's *Kino*, begun in the late 1930s, remained unpublished until 1960, and even then was turned down by American publishers. It is important to note here as well that the conflict embodied in this brief encounter with Macdonald also had important personal consequences for Leyda: it initiated a series of reactionary attacks on his work by Seymour Stern in *The New Leader*, leading to his forced resignation from the Museum of Modern Art in the Spring of 1940.[33]

What the entire episode also suggests, in a much broader context, is that the complexity and contradictions of Leyda's defence of Soviet film in the late 1930s reflected many similar contradictions encountered in Eisenstein's work during the same period. Embracing these contradictions as an opportunity for historicising Leyda's contribution seems particularly important as we seek a dynamic, rather than a static understanding of his scholarship.

Chapter 3

Eisenstein's early films abroad[1]

Kristin Thompson

INTRODUCTION

The circulation of Eisenstein's early films outside the Soviet Union is an important issue for at least two reasons. First, we would like to be able to gauge the conditions which allowed his films to influence other film-makers. Second, the success that greeted *Potemkin* in particular seems to have had a significant impact on Soviet production practice, and almost certainly it made the radical montage style more acceptable to officials there.

I shall concentrate here on the 1920s, and particularly on *Potemkin*'s impact in Germany and the USA; these were the most important foreign markets in which Eisenstein's films were given relatively successful commercial releases, and in both cases *Potemkin* paved the way for subsequent imports of Soviet films.

The standard account of *Potemkin*'s early career claims that only after the film became an enormous hit in Berlin did Soviet audiences become interested in it.[2] One thing I hope to do here is put its German success into some perspective and briefly suggest what impact it may have had on Soviet film-making policy. In looking at *Potemkin*'s American career, historians have concentrated on the New York première and the film's censorship problems. I shall try to flesh out such accounts by looking at how the film entered the growing art cinema market in America and played successfully in smaller American cities. Finally, I shall conclude with a very brief set of examples suggesting that Eisenstein's early films quickly became classics, being revived in a variety of situations, running from art cinemas to 16mm screenings by leftist workers' groups.

My focus is thus selective, but I hope to suggest at least one general conceptual point. From our modern perspective, historians often tend to create a split between commercial films and avant-garde films, with the assumption that avant-garde films tend not to be popular successes. Yet the 1920s was a decade during which the alternative institutions of the art cinema were just beginning to be created. To a surprising degree,

Figure 14 The business of propaganda: a claim that 300,000 spectators had seen *Potemkin* at the Artistic cinema (recently renamed the 1st Goskino) by the fourth week of its run.

stylistically radical films made in France, Germany, the Soviet Union and other countries were produced, distributed and exhibited successfully within existing commercial cinema institutions. Eisenstein's films demonstrate how the Soviet cinema was seen abroad in a variety of institutional situations.

BIG BOX-OFFICE IN GERMANY

Of all major foreign markets, Germany was the most sympathetic to Soviet films, and it provided the conduit through which many such films passed to other countries. *Potemkin* was far more successful in Germany than in any other foreign market, and it was the one Soviet film which prepared the way for exports.

Prior to *Potemkin*'s Berlin première in April 1926, most Soviet films had failed to penetrate the German market. In mid-1922, one of the famine documentaries was shown, being reportedly the first Soviet film to appear in Germany.[3] *Father Sergius* showed in early 1923, but the first Soviet film to achieve commercial success in Germany was *Polikushka*, in March of that year.[4] *Polikushka* was released by Germany's leading film company, UFA, and the film's popularity was apparently due primarily to the performance of its star, Ivan Moskvin.

Polikushka did not, however, create a general interest in Soviet films in Germany. Other Soviet films were released over the next two years, without notable success. These included *The Palace and the Fortress*, *The Cigarette Girl from Mosselprom*, *Aelita* and *The Station Master*. Although these were trade-shown in Berlin, only *The Station Master* seems to have had any commercial distribution, probably due mainly to Moskvin's continued popularity.[5]

Potemkin's spectacular career in Germany changed the situation considerably. The film's initial censorship difficulties in late March and early April of 1926 are familiar enough not to need outlining here. With cuts totalling about one hundred feet, the film was passed for public exhibition on April 10.[6] It premièred on 29 April at the Apollo Theatre in Berlin and met with unprecedented success. By mid-May the film was in general release and played all over Berlin, repeating its initial success and selling out consistently.[7] A description from the Berlin correspondent of the Parisian arts journal *Comœdia* suggests how intense *Potemkin*'s impact was on the intelligentsia:

> It is no exaggeration to say that over the last three weeks, the Russian film *Battleship Potemkin* has revolutionized Berlin. Every stranger who disembarks and asks what there is to see in the capital of the Reich is invariably told: 'Go see *Battleship Potemkin*.' Nothing else is discussed in the salons. In the course of the season which is ending, not a single

film, not a single play has approached the success of this Bolshevik propaganda film, which is showing simultaneously in twenty-two cinemas in Berlin.[8]

To put this statement in context, the total number of cinemas in greater Berlin in 1925 was reported in one source as 342 and in another as 382.[9] In the provinces, *Potemkin* repeated its initial success, with sold-out houses in Frankfurt, Mannheim, Dresden, Dusseldorf, Hamburg and other German cities.[10]

The question remains as to how big *Potemkin*'s German success really was and how it affected Soviet production and export. There are indications that *Potemkin* was an enormously popular film in Germany, perhaps even the top box-office hit of the 1925–6 season. Heinrich Fraenkel, the German correspondent for *The Bioscope*, reported in July that *Potemkin* had 'achieved by far the biggest box-office success of the last season in Germany'.[11] Other sources support this claim that *Potemkin* was the top grosser of the German season, which would have lasted from September 1925 to May 1926. An article in *Comœdia*, published in August 1927, summarised the past two seasons in Berlin:

Last summer, the cinematographic season in Berlin ended with the triumphant success of a Russian film, *Battleship Potemkin*. Several weeks later, the next season began with the triumph of an American film, *Ben Hur*. No German film has attained anything like the success of these two foreign works.[12]

Prometheus, *Potemkin*'s German distributor, ran an advertisement for its Soviet releases for the 1926–7 season, proclaiming: 'We brought you the greatest box-office hit of the past year, *Battleship Potemkin*.'[13] Difficult though it is to imagine from a modern perspective that *Potemkin* could be a hit comparable to *Ben Hur*, it would seem that this was the case in Germany at least.

The film's German success quickly led to sales in other foreign countries. As of 1 July, the Soviet Trade Delegation in Berlin reported that *Potemkin* had already made $20,000 for Goskino within Germany. Deals had been made with other foreign countries, guaranteeing the following minimum fees: Austria, $2,500, Czechoslovakia, $3,500, Scandinavia, $4,000, the UK, $16,000.[14] By the autumn of 1927, *Potemkin* had reportedly been sold to thirty-six different countries, a record second only to that of *The Station Master*, with thirty-seven.[15] By spring 1928, Eisenstein's film had slipped to fourth place among Soviet exports, with sales to thirty-eight countries.[16]

The question remains as to what these figures imply about *Potemkin*'s actual success and its impact on Soviet film policy. I would like to make a few suggestions on these topics, though these must necessarily be very tentative and speculative. If we assume that *Potemkin* sold to nearly forty foreign countries, and that a conservative estimate of the average price for the distribution rights would be around $3,000 per country, it seems possible that the film brought in over $100,000 through these sales. In Germany alone, Goskino's share of the grosses was $20,000 for the first two-and-a-half months of *Potemkin*'s release; although the film was temporarily withdrawn during its second major censorship battle in July, it then continued to circulate in Germany for at least a year. There was no other foreign market where *Potemkin* enjoyed this degree of success, but it seems conceivable that the film's total income abroad was in the range of hundreds, rather than tens, of thousands of dollars. Clearly *Potemkin* brought a considerable amount of money to Sovkino.

In early 1928, Konstantin Schvedchikov's report on the film industry of the Soviet Union stated that before the 1926–7 season, Soviet films as a whole made no profit, and that they brought a profit of about 10 per cent in the 1926–7 season.[17] *Variety*, in outlining the Schvedchikov report, gave the average cost of production for a Soviet feature as $35–40,000.[18] It is virtually impossible to determine equivalencies between dollars and roubles for this period, but the *Variety* figure at least seems plausible; an average feature film made in Western Europe at this time would typically have cost in this same range. Rough though these estimates must be, it seems probable that *Potemkin* made back its costs several times over.

Moreover, it must have done so in a remarkably short time. In late 1926, a study of Soviet production declared that films typically took a long time to amortise their costs: often twelve to sixteen months, occasionally as long as two years. Given that *Potemkin*'s first Soviet run was in January of 1926 and its German success began in April, it may well have begun to make a profit within six months of its release.[19] *Potemkin* also created a fascination with Soviet films in Germany. Over the next few years dozens of films were imported, and many were successes – though few achieved anything like the popularity of *Potemkin*.

It is not surprising, then, that the exportation of *Potemkin* and the Soviet films that followed it seems to have galvanised the Soviet industry. At the beginning of 1927, the *Lichtbildbühne* stated that the success of *Potemkin* abroad had been used 'to secure new capital for state film production'.[20] In a 1927 interview, Alexander Ivanovsky, director of *The Palace and the Fortress*, credited the recent exportation of films to Germany and the USA with permitting the Soviet industry to import lighting equipment; such importation finally solved what had been a major problem for the studios.[21]

In mid-1927, the Moscow correspondent of the *Lichtbildbühne* wrote an article which reflects a major change in official Soviet policy in the area of film-making. This article is worth quoting at some length, in part because it singles out Eisenstein for special mention:

> We have witnessed a remarkable process here. Film, which has by no means held a great interest for the Soviet authorities, has suddenly

advanced into the centre of attention. This change has been caused especially by the enormous success of the Russian film in Germany, which has been reported by all the newspapers in glowing terms. While previously little attention was paid to the fiction film, and the interest in film in the departments of Lunacharsky (People's Commissar for Education, etc.) was almost solely in the educational film for the peasant population, the fiction film has now gained a political attractiveness. I had the opportunity to speak with a person who is also well known in Germany, which is particularly interested in the political effect of the Russian film. I was told:

'We have had no money for amusements. As long as the fiction film meant nothing in our public affairs, we could not allow ourselves the luxury of film production. Moreover, and we do not wish to deny it, we made many mistakes in the production process and did not always approach the right people. Now circumstances have completely changed. The success of our films abroad has shown us that they represent the artistic and spiritual resources of our people and that they create a sort of silent, nonpolitical propaganda for Soviet Russia. That makes it worthwhile for us to raise film production to a new, high level, which in turn makes substantial expenditures urgent. If you watch the work in the studios, you will notice that it has less to do with political propaganda films than with cultural propaganda. We want to serve Russian art, naturally without being able to interfere in the private lives of our artists by making rules concerning the types of work they do.

It is a fact that political subjects are declining. The die-hards, like Eisenstein, naturally will not swerve from their concerns. Eisenstein's plans are aimed, after all, exclusively at producing films that display the lives and sufferings of the Russian people, free from all constraints of acting and aesthetic construction. He wants to work again without stars, heroes, or "romance" '.[22]

It is hard to imagine this remarkable description of the new policy in the Soviet film industry being given even a year later than mid-1927. Still, it gives some indication of Eisenstein's importance in that industry and suggests how *Potemkin*'s foreign success helped make the radical style of the Soviet montage films acceptable to officials.

Eisenstein's other works were among the many Soviet films that made their way to Germany in *Potemkin*'s wake. Recent accounts suggest that *The Strike* was a complete failure in Germany in 1927. I have, however, found a number of contemporary references to the film indicating that it may have done average business.[23] *October* was more successful, premièring as *Zehn Tage, die die Welt erschütterten* on 2 April 1928. It ran for three-and-a-half weeks, until 26 April; at that point it went into general release and was booked into 120 Berlin theatres.[24]

It was *Potemkin*, however, that remained the touchstone film for the Germans. Later Soviet films were often compared to it, and most were found wanting. For example, about one third of the *Lichtbildbühne*'s 1927 review of Room's *The Bay of Death* was actually devoted to Eisenstein:

> Every time that a new Russian film arrives here, its première is eagerly anticipated, and we hope for a new revelation of Russian film art. Eisenstein's *Potemkin* – not its political themes but its cinematic artwork – again becomes alive for us and compels comparisons with its elementary power. For us, Eisenstein has become a landmark of everything that is distinctive in Russian film. And we can only state once again: He came to us too early! Had we not seen his *Potemkin* yet, we would take a number of Russian films shown here recently and, on a purely artistic basis, would perhaps have evaluated them differently than we have actually done.[25]

On the other hand, had it not been for *Potemkin*, many of those films might not have reached Germany at all.

EISENSTEIN'S FILMS IN THE USA

Potemkin was a breakthrough film for introducing Soviet cinema into the USA as well. Although a few Soviet films had been shown prior to *Potemkin*'s première in late 1926, none of them had been seen widely or had been commercially successful. After that première, American interest in Soviet films gradually increased.

The relation of *Potemkin*'s American release to the founding of Sovkino's American branch, Amkino, in November of 1926 still needs to be researched, but it is clear that there was a connection. By June of 1926, Sovkino's New York representative, Leon Zamkovsky, was reportedly holding trade shows of *Potemkin* in New York, looking for an American distributor.[26] For example, it was shown to an invited group on 31 August, where distributors were reportedly dubious about the film's commercial prospects.[27] These trade shows failed to find a distributor for *Potemkin*. Possibly partly as a result, in November 1926, Amkino was formed; during that month, the American première of *Potemkin* was announced for early December, at the Biltmore Theatre in New York.[28] Amkino was to distribute the film in the USA.[29]

During the 1920s, it was extremely difficult for imported films to break into the American market. It was therefore common practice for a foreign company that hoped to find American distribution to rent a theatre in New York and hold a première run, usually hoping that the film's success would attract a distributor. According to a *Variety* report published four weeks after *Potemkin*'s 5 December première, Amkino had apparently paid an unusually high rent for the Biltmore but still did better business than it had expected. Still, Amkino was apparently reluctant to gamble on the film's success beyond four weeks, when an American entrepreneur took over:

> 'Potemkin', the Russian special feature picture at the Biltmore, New York, has extended the booking another four weeks. The film sponsor is guaranteeing $5,000 weekly for the bare walls but is said to have shown a profit.
>
> Starting this week and for the remainder of the engagement, 'Potemkin' is under the management of Ralph Shoflar. It appears the Russian management did not care to take a chance on the extended booking.[30]

Shortly after *Potemkin*'s New York première, Zamkovsky described in an interview how Amkino 'was founded for the purpose of purchasing motion picture equipment and also of acquainting the American public with the production of Russian studios'.[31]

That process proved to be only gradual, but Soviet films did make headway in the American market. *Potemkin* was the only film Amkino released in the USA during 1926. It premièred two in 1927: *Polikushka* and *The Legend of the Bear's Wedding*.[32] The number of Soviet releases increased in later years, however, with eight in 1928 and twenty-one in 1929.[33] Moreover, a small number of Soviet films were released in the USA by independent distributors; mostly notably, in 1928, Hammerstein-Selwyn distributed *The End of St Petersburg*, *The Golden Dawn* and *The Mother*.

One reason that *Potemkin* and subsequent Soviet films succeeded in the USA is because their releases coincided with the rise of the institution of the art cinema there. The first successful organisation in America devoted to showing artistic films, especially imports, was Symon Gould's Film Arts Guild. The Guild was founded in 1925 and in the spring of 1926 it began holding regular screenings in the Cameo Theater in New York.[34] Over the next few years, a series of similar small cinemas opened in other American cities. Initially their staple fare consisted largely of German imports, but during the late 1920s and early 1930s, they increasingly showed Soviet films as well.

Such cinemas provided a small but enthusiastic intellectual audience for Soviet films outside New York City. During 1927, *Potemkin* and its successors did well in such venues. In Washington, DC, for example, *Potemkin* drew crowds at the newly-opened art house, the Little Theatre. *Variety* described how Eisenstein's film 'not only had the customers lined up for a block, but had every allowable standing room space filled practically every show'. Despite its tiny 225-seat capacity, the Little grossed a respectable $2,000 in *Potemkin*'s short two-and-a-half day run.[35] *Potemkin* was the first film shown when Chicago's Playhouse went over to an art-house policy in September of 1927; as *Variety* put it, 'First week of house's conversion to people with brains; $5,400; looks like it has a good chance'.[36]

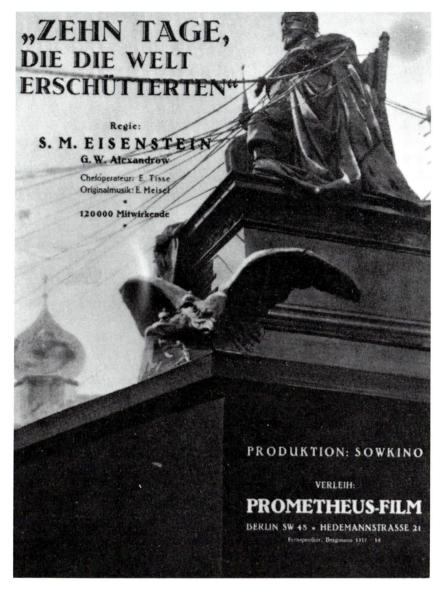

Figure 15 Prometheus-Film's advertisement for *October*, shown in Germany under its usual foreign title *Ten Days That Shook the World*, claimed a cast of 120,000.

Potemkin consistently did well in New York, being revived at the Cameo several times. In September of 1927, *Variety* reported: 'Around three or four times now, but management thinks well enough of it to hold over'.[37] It became a standard double-feature item for the Cameo, showing with *The Last Laugh* in mid-1928 and again with *Ivan the Terrible* (i.e., *Wings of a Serf*) about a month later – each time to average business.[38]

The Cameo, under the management of the Film Arts Guild, held the première New York runs of many Soviet films, and other little cinemas soon appeared. New York's third art-house, the Fifty-Fifth Street Cinema, opened in mid-1927 with *The Legend of the Bear's Wedding*.[39] Late that same year, New York's Fifth Avenue Playhouse Group opened branches in various American cities; its Cleveland house, the Little Theatre of the Movies, showed *Potemkin* as its first feature.[40] When the Little Carnegie Playhouse opened in the autumn of 1928, the American première of *Ten Days That Shook the World* was among its first presentations.[41] The film did good business there and ran for four weeks.[42] It quickly moved to the Cameo for a second run at the end of 1928.[43]

I should note in passing that not all Soviet films played only in art-houses. A few made their way into regular commercial cinema theatres. *Potemkin*, for example, played a down-at-heel Baltimore theatre in the spring of 1927; *Variety*'s inimitable prose describes how local intellectuals turned out in droves:

> The Embassy furnished the box-office sensation last week. Just about the time the public had forgotten the location of this house and local film people were wondering when the crepe would be hung on the door the long-neglected ticket machines began grinding out paste-boards so fast that the ticket-seller's dress was scorched by the overheated machinery. 'Potemkin' was the magnet.[44]

Such scattered clues in *Variety* suggest that Soviet films, by Eisenstein and others, made their way beyond Broadway, and that they were often successful in other cities in the USA.

INSTANT CLASSICS

I have concentrated on the commercial successes of Eisenstein's early films, but of course they met with censorship and other obstacles in many foreign countries. Nevertheless, they also had a broad impact that cannot be gauged by commercial popularity alone. I would like to close by emphasising that the contemporary impact of these films did not end with their first screenings in various countries. In those places where they were allowed to be shown, they typically became classics at once. This often meant, as we have seen with the US market, that they were revived in art and repertory cinemas; in addition, in some countries, left-wing groups circulated them extensively. I shall give a few examples of such practices here.

Not surprisingly, revivals of Eisenstein's films quickly occurred in Germany. In April of 1928, the newly-opened Kamera cinema, Berlin's first art house, ran *Potemkin* for one week; this revival was apparently timed to coincide with the première of *October*.[45] Various local branches of the main socialist cinema club in Germany, the Volksverband für Filmkunst, sponsored screenings of Soviet films by Eisenstein and others.[46] In the Netherlands, a leftist group called the Institut voor Arbeidersentwikeling gave a number of screenings of various films during the 1927–8 season, showing *Potemkin* 137 times.[47]

In Britain, where censorship problems delayed the releases of Eisenstein's early films for years, the extensive network of film societies and workers' clubs meant that the Soviet classics eventually were widely seen. For example, the Workers' Theatre Movement formed a 16mm distribution section called KINO in December of 1933. The first print acquired, of *Potemkin*, paid for itself in the first two months of bookings, and the group went on to acquire *The General Line*. By the winter of 1935, KINO had nine Soviet features and various shorts in distribution; another London distributor, the Progressive Film Institute, had films by Eisenstein and other Soviet film-makers available in 35mm.[48] In 1934 and 1935, the Forum Cinema in London held Soviet film seasons, including *Potemkin*, *October* and *The General Line*.[49] In the USA, according to Russell Campbell, Soviet films such as these were shown in 16mm in rural areas during the 1930s by small leftist groups like the Farmers' Movie Circuit.[50]

These brief examples should suggest, as I indicated at the outset, that Eisenstein's films, though part of what we would now consider an avant-garde movement, drew upon a wide range of cinematic institutions for their dissemination abroad. Some of these institutions were overtly commercial, while others were anything but. As a result, even though the films were banned in many countries, they managed to reach a surprisingly large and heterogeneous audience, ranging from Berlin's intellectual elite to farmers in the USA.

Chapter 4

Recent Eisenstein texts

INTRODUCTION: EISENSTEIN AT LA SARRAZ

Richard Taylor

Eisenstein's attendance at the Congress of Independent Film-Makers, held in the rather unlikely setting of the château of La Sarraz in Switzerland in September 1929, is well known but not well documented. We know that he was accompanied by his assistant Grigori Alexandrov and the cameraman Eduard Tisse and that the Congress was also attended by Walter Ruttmann, Hans Richter, Béla Bálazs, Léon Moussinac, Ivor Montagu and Alberto Cavalcanti among others. We know that one of the highlights of the Congress was the impromptu production of a film, *The Storming of La Sarraz*, a rather light-hearted allegory depicting the triumph of independent cinema over commercial dominance.[1]

The film however was accidentally lost and only tantalising photographs remain showing Moussinac as D'Artagnan or Eisenstein as Don Quixote. Until recently it has also seemed that no record of the discussions had been kept either. It appeared that one of the most extraordinary meetings of minds in the history of cinema had to all intents and purposes been lost to posterity.

Fortunately that was not after all the case. Naum Kleiman, whose knowledge of the Eisenstein heritage is unparalleled, has recently uncovered two manuscript sources in the TsGALI archive in Moscow, where the Eisenstein papers are held. Both manuscripts were written in German: one comprised the notes Eisenstein made for his La Sarraz speech while still in Berlin and the other was a fuller version that was written up when he returned to Berlin after being expelled from Switzerland as an undesirable alien. Kleiman has used his extensive experience of Eisenstein's writing method to combine the two manuscripts and the version that follows, 'Imitation as Mastery', is the result of that combination.

We cannot of course know whether Eisenstein did actually deliver the speech in this form at La Sarraz, just as we do not know for certain whether the Congress film ever existed: Hans Richter for one suspected that Eisenstein had told Tisse not to load the camera because they did not have enough money to pay for the film, but then others have alleged that Richter himself lost the film canisters on a train. But 'Imitation as Mastery', whether delivered or not, marks an important stage in the development of Eisenstein's thought at a time when he was still savouring the first excitement of his prolonged stay abroad and when the advent of sound, which he had left the Soviet Union to study, seemed to many to threaten the old film world, both in its theory and its practice, with complete collapse.

Eisenstein had reacted to protect the centrality of the montage concept in his own theory of cinema just over a year earlier with the celebrated 'Statement on Sound', first published, interestingly enough, in Berlin.[2] (It was Eisenstein who actually wrote the 'Statement' and it really represents his views, but Pudovkin and Alexandrov signed it too.) Montage, the 'Statement' argued, must be applied to sound as well as image: the threatened dominance of the 'talkie', where sound was used merely to illustrate the image, was but one alternative. Orchestral counterpoint, where the two conflicted, offered much greater potential.

Eisenstein devoted considerable attention to the problem of finding a common denominator between sound and image so that some kind of system of audio-visual montage could be elaborated: it was one of the main themes of his articles, 'An Unexpected Juncture', published in August 1928, and 'Beyond the Shot' and 'The Fourth Dimension in Cinema', both written in 1929.[3] Without the achievement of such a common denominator, it would have been impossible to continue with Eisenstein's developing notion of the 'attraction' in sound cinema and the whole idea of a non-linear narrative intellectual cinema would have foundered.

'Imitation as Mastery' represented part of Eisenstein's attempt to avoid this fate and to look forward to the ideas he was to develop in his increasingly complex montage writings of the 1930s and 1940s. The central thrust of the argument, as Mikhail Yampolsky makes clear elsewhere in this volume,[4] was that when art imitated reality it had to imitate not the reality of surface appearance (photographic reality) but the reality of inner essence (the essential bone-structure). That inner reality did of course include all the associations connected with the objects depicted in a particular sequence that gave those objects their quality of *attraction* and made them *effective* in an artistic (and also a political) sense. Two obvious examples from Eisenstein's silent films would be the Odessa Steps sequence in *Potemkin*[5] or the series of images of different deities in *October*.[6] Sound added other layers to the bone-structure of the film and would provide the film-maker with an almost endless combination of possible uses for an increasingly sophisticated delineation of montage types. In 'The Fourth Dimension in Cinema' Eisenstein distinguished metric, rhythmic, tonal and overtonal montage as major groups.[7] We can cite plenty of examples of his own attempts to use these various types of audio-visual montage from his two completed sound films, *Alexander Nevsky* and *Ivan the Terrible*. One obvious instance that Eisenstein himself analysed is provided by the Battle on the Ice in *Nevsky*, perhaps the most famous single example of his collaboration with Prokofiev.[8]

It is important to remember that sound did not represent for Eisenstein as it did for others a complete break with silent film. After all many theatres showing silent films had employed at least a piano accompanist and sometimes a full orchestra and the music they performed was not always mere improvisation. Edmund Meisel wrote specific scores for both *Potemkin* and *October*, which Alan Fearon has in recent years restored with the support of the British Film Institute. Nobody who has seen these films with the scores in live performance can doubt the influence that Meisel's music must have had on Eisenstein and the corresponding influence that Eisenstein's ideas must have had on Meisel. There is a far greater continuity between *Potemkin* when performed in this version and the practice of orchestral counterpoint in sound film than is generally appreciated because the score brings out the inner essence of the images rather than merely illustrating their surface appearance.

The ability of cinema to extract this inner essence through the use of both sound and image, as in the examples cited above, confirmed for Eisenstein its potential superiority over other art forms. The construction of a film from units of attraction linked by a dialectical conflict between the inner essence of each unit rather than the superficial similarities between the external appearances of successive objects offered an escape from the impasse of linear 'literary' narrative, a way for independent film to storm more than the château of La Sarraz.

The concerns articulated in this 'lost' document have a far broader and more lasting relevance for art than the more famous lost film. Art should, in this view, be more than a mirror, just as it should be more than merely Trotsky's hammer. 'Imitation as Mastery' confirms that Eisenstein was both a product of his time and a provocative and original thinker far ahead of it.

IMITATION AS MASTERY

Sergei Eisenstein[1]

Imitation . . .
   According to Aristotle, the basic principle of artistic creativity.[2]
   Like the creative urge itself therefore, also the key to mastery of form.
   This basic idea of imitation as means to mastery crops up in the oldest ideologies, in the magic ideologies of the most ancient peoples.

The sun goddess of the ancient Japanese, Uzume, suddenly hides in a cave.[3] The world is plunged into darkness. Prayers are to no avail. . . . Even the gods are in despair. Then someone has the brilliant idea of holding up a mirror in front of the capricious goddess. Uzume's likeness appears in the mirror. The goddess is plunged into self-contemplation and follows the mirror out of her dark cave . . .

That is how the mirror enters Japanese culture.

Catherine de' Medici has her court magician make wax models of her enemies. Then she pokes out their eyes with needles. Cuts up their bodies and limbs. She does it to make them unhappy. . . . She does it only when she cannot, fortuitously, make these poor people unhappy in any other way!

Nowadays any old tart imitates her!

When her Fritz, Paul or Lude leaves her in the lurch, she cuts his photo across the face with her scissors. And tears his likeness to shreds.

There is no way in which the peasants of Normandy can be persuaded to have their photographs taken.

Caution is the mother of all porcelain dishes!

The tyrannical demi-urge of the Bible, Jehovah, knew that when he issued his first commandment, which was also [a] first prohibition: 'Thou shalt not make unto thee any graven image etc.'[4]

But this mastery, the magic one, is a mere fiction. Because magic imitation copies form.

And the event as such remains as intangible to it as the pale reflection in the empty mirror.

Nonetheless imitation is the way to mastery.

But imitation of what?

Of the form that we see? No!

Catherine de' Medici needed a lot more than wax models to defeat her enemies.

Fritz meets his new Minne unscathed.

And the sun rises every morning whatever happens to go to sleep again in the evening.

No mirror is of any assistance in these cases! So – away with form as model! What then remains?

Principle remains.

Mastery of principle is real mastery of objects!

Principle or form?

Anyone who sees Aristotle as an imitator of the form of objects mis-understands him.

Like a cannibal.[5] The idea of cannibalism runs deep as well. How, where and when does a drive like that arise?

'Man is what he eats.'[6]

We read that every week in all the illustrated magazines! And that, it seems to me, conditions the instinct that drives us to consume our own likeness.

Our deep-seated instinct for self-preservation leads us to use as food what we ourselves consist of.

In instinctive primitive form there is however no distinction between external attribute, internal content and principle. It is all the same, so you eat what you see. If you eat your own likeness, you live forever.

This atavistic cannibalism is also evident in the highly intellectualised mythology of the Greeks.

Chronos (Saturn). Eternity. Immortality. . . . And Chronos . . . devours his own children.[7]

His likeness would be one. His children two. Is there a third in the mythology? What would remain? Devouring oneself after devouring one's own children.

India has the god Brahma. The god is depicted sucking his own foot. The phallic symbol is crystal clear: Brahma, who is also the god of eternity and immortality, is devouring his own *sperm*. His own children. His own likeness. Something other. That is just a step-by-step development of the same principle.

Brahma represents it in all its clarity.

But . . . were the wretched Indians really so wrong? What was the starting point for the Steinach and Vorontsov method of rejuvenation?[8] None other than self-fertilisation. The realisation of the symbolism of Brahma?

There is a great confusion between Brahma and Steinach, between different conceptions of the life-principle, caused by the false conception of the formal. Chronos. Cannibals.

Gilles de Retz, the child murderer: Retz too was seeking a means to eternal life.[9] And he expected to find the solution through sacrificial offerings of his own likeness!

The sacrifice of one's own image in the form of a human likeness in order to achieve eternal life: does not the same idea also lie at the basis of the Christian myth? . . .

So we have Steinach and Brahma. If the greatest mystery of immortality is addressed in this instance, then the most that medicine has to offer us is conceived in accordance with the same principles.

I was overwrought. Had a headache and so on. The doctor prescribed glycerine phosphate. I wanted to know what it was made of. Æsculapius explained to me that it was the same stuff that parts of the brain were made of . . .

How many people take blood cures . . .

How many mineral cures . . .

The age of form is drawing to a close.

We are penetrating matter. We are penetrating behind appearance into the principle of appearance.

In so doing we are mastering it.

Symbolism in myth is giving way to analysis of principle.[10]

Marx overthrows the magic of the cosmic concept through economics. He demonstrates how it is conditioned.

Marx does this through economics.

Marxism does it through history.

If you know how it is conditioned you can get right inside it. Make new history. Build a new life.

The burial-place of the pharaoh. Countless slaves. Oxen. Grain. Poultry. And it is all . . . painted! The difference between form and reality is non-existent.

It is enough to draw all these things.

The pharaoh will have them with him in the other world as reality.

It is true. Nowadays half the world lives according to the same system. It sells, buys and sells again – objects that likewise only exist on paper. Nowhere more than in the film business.

But they call that speculation.

And it is one of those dishonest things!

Art is already familiar with the same phenomenon. First and foremost the art that is closest to real life: architecture and applied art.

In the dreadful era of *art nouveau* architecture too imitated nature. Houses stretched out like lianas (I almost said like Liane Haid![11]). Balconies became flowers, lamps fruit, pillars became hunchbacked maidens, and so on. It needed the advent of a Le Corbusier, a Gropius or a Bruno Taut[12] to show the way to imitate nature: to investigate utility, the principle of the structure of plants. To grasp the logic of the arrangement of the body, not to ape its proportions but likewise to investigate the logic of its design structure.

The bust of Queen Marie-Antoinette.

In its form wonderfully suited to its precise purpose. Shaped in glass and used as a punchbowl, it was probably not the most suitable form for a vessel. Look it up in Ed Fuchs's monumental work on the history of manners.[13] There you will see the nonsense that Frenchmen produced as recently as the eighteenth century: the photo of the famous punchbowl. Nobody will imitate that now!

But in film we are still playing Marie-Antoinette. Admittedly Marie-Antoinette is sometimes called Dubarry, Lady Hamilton or Tom Mix.[14] The names change. The essence remains the same. The focus is exclusively directed towards the actor.

The task of film? Years ago I called it the Luna Park of our emotions.[15] Of the emotional conditions into which the audience is pitched. Entertainment film is stuck there. For true film this is just a means to drill the intellectual thesis through the emotions into the audience! And the role of the actor was a means to convey emotion.

The actor was and is the most direct object of imitation. We never know precisely *what* is going on inside another person.

We see his expression. We mimic it. We empathise. And we draw the conclusion that he must feel the same way as we feel at that moment.

The actor shows us how to feel.

That's fine. Why then rack your own brains! Everything is all so straightforward.

It is certainly the most straightforward way. But also the most restrictive.

Utilising the individual, he must break down the barriers as soon as it turns into the social-monumental.

The protagonist becomes the mass. Thus mass film arises.

But film cannot stand still either.

The depiction of mass movement is not yet an end. The mass, as dramatic actor, must once again give way.[16]

A new demand arises: to give pathos to everyday life. After the pathos of the bloody years of struggle comes the pathos of construction. The epoch of reconstruction.

In *Potemkin* it was simple. Pathos in form was at the same time pathos in treatment. Content and form coincided.

A concrete example of giving pathos to everyday life: the separator in *The General Line*. And pathos. The principle of construction is derived from the pathos of the situation. Eroticism is far too strong a force not to be utilised. It is 'delocalised'. Not a love *situation* but a treatment of the subconscious. *The General Line* once more.

That is dealt with fully in my book.[17]

All well and good. But do we need that?

Yes!! Film in its present state is worse than chained. On the technical front it is developing. But it always stays the same. What is conclusively acquired in school and drummed in emotionally is simply used by art: the fear of concentrating a problem. The fear of the new. The fear of a new coherence. Only new forms can elicit new *questions*. And new questions can only throw up a new social system.

And that is the role of Soviet film in film culture. I do not believe that we are particularly gifted. But the new social situation creates new problems. Anyone who wants to stand at the summit of monumental life in Russia must immerse himself in these problems emotionally. And traditional form will not help him. There must be a new basic principle.

We have to create new forms because we *need* them. That is the difference between our avant-garde and the other. Objectivity etc.[18] The emergence of associations. . . . Rastelli at the wireless receiver.[19]

The film of fact.

'Factual' play (illusion).

Play with facts (montage of visible events).[20] The creation of a new world.

Only now do we see that the fear of the sycophants was well-founded! We must seize the principle of nature and the new technological man will become Almighty in the sense that the Bible attributes to the Almighty.

Berlin, September 1929

Translated from the Russian by Richard Taylor

SOME PERSONAL REFLECTIONS ON TABOO[1]

Sergei Eisenstein

I like M.

Today I catch myself drawing her from memory. And suddenly I realise why in ancient religions people were not supposed to depict the images of their deities.

Jehovah's bass voice boomed from the cloud-covered heights of Sinai, 'Thou shalt not make to thyself any graven image, nor the likeness of any thing'.

In Persian miniatures and other examples of religious painting the central deity has a blank spot instead of a face.

The name of God was taboo to primitive peoples.

It could not be spoken aloud. This reflected the limitations of the mode of thought of primitive man. Name and being were the same thing – identical. To name a name was to summon up the being. To name Him was to draw Him to oneself.

So what . . . ?

I think that it is possible to go further.

Let me say something about depictions from my own experience of life.

I liked a girl called K. Getting to know her was a very slow and difficult process. Surprisingly I draw quite quickly. In the drawing I achieve a reflex immediacy which translates the idea/conception straight into the drawing. That is how Alexander Ostrovsky taught the actor's craft, using the very same term 'reflex'!

In pursuit of immediacy I am trying to think in strokes. For that reason I have stopped using a rubber or making an outline sketch.

For a long time I have been trying to capture K. on paper from memory. Just as unsuccessfully as on the other side of the paper. At last, I have managed it. And I captured the character of her appearance at the moment when . . . well, you know when. But it was by no means because of this. No! It was simply that both lines of depiction, developing uniformly, reached their conclusion at the same moment. The model submitted both on paper and in the psychology of consent.

Figure 16 Photograph sent by Eisenstein to Ivor Montagu from Mexico in 1931: 'Makes people jealous!'

I remember that it was the same on at least three other occasions (L., V. and E.). The moment the image was captured on paper, the subject submitted psychologically.

This seems almost like magic operating. What is more, beforehand, before there was a lifelike depiction on paper, I had no success whatsoever!

What curious devilment!

But I think that the drawing here repeats the gradual pace of capturing the features of the model herself. We come to resemble those we love. Do we not sometimes catch ourselves reproducing the person we love in our gestures and intonations, our movements and manner of thinking?

Isn't this why the English language, in order to distinguish the first stage of love, i.e. the stage preceding fusion (love), has preserved the term 'like', which simultaneously conveys the sense of 'I like' (something less than 'I love') and 'I resemble'?!

Isn't this glaringly obvious from women in love?

Don't they think our thoughts, speak our turns of speech, use our words?

Wasn't I right to make Anastasia in my *Ivan the Terrible* speak about the state and power with the words originally used by Ivan? The objectivisation of the features of the loved one in oneself is a characteristic of women.

Men apparently externalise. On to raw material. On to their surroundings. On to the heroine of a novel. A woman's image on the screen. Drama. Elegy. And . . . drawing.

But complete objectivisation is possible only in the case of complete (psychological) identification with the image of the model. This is the moment of simultaneous perception of her within oneself. This is the fusion. From this derives complete knowledge.

We do however remember what it means to 'know' one's wife in the biblical sense. It does not just mean to fuse with her. But, from the position of an admirer – to possess her.

You can only imagine another person at the second stage. After the first stage in which at first you mimic the model. You reproduce her subjectively in yourself in order to return her once again to objectivity, as an image on paper.

It is only when this process of mutual penetration – getting inside the model and accepting her within you – is achieved that the image will come on paper.

For the image is precisely the combination of features that, when we perceive it, forces us to recreate the original. It is not, however, a depiction which reflects in a dead and precise way existing detail.

Thus the image on paper is a reliable indicator of the fact that this mutual penetration, with its accent on the man as the active originator, has already happened.

Figure 17
Women in love
'think our
thoughts . . . .
use our words':
Anastasia and
her nemesis in
Ivan the Terrible.

The drawing is not a magic key to fulfilment, but an indicator of the degree of 'crystallisation' of the relationships.

'Relationships' because this is possible from one side. The degree of penetration is furthermore an indicator of the defensive position of the besieged citadel, the degree to which and to what extent the attacking forces have been admitted into it.

That is probably why we are not allowed to depict the image of God.

To depict Him means to amalgamate with Him.

To possess Him.

To stand in His place. . . .

22 January 1943

Translated from the Russian by Richard Taylor

Part II

Eisenstein's roots

Chapter 5

Eisenstein and Russian Symbolist culture

An unknown script of *October*

Yuri Tsivian

This chapter represents yet another attempt at a textual analysis of Eisenstein's *October*, a film which has been analysed over and over again at the risk of some sequences being over-interpreted. Nevertheless I have two good reasons for approaching the subject again. One is that almost all analyses of *October* tend to regard the film as a closed textual entity, with little or no attention being paid to whatever extra-textual connotation a particular sequence might have. Either *October* is totally impervious to its cultural milieu or we are not prepared to read its text in a broader cultural context. It seems that we are too used to thinking of Eisenstein as a Constructivist artist to admit that some of his constructions might be open-ended and susceptible to more traditional patterns of contemporary thought. In this respect Eisenstein's contemporaries were occasionally more acute than modern film historians. In 1928, when the newspaper debates about *October* were at their peak, Eisenstein was routinely accused of being a 'Symbolist in film'. Adrian Piotrovsky, Eisenstein's fiercest critic and one of the most educated men of his time, wrote in an article entitled '*October* Must Be Re-Edited' about what he called the 'stylistic discord' of the film:

> When the statues, the crystal and the porcelain begin to fill the screen persistently we are reminded not just of the symbolism of the Tsar's palace and of autocratic Petersburg that derives from Blok and Bryusov but also of the closely related line of Russian aestheticism that is associated with the World of Art group. Thus, beneath the Constructivist exterior of a materialistically conceived *October*, there lurk the vestiges of the decadent and outdated styles of our art.[1]

Historical criticisms like this should not perhaps be discarded as false but rather restated in less accusatory terms to account for the genuinely polystylistic structure of *October* and, in particular, for those motifs in it that refer back to the literary tradition established by Russian Symbolist writers.

A second reason why I think some well-known sequences from *October* should be reconsidered is that an unknown early version, which provides us with a significantly different editing concept, has come to light. It is the typescript reproduced here in English translation as an appendix to this chapter. The typescript, of which only the last part survives, obviously represents the last script version of *October*. It differs not only from the screen version but also from the literary treatment published in the six-volume Russian Eisenstein edition.[2] This latter version was not meant to be used during the actual shooting, despite the numbering of the lines, but to be read by other people: after all, the Party's Anniversary Committee did exercise tight control over the production. The script in the appendix is, by contrast, a working script. Its lines look more like mnemonic signs than narrative sentences. Often in the script Eisenstein uses actors' names instead of the names of characters and this indicates that he is referring to sequences that had already been cast and shot. Lines such as 330 ('326 again') confirm that we are dealing with an editing script. To judge by the physical condition of the typescript, it has already been worked with. It therefore seems plausible that a version of *October* existed which is quite different from the ones that we know, and the script in question is a kind of shorthand version of it. There is only one time when this version could have been made. As we know, Eisenstein was unable to complete the editing in time for the celebration at the Bolshoi Theatre of the tenth anniversary of the October Revolution so that only some fragments of the film were shown on 7 November 1927. After this screening Eisenstein was advised to change the montage conception, to re-edit the fragments and to shorten the whole film. At the same time he insisted on several days' additional shooting and this request was granted. It seems that this editing script was produced for the Bolshoi screening, the storming of the Winter Palace being one of the fragments shown on that day.

We are therefore dealing not just with a different montage version of *October* (familiar shots in unfamiliar cutting positions, script lines referring to unknown footage – all this would in itself provide enough material for a comparative study) but also with a version that pre-dates any of the screen versions, a fact which allows us to trace the genesis of each shot. Although the script requires more extensive textual analysis, I am going to touch only upon the points that link *October* to Russian Symbolist culture.

THE CASE OF THE PROVISIONAL GOVERNMENT

Let us consider script lines 428 to 431 in the appendix. The scene is the mortuary in the Winter Palace, omitted from the final version of *October*, although photographs from the Eisenstein Archive in Moscow displayed in the 'Eisenstein: His Life and Work' exhibition testify to the fact that the mortuary sequence was shot.

Why a mortuary? If we compare this editing script with the literary version and also with the screen version, we find that Eisenstein hesitated to the very last moment as to how he should treat the Provisional Government. Each different version provides a different solution. In the editing script under discussion line 431 reads 'Torpid government'. In the literary treatment we find a slightly different epithet: 'Petrified government.'[3] The difference is not as negligible as it might appear. Eisenstein was very particular about the exact wording of script lines: suffice it to recall his classroom analysis of the distinctly different treatments required by the apparently synonymous script lines 'Dark window' and 'Unlit window'.[4] The 'petrification' of the Provisional Government looks a particularly apt remark for *October* because it fits perfectly into Eisenstein's general design of stone images in the film and seems to anticipate the observation made by Marie-Claude Ropars-Wuilleumier that the statues in *October* represent forces hostile to the Revolution.[5] What is more, the remark is reminiscent of Symbolist theatre, and in particular of Alexander Blok's play *The King in the Square*, written soon after, and under the impact of, the revolution of 1905. The *coup de théâtre* in Blok's play lies in the fact that the King, who is permanently present on stage (the other characters keep addressing him in the hope of getting an answer), turns out towards the end of the play to be a stone idol. Let me quote Blok's stage direction for the concluding scene:

> At that very moment the infuriated crowd pours out on to the steps behind the Poet. The columns shatter from below. Wailing and shouting. The terrace caves in, taking the King with it. . . . In the red glow of the torches you can clearly see people down below scouring around searching for bodies, holding up a stone splinter of a cloak, a stone fragment of a torso, a stone hand. You can hear cries of horror: 'The statue! The stone idol! Where's the King?'[6]

The opening sequence of *October* with the Tsar's monument being dismantled overtly alludes to this dénouement and both destruction scenes function within a more general inter-textual matrix, that of Pushkin's *The Stone Guest*, to which Eisenstein refers by making his statue nod before it falls.

This reference to Blok makes it easier to discern the outline of what appears to be Eisenstein's initial conception of the film in the literary treatment. By making *October* begin precisely where Blok's play ends and by inserting later the line 'Petrified government', Eisenstein seems to reaffirm the essentially Symbolist idea of history as a permanently alternating cycle between the petrification and destruction of power. Although this idea does not exactly pervade the overall structure of *October*, some sequences (such as the Kerensky–Napoleon metaphor) still bear the traces of Eisenstein's initial intention to turn the Provisional Government into statues. Curiously this cycle is worked out more explicitly in *The General*

Line, when plaster busts of Lenin threaten to substitute for revolutionary power.[7]

For some reason the line 'Petrified government' was discarded and replaced by 'Torpid government' in the editing script. Instead of transforming the image, Eisenstein now worked on it through its context. This is where the mortuary comes in. Lines 428 to 430 mention rows of corpses with numbers on their heels. Then Eisenstein abruptly cuts away to the shot of the Provisional Government (line 431), which this time is described as 'torpid'. The cut-in metaphor is quite obvious and like the one that Eisenstein had already employed in *The Strike*. The meaning here was probably related to the verbal cliché 'political corpse', which was current in newspapers of the time. It is small wonder that Eisenstein abandoned that as well.

The final version represents a return to some elements of the initial design. At one moment the audience sees empty suits on the screen instead of the Provisional Government.

As we can see, the metaphor has changed its locus and is back in the frame, instead of being on the cut. Once more a transformation is implied, this time disappearance rather than petrification.[8] Finally, this sequence also borrows from the vocabulary of the Symbolist theatre, the empty suit metaphor finding its extra-textual counterpart in *The Fairground Booth*, an earlier play by Blok staged by Meyerhold in 1906. In this play a trick somewhat similar to the petrification scene in *The King in the Square* was introduced. A council of mystics was permanently on stage watching the show. The moment the show takes an unpredictable turn, the mystics suddenly lose their identity:

> Harlequin took Columbine by the hand. She smiled at him. General collapse of mood. Everyone lifeless on the edge of their chairs. Coat sleeves stretched out and covered the hands as if the hands did not exist. Heads disappeared into collars. It was as if empty coats were hanging on the chairs.[9]

Eisenstein never saw Meyerhold's famous production of the play but for Meyerhold's disciples and for an entire generation of non-traditional theatre people *The Fairground Booth* was, as it were, a cult production and it was recalled over and over again in minutest detail by those who had seen it. That accounts for the reproduction of its key metaphor in *October*. In his memoirs Eisenstein recalls a session like this when a former participant in the production reminisced to Meyerhold's students:

> Nelidov, of the young idealists. Nelidov participated in the production of *The Fairground Booth*. And *The Fairground Booth* was to us as the Church of Spas Neriditsa was to ancient Russia.
>
> In the evenings Nelidov would talk about the wonderful evenings of *The Fairground Booth*, about the conference of mystics who look at us

Figure 18 October.
'Empty suits instead of the
Provisional Government.'

now from Sapunov's sketches in the Tretiakov Gallery, about the première, and about how Meyerhold, as the white Pierrot, stood like a stork with one leg behind the other and played on a thin reed pipe.[10]

The impression left by these stories was so strong that Eisenstein chose to use the empty suit metaphor from *The Fairground Booth* to describe his first meeting with its celebrated producer. This meeting took place in 1914 in St Petersburg when the 16-year-old Eisenstein attended a public lecture given by Konstantin Miklashevsky, a theatre historian who was later to become an émigré film-maker and the real author of the script for Feyder's film *La Kermesse héroïque*. Meyerhold was also there, sitting on the stage among the honoured guests. Twenty-nine years later Eisenstein took the trouble to recall the lecture:

> The chairman's table was in the depths of the stage, dignified, like the mystics at the start of *The Fairground Booth*, but I remember and see only one of those seated at it. The others have vanished into the slits of their own cardboard busts, disappeared in memory, as those in *The Fairground Booth* disappeared.
>
> The only one – you have guessed it – the divine! The incomparable! Mey-er-hold.
>
> It was the first time I had seen him. And I was to worship him all my life.[11]

If we agree that, inter-textually, eye-witness accounts may be at least as influential as seeing with one's own eyes, the empty suit metaphor in *October* may be regarded as an attempt to recreate on film the impression that Eisenstein had missed twenty years earlier as a theatre-goer. The idea of early impressions being reproduced in his later films was among Eisenstein's favourite themes when discussing his own work: suffice it to recall *October* and the 'forbidden' passages from Zola, or the Teutonic knights from *Alexander Nevsky* and the anecdote about Eisenstein's mother's nasty habit of frightening her son by motionless grimaces. If Eisenstein's predilection for Symbolist imagery needs any psychological motivation at all, it may be traced back to two figures Eisenstein regarded as 'incomparable' and 'divine' from his early days and for the rest of his life: Vsevolod Meyerhold from Symbolist theatre and Andrei Bely from Symbolist prose.[12]

THE 'INTELLECTUAL' TOPOGRAPHY OF THE TSARINA'S BED-CHAMBER

The rest of the discussion will be confined to the scene introduced by the intertitle 'The Tsarina's bed-chamber'. When we compare two versions of the scene, the first thing that strikes us is the considerable divergence between the editing patterns. The editing script version (lines 365–422) looks less 'intellectual' (in the specifically Eisensteinian sense of the term) and more diegetic. This suggests that the 'intellectual' sequences in the film are due mainly to a later re-editing when it was decided to release *October* as one film instead of two. If we examine the chase in the Tsarina's bed-chamber from the continuity point of view, we see that the only continuity conditions that are strictly observed in the screen version are correct matches on movement, whereas constant eye-line mismatches and directional mismatches make the space of the bed-chamber vague and indeterminate.[13] Sometimes we cannot even tell for sure how many characters are participating in the chase: some cuts seem quite continuous because of a good match on movement, despite the fact that two different characters are made to pass as one.

From what we can tell from the script version, this editing style was not something carefully planned in advance. It seems that the occasional 'trick cuts', which are meant to make the sequence look more or less coherent at the expense of its diegetic clarity, are a kind of emergency device Eisenstein used to cope with excessive footage. This becomes quite evident when we look at the editing script. In it the chase was supposed to be an extended event taking place in several rooms in succession: the bed-chamber (lines 366–8 inclusive), the prayer-room (369–72 inclusive), two lavatories – one semi-circular (387), the other right-angled (388), the linen-room (379–94) and the trunk-room (395–422), which is not named directly in the script but is referred to in other documents. The six rooms were meant to form a realistically motivated space, a space that directly corresponded to the pro-filmic interior architecture of the royal bed-chamber (which was in fact a whole apartment rather than a bed-chamber) in the Winter Palace. There were to be no inconsistencies like the lavatory pan in the bed-chamber, which the audience is forced to believe in when watching the screen version where a mere turn of the sailor's head creates a spatial contrast as scandalous as those in *Un Chien andalou* by linking objects which simply cannot coexist in one room, like icons and a bidet.

When we maintain that no such spatial inconsistencies exist in the editing script version, this does not mean that the editing is less conceptual there. The real difference is that the editing script version is more deeply rooted in the diegesis. When Eisenstein wanted to confront the world of religious objects and the world of human biology, what he tried first was something any run-of-the-mill film director would think of: in the editing script version the women soldiers hiding in the prayer room exchange fire with the sailors hiding in the lavatory (lines 371–6). Script lines 381–6, which describe the sailor looking around him, show that the conceptual juxtaposition of objects is already all there, except that spatial boundaries are not violated. Toilet requisites, meaning towels or toilet paper (line 384), look perfectly natural in a linen storage room, but Eisenstein still thinks it necessary to insert an orientation mark – 'Opens a door: a lavatory' (lines

387–8) to enable him to cut in a lavatory pan. That is where the fine distinction between conceptual and intellectual montage lies: in later versions all the openings of doors are omitted. There is no prayer room and no lavatory in the screen version. What we have instead is a single formless room which is called 'The Tsarina's bed-chamber' but which looks more like a junk shop than a royal parlour.[14]

What should be emphasised once again is that what we see in the editing script and what we see in the final screen version are different stylistic layers, the second layer arising from the need to compress the first. 'Intellectual montage' was born from the attempt to cover the action at a very rapid pace, rather as a digest does. In order to do this, Eisenstein had to strip the diegetic space of many of the orientation marks required for the continuity editing and to 'replace' them with differentiating features he called 'intellectual'.

In a sense it was an innovation forced on him by circumstances, by the situation that Viktor Shklovsky thought was the main impulse for the early history of Soviet cinema. Shklovsky was fond of repeating anecdotes about Kuleshov's short-shot cutting being invented because no full-length film stock was available at the time so that cameras had to be loaded with old laboratory offcuts. Another of his stories rings more true. Because of the same problem Sanin's *Polikushka* was shot on old pre-revolutionary stock which had long been out of use because of its so-called 'haze', a finely meshed web of cracks in the emulsion. This haze made European audiences enthuse over what they thought was highly sophisticated soft-focus photography![15]

When he strung together a sequence according to the 'intellectual' principle, Eisenstein was operating with the debris of the coherent diegesis he himself had observed while shooting and editing the first version. This means, as far as textual analysis is concerned, that sequences like this in *October* should be analysed with caution, layer by layer. It would be useful to try to reconstruct the initial diegetic situation which a particular shot was primarily conceived as part of. Contrary to what we might expect, the 'intellectualisation' of editing patterns was a double-edged sword: brought too close to the foreground, the symbolic connotation of some objects threatened to become practically unreadable. To understand why they are there at all one should try to build them back into the context that they have lost. This may be illustrated by the case of the china eggs, an image whose semantic potential was gradually reduced to the point where it vanished altogether.

THE EVOLUTION OF THE EGG SYMBOL

When Eisenstein and his team were first shown into the Tsarina's bed-chamber they were stunned by the sight of huge painted eggs made of china. There is an entry in Eisenstein's shooting diary for 14 April 1927: 'The bed-chamber alone contains 300 icons and 200 china Easter eggs. It dazzles you. A bed-chamber that psychologically a contemporary could not stand. It is intolerable.'[16] If we compare the number of lines devoted to eggs in the editing script version with the number of egg shots in the screen version, we see that the ratio is eight to two, or even eight to one, since the two shots are 'concertinaed' into what amounts to a single cutting position. In the sonorised version re-edited by Alexandrov the egg shots were cut out altogether, probably because, thirty years after the film was made, Alexandrov was uncertain of what the egg image was meant to signify. We have to trace the history of the egg sequence back to the editing script in order to restore its meaning.

Script line 382 reads 'Icons. Eggs. Crosses'. It corresponds to a series of similar shots in the film. We recall that these shots mark the beginning of the sequence illustrating the sailor's inner monologue while he is examining the details of the royal bed-chamber. The sequence is edited according to an apparently simple pattern. Religious objects are juxtaposed to objects that remind us of human genitals: a bidet, a lavatory, and so on. Eggs as a symbol for Easter belong to the religious sequence.

Two script lines have no counterpart in the screen version:

414 The sailor with the St Nicholas egg in his hand.
418 Nicholas II's eggs roll.

What is intended here is a double pun. First, there is a play on the homonym of the Tsar's name and that of his patron saint. Second, the Russian word for eggs, *yaitsa*, has a double meaning. The second meaning is a contemporary colloquialism for testicles, so that a more apt translation of line 418 would be 'Nicholas II's balls roll'. The pun makes the egg image not the fixed image it appears to be earlier in the script but a cluster of two meanings that are crucial to the sequence: eggs stand both for religious objects and for male genitals, representing the two extremes which were believed to determine the politics of the last Russian Tsarina, her frantic sexuality and her fanatic religiosity (cf. the popular image of Rasputin as a saint and a sex-machine at the same time).

Lines 416–46 link the theme of genitals with the theme of the Revolution. In his recent study François Albera has demonstrated how Eisenstein built into *October* two early impressions from his childhood: the scene from Zola's *Germinal* in which revolutionary women march brandishing the genitals of their castrated oppressor; and Marie-Antoinette's head impaled on a soldier's pike, which shook the young Eisenstein when he saw it in a waxworks.[17] Albera's study is well grounded in Eisenstein's own post-analyses and he is quite right when he states that for Eisenstein the very essence of the Revolution was symbolised by the decapitation/castration of the ruler.[18] It is in this context that the script lines that deal with Nicholas's rolling balls (418, 422) or the scene in which the same eggs/balls are stolen by a woman from the Tsarina's bed-chamber (line 446) should be situated.

The egg image also figures in the sequence in lines 401–14. Let us take a closer look at what is happening in this sequence. It is a short episode absent from the final version of *October*. Some cadets are trying to disarm a revolutionary sailor but the sailor tricks them into dropping their guns. This apparently straightforward little narrative is constructed so as to convey a double meaning and the very technique of its narrative construction bears a strong resemblance to what Russian Symbolist writers did in their prose and plays.

Because of a defect in the typescript line 403 is partly illegible: we cannot therefore know what the sailor is groping for. The next time we see him (line 405) he is about to throw whatever it was that he was groping for in line 403. Then we see him standing in a whirl of feathers with a bomb (line 410), the disturbance being caused by the salvo from the *Avrora* (line 406). The next time we see him the object he has in his hand is not a bomb but an egg (line 414). If we assume that the defective line 403 reads something like 'The sailor jumps aside and gropes for a china egg behind him' the story becomes fairly connected: the sailor threatens his enemies with a make-believe bomb which is actually an egg; the salvo comes in time to play the part of an explosion; the cadets drop their rifles. This would be the outcome if you were programmed to read the sequence horizontally. But this kind of reading would not seem natural to anyone raised on Russian Symbolist culture. For a Symbolist, and for any of his readers, a text is a puzzle to be read both across and down. You do not read Andrei Bely's *Petersburg* to learn how a young man tried to blow up his father with a bomb. The typical reader of this novel looks for vertical correspondences, such as why the bomb is repeatedly linked to the hero's chronic flatulence on the one hand, and to tinned sardines on the other. These are the substitutions through which a Symbolist writer is expected to communicate his 'timeless message'. Eisenstein, in his effort to make objects mean more than they do mean, draws much of his narrative technique from Symbolism. With his usual insight Osip Brik noted this as far back as 1928: '[Eisenstein] takes the principle of the creative transformation of raw material to the point of absurdity. In their time the Symbolists in literature and the "Non-Objective" painters did the same and this work was a historical necessity.'[19] Among the 'vertical' substitutions inviting the audience to read the sailor story from the editing script in a Symbolist way (the salvo from the *Avrora* substitutes for the bomb blast, the feathers imitate an explosion) the egg–bomb substitution is especially significant. Performed at the diegetic level, it parallels another substitution functioning at the level of discourse, namely the cut that Eisenstein has commented upon in his *Film Form*.

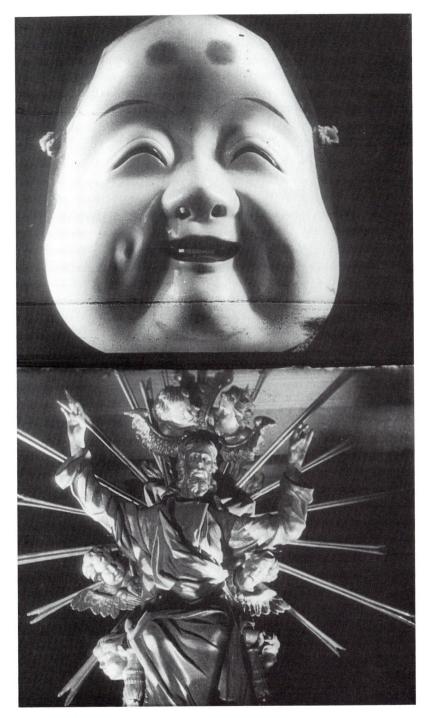

Figure 19 October: the 'graphic conflict' of egg (Uzume) and bomb-burst (Christ).

Eisenstein used this cut from *October* to illustrate his idea of 'graphic conflict' (two objects juxtaposed generate an idea or an 'image' that is external to both). He insisted that the star-like Baroque Christ figure produced the effect of a bomb burst.[20] To make sure that the trick works Eisenstein repeats the cut several times in succession.

The egg simile seems quite clear, an egg being a graphic equivalent of all that is perfectly self-contained. Then why not use an egg as the first element of the cut? It seems that neither of the elements forming the 'graphic conflict' is fortuitously chosen here. Just imagine an egg instead of the oriental mask and, say, a starfish instead of the Christ figure and you will have a *Ballet mécanique* instead of *October*. To anyone acquainted with Symbolist imagery the image of an exploding oriental head has a familiar ring. The symbol of a human skull filled with dynamite is one of the early literary metaphors for revolution. Implicitly it goes back to Dostoyevsky's idea of revolution as madness, a malady of the brain. The idea was developed by Andrei Bely in his *Petersburg*, a novel about the 1905 Revolution, where it figures as the hero's fixation. Probably, as Roman Timenchik has recently observed, Dostoyevsky's idea had to travel via England in order to acquire the form of an exploding head. Let me quote an anarchist speech from G. K. Chesterton's *The Man Who Was Thursday*, the novel which was translated into Russian before Bely began work on his *Petersburg*:

> Dynamite is not only our best tool, but our best method. It is as perfect a symbol of us as incense of the prayers of the Christians. It expands; it only destroys because it broadens. 'A man's brain is a bomb,' he cried out, loosening suddenly his strange passion and striking his own skull with violence. 'My brain feels like a bomb, night and day. It must expand! A man's brain must expand, if it breaks up the universe.'[21]

In an article written in 1918 Bely provided a similar commentary on his *Petersburg*:

> Our freedom dares us to fly up over the fire of our heart to the limits of the skull and to rupture those limits. Nikolai Apollonovich senses within himself the need for that rupture, like a bomb inside him, but he has no desire for it. . . . The skull will be smashed: the bright Dove of Advent will descend into the orifice of our own ruptures.[22]

Buddhism vs Christianity; stasis vs ecstasy; fatalism vs mutiny; stagnation vs explosion – these oppositions equally dear to Russian Symbolist thought and to Eisenstein as a philosopher of art (especially in his *Non-Indifferent Nature* period) cluster round the cut where the Japanese mask of the goddess Uzume explodes into the image of Christ. It seems that the egg/bomb substitution in the sailor story relies upon a very similar set of ideas. Structurally the sequence is built round the salvo from the *Avrora*,

Figure 20 Boy by/on throne: a jump-cut in *October*.

the pivotal point of the uprising. Semantically it centres round the idea of explosion. The egg/bomb correlation connects violence with procreation, a coalescence that is quite natural for a film that is an apologia for the Revolution. A shot of a peasant boy rejoicing on the Tsar's throne, which marks the climax of the screen version of this sequence, comes in the editing script version immediately after the burst of feathers, suggesting, in a somewhat Méliès-like fashion, that the boy emerges from the explosion. In the screen version the idea of revolution as explosion is reinforced at the discursive level by the famous jump-cut 'boy by the throne/boy on the throne'.

By violating the rules of continuity editing Eisenstein intended to take this moment out of ordinary, serial, experientially-motivated time. Diegetically the idea of marking historical moments and projecting them, as it were, into eternity is expressed in *October* by the obsessive use of clocks. In the passage from script to screen we can clearly see how the mechanism of intellectual cinema is made to work. In order to define the moment of revolution (burst, leap) as opposed to evolution (gradual, eventless development) Eisenstein dropped the diegetic symbolism of the exploding egg and proposed its discursive equivalent, a jump-cut.

EISENTSTEINIAN BAWDINESS

In his analysis of *October* David Bordwell has illustrated how important paronomasia (or punning) is to the understanding of what a particular sequence means.[23] The eggs/balls semantic shift demonstrates that this is also true of the sequence in the Tsarina's bed-chamber. The apparently simple pattern of the sailor's inner monologue while he is examining the bed-chamber turns out to be not quite as simple when we apply verbal codes to decipher it. The very first shot of this little scene bears an inscription within the shot that is open to a double reading.

The word 'Amur' on the sailor's hat is historically correct because there were sailors from the warship *Amur* among those who stormed the Winter Palace. But it still looks like a pun. Apart from the inevitable Francophone associations, to a Russian ear it means:

1 a river in Siberia;
2 the warship bearing that name;
3 Eros (or Cupid), the armed god of love.

The last meaning may pass unnoticed in the screen version but not in the editing script version, where it was substantiated by a number of other shots. We know from his drawings how fond Eisenstein was of visual puns on weapons and sex. A frame from an earlier reel of *October* may serve as a reminder that in this film erotic metaphors were also used to signal some points in the historical narrative.

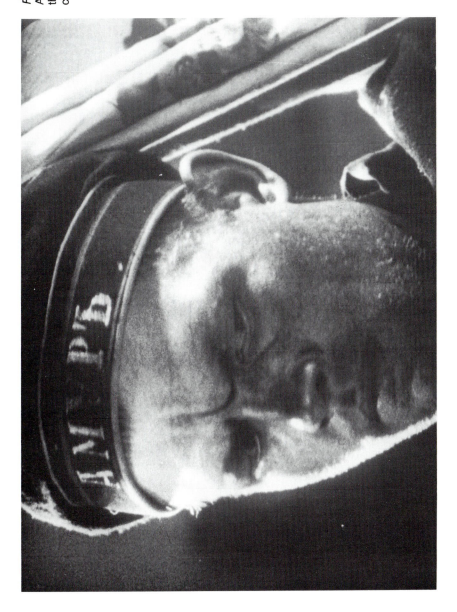

Figure 21 October. A sailor from the 'Amur' in the Tsarina's bed-chamber.

Figure 22 Machine gun and male Caryatid combine in one of the many powerful erotic metaphors created for, though in this case not used in, *October*.

It may be that the sailor inspecting the Tsarina's bed-chamber was also initially conceived as a mythological figure of an armed lover. There is a line in the script that is missing from the film: the sailor looks at a bidet and then, disgusted, he wipes his bayonet (line 393). As François Albera has demonstrated, a similar metaphor of a bayonet (in close-up) ripping a pillow (intercut with two women soldiers gasping) still exists in some versions of *October*, indicating that at its metaphorical level the sequence in the Tsarina's bed-chamber implies the notion of rape. The very fact that in other versions this close-up has been omitted is eloquent testimony to the fact that for some censors the implication has been too transparent. Another missing line (400) maintains the metaphor: after the sailor has discovered the women in one of the trunks we are shown pieces of linen flying through the air and then the sailor saying 'Ugh!' and lighting a cigarette in what must be understood as a post-coital gesture.

We might ask why Eisenstein was so insistent on making this point. The question is not that simple, particularly as, immediately after the Winter Palace was seized, persistent rumours circulated that acts of rape and violence had taken place during the assault. Was Eisenstein implying that the rumours were well-founded? After all, Kerensky did summon the Women's Shock Battalion to defend the Palace and the mutinous sailors who led the attack could not exactly be called the most disciplined element of the Revolution.

In order to resolve this question we need to pose a more general question about Eisenstein's attitude towards historical accuracy. Some of his contemporaries, especially those who belonged to LEF, criticised *October* for its lack of historical authenticity. Sergei Tretyakov wrote in his review that in the film the ragged sailors of 1917 looked as smart as the naval officers and concluded: 'If he is familiar from his own experience with the epoch depicted on the screen, the viewer will be divided between his own memory and the directive from the screen.'[24] Let me quote another review, this time by Osip Brik:

> Everyone knows that the battle for the wine-cellars after the Revolution was one of the murkier episodes of October and that the sailors not merely did not smash the cellars but tried to drink them up and refused to shoot the people who had come to take the wine. . . . But when a real sailor efficiently smashes real bottles the result is not a symbol or a poster but a lie.[25]

Tretyakov and Brik, both adherents of the LEF doctrine of the 'literature of fact', imply that Eisenstein tries to replace real history by political mythology. The reproach is not totally unfounded, but this explanation does not account for all the deviations from actual facts that we can detect in *October*. It would be more correct to say that what Eisenstein particularly favoured was not exactly political but rather popular mythology, a system of rumours and common talk that spread like wildfire immediately after the October Revolution. It is not a question of incompetence: first-hand information in the form of memoirs written specially for the occasion was at Eisenstein's disposal before the shooting started. Kerensky's flight from Gatchina serves as a good example. In John Reed's book *Ten Days That Shook the World* (*October* was first conceived as a screen version of the book but the idea was discarded and the book itself soon forbidden because there was too much of Trotsky in it) Kerensky's flight was de-scribed as being a success because Kerensky was disguised as a sailor. The story is perfectly true and is based on the evidence of the man who came to arrest him. But what Eisenstein was going to use instead was an apocryphal story according to which Kerensky fled disguised as a nun. In his literary treatment Eisenstein commented: 'Bonaparte in a skirt'.[26] Eisenstein needed the false story because it was better suited to what he had in mind at the metaphorical level: first, the Kerensky–Napoleon simile – the famous sequence of the 'two Napoleons'; next, the ambiguous sexual status Eisenstein had already ascribed to Kerensky with the intertitle 'Alexander Fedorovich in the Apartments of Alexandra Fedorovna' (an imputation that can easily be refuted since in reality Kerensky lived in the apartments of Alexander III).[27]

The rape story is of a similar kind. The Press of the day was full of rumours that the women defenders of the Winter Palace had been raped by the attacking crowd: we also read about it in Chapter 5 of Reed's book. The City Council ordered an immediate investigation into the allegations. It was to be supervised by the Mayor, Schreider, a man of stern democratic principles and great personal courage. On the night of the storming of the Winter Palace, followed by a group of unarmed civilians, he had tried to stop the revolutionary crowd and save the Provisional Government: Eisenstein caricatured him in the sequence where the old man confronts the bridge patrol. The enquiry found that the newspaper scare story was totally unfounded. When they were summoned to the public hearing, the women soldiers testified that no harm had been done to them, except that all 136 of them had been disarmed and sent back to the Pavlov barracks. Nonetheless, as in the case of Kerensky's disguise, Eisenstein preferred the popular legend to the true story, even though the former might seem detrimental to the character of the victorious power. He did this for the sake of the all-embracing metaphor that underlies every key sequence in *October*: the Revolution portrayed in terms of erotic conquest.

Curiously, popular mythology and the actual historical setting of October 1917 provided Eisenstein with a set of coincidental details to play upon: the Winter Palace defended by women against the virile force of the revolutionaries was, by virtue of accidental irony, counterbalanced by the fact that the Smolny Institute, the headquarters of the revolutionaries and the base for the attack, was known as a former school for fashionable young ladies of the nobility. The mutual travesty of opposing palaces did not escape the Press of the day: a photograph appeared showing Trotsky's (later Lenin's) room in the Smolny flanked by two Red Guards with a sign on its door reading 'School-Marm'. All this constituted the popular mythology of the Revolution reflected in common talk, cartoons and the topical satire of the daily press and echoed later in Eisenstein's *October*. Here the Winter Palace was further travestied by making Kerensky an effeminate character: the famous sign 'School-Marm' was also used to decorate the door of the Menshevik faction. We can go even further and assume that for Eisenstein the architectural body of the Winter Palace was itself a huge metaphor for femininity. The idea might not seem too far-fetched if we remember that Eisenstein was an attentive reader of Otto Rank's psychoanalytical works, and also that in popular consciousness the last twenty years of the Romanov dynasty bore all the signs of 'petticoat rule'. In this case it is no wonder that the climax of the film is signified by, of all places, the Tsarina's bed-chamber. To crown the gag, it should be added that the corridor through which the revolutionary crowd penetrated the Winter Palace, now called the October Corridor, was then known as 'Her Majesty's Personal Entrance'.

The extent to which the Winter Palace is conceived as an important character in the film may be illustrated by the famous sequence with Kerensky and the peacock. The sequence intercuts Kerensky entering the royal apartments with a clockwork peacock turning. Usually the peacock shots are interpreted as non-diegetic inserts providing a simile for Kerensky's arrogance. This reading is obviously too simple. Noël Burch once remarked that the movement of the peacock

> is so tightly meshed into the movement of the door itself that it resists any reduction to a single signifying function. A naive reading, predicated on the inviolability of diegitic space/time, might conclude that this is an automaton set in motion by machinery which connnects it with the door.[28]

We should ask: what was the reading envisaged by Eisenstein? To find out, we need to look more closely at the sequence. Kerensky pauses in front of the door; the peacock turns its back on the audience and opens its tail; Kerensky opens the door and enters; the peacock turns 'about face' again so that it is now facing the audience; then we see a padlock in close-up. None of the readings that pursue the Kerensky–peacock simile can account for the padlock, which seems to have no function in either diegetic or contextual terms. What Eisenstein had in mind was not so much to provide a simile for Kerensky himself as for the Winter Palace that the new Prime Minister was moving into. Eisenstein's idea for this sequence was not to ignore diegetic space but to construct an 'imaginary space', much in the spirit of Kuleshov's experiments. By operating through the dynamics of movement and by trying to manipulate different shot scales so that the audience is forced to believe that the peacock in close-up is much bigger than Kerensky in full shot (an assumption that did not work in practice), Eisenstein was hoping to achieve the effect of Kerensky entering the peacock's arsehole. The idea did not quite work out, not only because shot scales were too resistant to be manipulated in this way, but also because the action is too slow. If you try to project the sequence on the editing table using the rewind speed of over thirty-six frames per second, you suddenly witness Eisenstein's design coming to life. Kerensky is 'devoured' by the peacock through its arsehole, on which a padlock is then 'suspended'. The Winter Palace has entrapped its Prime Minister.

Let us return to the sailor's inner monologue in the Tsarina's bed-chamber: one more verbal pun seems to need a commentary. There is a shot reproducing a photograph of Nicholas II in close-up, his head slightly off-centre so that the viewer can decipher an inscription on it.

The inscription reads 'Nicky the falconer' and is immediately followed by a shot of a chamber-pot. This juxtaposition is affirmed with the insistence that is characteristic of Eisenstein when he is determined to drive his point home. The cut is repeated three times with the only difference that the photograph is now shown in full.

The joke implied by the first cut lies in the juxtaposition of the idea of duck-hunting with falcons – the favourite outdoor entertainment of the Russian Tsars dating back to Ivan the Terrible – and a special type of chamber-pot that is shaped like a duck and is also called a duck (*utka*) in Russian. When the cut is repeated the second time the verbal pun turns into a visual one: the royal eagle on the Tsar's hunting outfit enters into an interplay with the hygienic 'duck', bringing the two notions into what Eisenstein used to term a 'conflict' of high and low on an axiological as well as a plainly spatial scale.

We should not be too tempted to interpret Eisenstein's puns psychoanalytically. All that is going on in the Tsarina's bed-chamber has very clear cultural origins. Jokes about the Tsar and his chamber-pot were already encoded in the Russian euphemism *kuda tsar' peshkom khodil* 'to go where the Tsar went on foot' and belong to the old Russian tradition of what we might call 'royal bawdry'. This was particularly popular with the leftist theatre of the 1920s: the Emperor on his chamber-pot in Meyerhold's *Earth Rampant* and similar scenes in Eisenstein's *Wise Man* and in Igor Terentiev's *The Government Inspector*.[29] When in November 1917 Larisa Reisner, the famous woman commissar, went on a tour of inspection of the Winter Palace, she could not resist the temptation to make a joke about Kerensky being thrown off 'if not the throne then the stool of Nicholas II'.[30] All this, including the sequence in the Tsarina's bed-chamber from *October*, seems to stem from a real event in Russian history, when

Figures 23 and 24 'Eisenstein was hoping to achieve the effect of Kerensky entering the peacock's arsehole.'

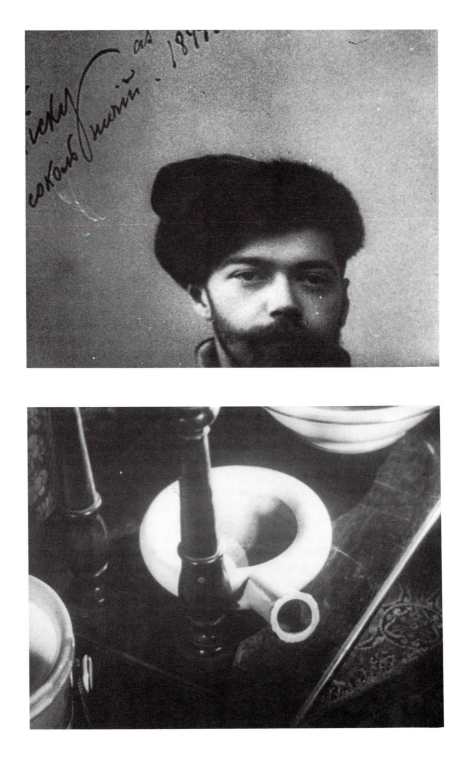

Figures 25, 26 and 27 The repeated montage juxtaposition of Tsar and chamber-pot evokes first a verbal and then a visual pun.

Catherine the Great was found dead in her private lavatory. The event was immortalised by Pushkin in a poem:

> The dear old lady lived,
> Pleasantly and somewhat prodigally,
> She was Voltaire's first friend,
> Gave orders, burned fleets
> And died, sitting on her bed-pan.[31]

The joke is based upon a pun on the Russian word *sudno*, which means both a ship and a bed-pan, the two notions also being juxtaposed in Eisenstein's *October* in the sequence where the revolutionary sailor examines the Tsarina's bed-chamber.

Finally, the very idea of a character's inner monologue based on a network of puns comes from Symbolist prose. Eisenstein himself defined this method in the following way: 'The elements of the *historiette* itself are thus chiefly those which, in the form of puns, provide the impulse towards abstraction and generalisation (mechanical spring-boards for patterns of dialectical attitudes towards events).'[32] Eisenstein and his later commentators justly link this technique to James Joyce. Contemplating his famous project for a screen version of Marx's *Capital*, Eisenstein wrote, 'Joyce may be helpful for my purpose: from a bowl of soup to the British vessels sunk by England'.[33] Nevertheless Joyce's influence can hardly be relevant to *October*: according to all the evidence, Eisenstein read *Ulysses* in March 1928. It seems that Joyce's impact on Eisenstein was as great as it was because the ground had already been prepared. The stringing together of sequences according to free verbal association can be found in Bely's *Petersburg* as well as in *Ulysses*. Let us take the example of the bowl of soup: it may seem Joycean, but Eisenstein's method of working with the technique of inner monologue looks very close to Bely. Even some details coincide: in *Petersburg* there is an episode where the hero is sitting over his plate of soup trying to find a topic of conversation. His mind wanders, its starting point being the sight of pepper in the soup:

> And in his loving son's head senseless associations began whirling about.
> 'Perception . . .'
> 'Apperception . . .'
> 'Pepper . . . not pepper but a term . . . terminology . . .'
> 'Logy . . . logic . . .
> And out whirled:
> 'Cohen's theory of logic . . . .'[34]

Eisenstein's 'intellectual montage' works in the same direction from everyday trivia 'towards abstraction and generalisation':

> Throughout the entire picture the wife cooks soup for her returning husband. . . . In the third part (for instance), association moves from the pepper with which she seasons food. Pepper. Cayenne. Devil's Island. Dreyfus. French chauvinism. *Figaro* in Krupp's hands. War. Ships sunk in the port. (Obviously not in such quantity!!) N.B. Good in its non-banality – transition: *pepper – Dreyfus – Figaro*.[35]

In the early 1930s Eisenstein had a conversation with Bely on which he reports in an unpublished part of his memoirs.[36] When asked about Joyce, Bely admitted to never having heard of him. The most curious thing about this is not Bely's confession but Eisenstein's sense of surprise at hearing it. It demonstrates the extent to which the literary technique of Bely and Joyce was experienced by Eisenstein as a joint impulse towards the revision of the narrative technique of the film medium.

MESSAGE AND VOCABULARY

All present-day research on Eisenstein, as well as the press controversy about him immediately after *October* was released, seems to develop in two directions. Some studies concentrate on him in the context of the Constructivist endeavours of Russian and European art in the 1920s: this approach is more characteristic of the French school of textual analysis. Others investigate Eisenstein in the context of more traditional culture and discover that his work fits there perfectly as well. As Susan Sontag has written: 'Eisenstein, who saw himself in the tradition of Wagner and the *Gesamtkunstwerk* and in his writings quotes copiously from the French Symbolists, was the greatest exponent of Symbolist aesthetics in cinema.'[37] The question may arise – and it did actually arise after this paper was presented at the Oxford Conference – as to which approach is more relevant, or, to put it more bluntly, as to what Eisenstein really was: an avant-garde film-maker or a traditionalist? This question has no single answer that is equally valid, say, for *The Strike* and *Ivan the Terrible*. In the case of *October* it is useful to distinguish between its image vocabulary and its message. You can control your message but it is more difficult to control your vocabulary, which is something you absorb from your cultural milieu before you are capable of criticising it. The October Revolution was not the first Russian revolution but the third, the first being the revolution of 1905. In 1905 the Russian literary scene was dominated by the Symbolists and it was they who established the basic symbolic vocabulary for this and for any subsequent revolution. Eisenstein was not a Symbolist as far as his message was concerned, but he used Symbolist vocabulary to formulate his message. His films are largely defined by the discrepancy between their vocabulary and their message. One striking example is *Bezhin Meadow*, where atheist ideology is rendered through Christian imagery, above all in the sequence where a church is 'deconstructed'. The famous sequence of the gods in *October* is typical of the way in which the vocabulary of symbols is manipulated to refute the meaning of the message. The principal point of controversy between Eisenstein and the more dedicated Constructivists, especially Vertov, was that for a Constructivist vocabulary determines message. Vertov, a purist in his choice of vocabulary, reproached Eisenstein for betraying the cause of revolutionary art by using actors, traditional narrative components and symbols.

I should like to conclude by quoting Eisenstein's open letter to the German journal *Filmtechnik*, in which he responds to Vertov by proclaiming the principle of relativity for the vocabulary any film-maker is free to choose to make his message work:

> Whereas today the strongest audience response is provoked by symbols and comparisons with the machine – we shoot the 'heartbeats' in the battleship's engine room – tomorrow we might exchange them for false noses and theatrical make-up. We could switch to make-up and noses.[38]

Written in 1927, this statement presages and explains Eisenstein's creative evolution from the Constructivism of *The Strike* to the theatricality of his later films. For Eisenstein it was but a matter of vocabulary.

Translated from the Russian by Richard Taylor

APPENDIX: EISENSTEIN'S EDITING SCRIPT FOR *OCTOBER*

Final sequences: shots 326–476[39]

326 Crush in cramped premises

327 Empty corridor

328 Ditto. The Jordan Corridor

329 Maelstrom in the corridors. / The Jordan Corridor

330 326 again

331 From the crush to amazement. / Ante-chamber with people, details of Chinese dining-room

332 48 clock-faces

333 Portières

334 Details. The peacock

335 Stupefaction

336 Do not touch!

337 Tiptoeing. The Pavilion Room. Ante-chamber. Echoes. A suite of rooms

338 Ambush and shooting on the Jordan Staircase

339 Maelstrom at the Jordan Entrance

340 Shooting from the Peter and Paul Fortress

341 A hit beneath the balcony

342 An archway. Solitary bonfires. Near the archway and the Stock Exchange

343 By one of these fires . . .

344 . . . is sitting . . .

345 Panic in the Dark Corridor[40]

346 Attempt to form ranks by the emergency exit / or in the 1812 Gallery

347 The cadets retreat through the doors

348 The Red Guards advance. Mirrored doors

349 Richly decorated doors

350 The cadets barricade themselves in

351 The door is blocked with gold furniture

352 The door is broken open

353 The door is broken down

354 The panels are broken

355 Chase through Nicholas II's library

356 Panic in brassières / Billiards and chambermaids

357 Chase through Nicholas II's library

358 Rosenblatt and book

359 Volley from behind five samovars

360 Children's chairs / An officer like Skoradinsky

361 Volley from behind the toys. Bicycles

362 A sailor jumps over the model of Laura

363 Women of the shock battalion shooting from beneath the curtains of the bed-chamber / at the people running in the foreground

364 At the entrance to the bed-chamber an old retainer will not let the sailors in

365 NO TRESPASSING. THIS IS THEIR MAJESTIES' PERSONAL BED-CHAMBER

366 Women soldiers amidst the curtains

367 The sailors rush past the old man

368 The women soldiers fire a volley

369 They flee to the prayer-room

370 The sailors rush in

371 They search. Rush into the lavatory

372 The women lurking in the prayer-room

373 The sailors in the lavatory

374 The women get away

375 They shoot at the lavatory

376 The sailors run out

377 The feather-bed is pierced

378 They break out through the water-closet

379 They reach the linen-room

380 A sailor with a feather-mattress on his bayonet

381 He looks around him

382 Icons. Eggs. Crosses

383 The sailor

384 Toilet requisites

385 Photographs

386 Icons

387 They open a door: a lavatory (semi-circular)

388 They open a door: a lavatory (rectangular) / Cupboards by the bathtubs

389 The Winter Palace numbers 200 separate lavatories

390 The sailor

391 A statue

392 A bidet

393 Disgusted, the sailor wipes his bayonet

394 He rummages in the linen

395 Breaks the grating

396 Trunks

397 He finds the women amongst the linen

398 The women on their knees

399 The linen flying in the air

400 The sailor says 'Ugh!' and lights a cigarette

401 The cadets rush in through the door

402 The cadets take aim

403 The sailor jumps across to the wall / He gropes for . . . [41]

404 The cadets take a step forward

405 The sailor raises his hand threateningly

406 Salvo from the *Avrora* / two-gun /

407 Windows shatter

408 A whirl of feathers

409 Cows panicking

410 The sailor holding a bomb in the whirl of feathers

411 The cadets abandon arms

412 A storm of feathers

413 A boy jumps on to the throne

414 The sailor with the St Nicholas egg in his hands

415 Trunks full of medals are broken open

416 A basket full of eggs is overturned

417 Etuis, cocked hats, gloves

418 Nicholas II's eggs roll

419 Medals pouring out

420 The crockery is locked up in the pantry

421 The cadets reach the cellar

422 The eggs rolling

423 Shooting

424 in

425 the

426 cellar

427 In the pantry, the ice-boxes, dressers and kitchen are locked

428 Break-in into the mortuary

429 Corpses with numbers on their heels

430 *C o r p s e s*

431 Torpid government

434 Ovseyenko elbows his way through the Dark Corridor[42]

435 Fighting in the rotunda / The infirmary

436 Schreider's men leave the Duma

437 TO SAVE THE LEGITIMATE POWER

438 The cadets are ejected from the cellar

439 Schreider's men

440 Chichkov, Bulygin and Butylka. Soynikov, Ovseyenko

441 The masses rush forward / The Jordan Staircase

442 The sailors chase the robbers / Vidumkin and her sons

443 Movement in the rotunda

444 The cadets are disarmed / Hands up! / At the Jordan Entrance

445 The stolen items are found

446 Antonova stealing eggs in the ransacked bed-chamber

447 The sailors chase out the robbers / lots of them /

448 Soynikov and Nilov drinking

449 The sailors chase out the thieves

450 The sailors and Schreider's men by the Politseisky Bridge

451 The cadets holding out in the rotunda

452 Miniature soldiers / from the Alexandrovsky Palace

453 Schreider's men in ecstasies

454 Senseless / women's rage / 'Beauvais' women[43] / biting and scratching. / Shooting from the attic storey or from the crockery room. / A chambermaid

455 'Le printemps' and 'Les enfants'

456 The burglars press on

457 Frenzied fighting with bottles

458 A cuff[44]

459 Schreider's men sit down

460 Fighting with bottles after the flood

461 The treasures of the Hermitage intact

462 They burst into the room where the Provisional Government is sitting

463 The cellar flooding

464 Brutal arrest / Foreground shot of tea

465 Arrest

466 The report to the Congress

467 Schreider's men with sandwiches

468 Antonov sits down to take the minutes among the bayonets and rifles

469 The Congress rises as one

470 LENIN at the podium

471 CONGRATULATIONS!

472 A peasant, a worker, a soldier at the Congress

473 Sinegub turns up his collar and leaves[45] / A churchyard

474 Tracking shot of leaflets flying through the air

475 LONG LIVE THE WORLD REVOLUTION!!

476 48 clock-faces

THE END

Chapter 6

Eisenstein's theatre work

Robert Leach

There are generally agreed to be three main streams in twentieth-century theatre: Realism-Naturalism, usually associated with Stanislavsky; Surrealism and the 'theatre of the absurd', whose best-known practitioner was probably Artaud; and finally, 'public', political, social, epic theatre, generally linked with Brecht. The roots of this third, Brechtian theatrical form are usually sought in the theatre of German Expressionism, the work of Büchner and Wedekind, the fairgrounds and cabarets Brecht frequented as a youth, even (as a reaction) Wagner's grandiose theories. But actually the specific form was first and in some ways most clearly utilised in the theatre of the Russian Revolution by those who wished to create an 'October in the theatre'. Meyerhold should perhaps be regarded as the real founder of it, yet Eisenstein is probably the practitioner who most clearly crystallised it.

The form was developed simultaneously on three fronts: playwrighting, play production, and acting. And, although Eisenstein himself was primarily concerned with play production, each of the three is considered at various points in this chapter.

Eisenstein's major theatre work was all carried out under the auspices of the Proletkult, where he and Boris Arvatov determined to create an 'agitational-dynamic' theatre. For both of them, their first opportunity was the proposal to stage *The Mexican*, a story by Jack London. They approached the project with the mixture of diffidence and bravado which characterised the approach by Rivera, London's hero, to Kelly, the boxing promoter. Arvatov made a rough dramatisation of the story, and Eisenstein was appointed designer, jointly with Nikitin. The production was ostensibly by Valentin Smyshlyayev, but it was to be a collaborative work, an improvisation from Arvatov's script, which meant that others in the group contributed heavily to the finished creation.

None contributed more than the exuberant co-designer, Sergei Eisenstein. He devised a Cubistic set, consisting of cones and triangles, squares and cubes, and dressed most of the characters in fantastic, clown-like costumes which echoed the stage decorations. The exception was

Figure 28 The Mexican: a 1920–1 Proletkult exercise in 'agitational dynamics', co-directed and designed by Eisenstein.

Rivera, who had no make-up and wore a sombre cloak and hat. The acting style, which was arrived at democratically by the whole group, was grotesque and acrobatic, capitalising on the 'eccentrism' then fashionable, but perhaps more vividly and imaginatively employed than usual. It was a style which rejected 'psychologism' and was rooted in popular, lower-class entertainment.

But Eisenstein's most notable suggestion ran clean contrary to this style: it was to stage the climactic boxing match as a 'real event':

> We dared the concreteness of factual events. The fight was to be carefully planned in advance but was to be utterly realistic. The playing of our young worker-actors in the fight scene differed radically from their acting elsewhere in the production. . . . While the other scenes influenced the audience through intonation, gestures and mimicry, [this] scene employed realistic, even textural means – real fighting, bodies crashing to the ring floor, panting, the shine of sweat on torsos, and finally the unforgettable smacking of gloves against taut skin and strained muscles.[1]

In Eisenstein's phrase, this was 'real doing', and it was set beside the 'pictorial imagination' of the other scenes. These two strands – utilitarian and expressive – were the sharply contrasting acting styles through which Eisenstein constructed his future theatrical works.

The Mexican was sensationally successful but, for reasons too complicated to go into here, the group responsible for it did not produce another show for well over eighteen months. By then, Eisenstein had taken over as artistic director, having spent some months working at the extreme avant-garde theatre workshop of Nikolai Foregger and a year as a student at Meyerhold's Higher Institute of Directing (GVYRM), during which time he had assisted the Master (as Meyerhold was known to his students) in one of his most daring productions, *The Death of Tarelkin*. He had also seen Nemirovich-Danchenko's extremely predictable production of Ostrovsky's comedy, *Enough Simplicity for Every Wise Man* at the Moscow Art Theatre, and had presumably heard Lunacharsky's call for the Soviet theatre to get 'back to Ostrovsky' in 1923, putting away the more outrageous forms of 'eccentrism' (of which the production of *The Death of Tarelkin* was a notorious example) in favour of a more considered realism.

Eisenstein's response was his most famous stage production, a free adaptation by the poet Sergei Tretyakov of *Enough Simplicity for Every Wise Man*, out of which came, directly and immediately, his theory of 'the montage of attractions'.[2] Retitled simply *Mudrets* (*Wise Man*) it was probably the single most shocking, brilliant and challenging production in the Soviet Union during its post-Revolution 'golden age'. It was followed by two more productions of plays by Tretyakov – first, the 'agit-guignol', *Can You Hear Me, Moscow?*, and then the melodrama, *Gas Masks*, staged

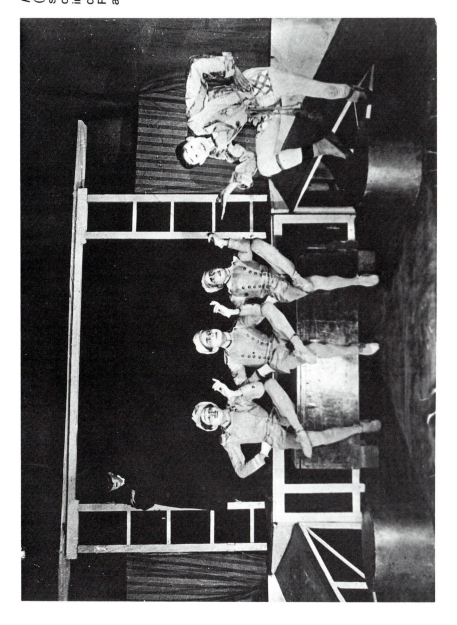

Figure 29 Wise Man (1923): 'the single most striking, brilliant and challenging production in the Soviet Union during its post-Revolution "golden age"'.

in an actual gasworks – before the group went on to make the film, *The Strike*, and never returned to the theatre, at least not as a group.[3]

Because of this migration to another medium, their contribution, and especially Eisenstein's, to the development of epic *theatre* seems to have been largely overlooked. Yet the method evolved for constructing a play, which is clearly visible even in parts of *The Mexican*, was highly original, and, I suspect, much more influential than has until now been acknowledged. It is a method which involves making a play as a 'montage of attractions', that is, creating a series of apparently self-contained scenes or episodes, each utterly different from the others, whose true meaning is only apparent when they are laid side by side and allowed to interact with the other scenes or episodes juxtaposed to them. Each scene is an 'attraction', that is, an 'aggressive moment in theatre',[4] which grips the audience in one way or another, and creates its own immediate response – suspense, titillation, laughter and so on – through the presentation of its content – symbolic, satirical, political or whatever. The greater the variety of kinds of scene, the better. In the terms of the early Russian Formalists, who were the avant-garde's close critical allies at the time, the method employs highly artificial 'devices' as its basic mode of operation, in order to 'make strange' its 'material'.

Following from this, it is the 'basic material', in Eisenstein's terms, which 'moulds' the audience 'in the desired direction (or mood)'.[5] This in turn demands a new approach to acting, and Eisenstein worked hard to develop a suitable training programme for the stage actor, one which could perhaps be revived, at least partially, with some profit:

> In the first place, it is a physical training, embracing sport, boxing, light athletics, collective games, fencing and bio-mechanics. Next it includes special voice training, and beyond this there is education in the history of the class struggle. Training is carried on from ten in the morning till nine at night. The head of the training workshop is Eisenstein.[6]

The programme may have owed a considerable debt to Meyerhold's Workshop, where Eisenstein had been studying, but it includes several original features and is clearly aimed at developing the actor's ability to 'jump' from utilitarian to expressive acting styles and back again at a moment's notice. The purpose of the jumps is to keep the audience on its toes, remind it that it is in a theatre, not lost in dreamland and direct its attention towards the theme and away from an all-absorbing psychology or fate. 'Down with the story and the plot!' Eisenstein wrote in 1924.[7] This method of acting was one of the tools he forged with which to do them down.

It is a method which enables the actor to cope, for instance, with the overt theatricality of Eisenstein's productions. This is initially seen in his finales. The climax of *Can You Hear Me, Moscow?*, for instance, is a play within a play (or rather, a pageant within it), while that of *Wise Man* is a film (*Glumov's Diary*). In *The Mexican*, it is a boxing match, a ritualised, or theatricalised, transposition of a fight, staged with what spectators found to be alarming, though compelling, realism. By thus drawing attention to the theatricality of the event at the moment of its climax, Eisenstein deliberately exploits the contradictions between reality and artificiality, thereby hindering the spectator's incipient desire to 'identify' with the fictional characters and replacing it with a means of establishing a new relationship with the world, and society, beyond the theatre.

This, of course, explains Eisenstein's own appearance at the end of the film of Glumov's diary, as it explains why in *The Mexican* the auditorium is extended right round the boxing ring, with actors playing the part of spectators opposite the real spectators. This is more than 'audience involvement', it is a disruption of the audience's normal role in the theatre. It is presaged in *The Mexican*, for instance, by the way the actors directly address the audience between scenes, sometimes 'in character', sometimes directly as themselves. In *Wise Man*, fireworks exploded under the spectators' seats at the end of the play, in *Can You Hear Me, Moscow?*, the cast turned to the audience to demand: 'Are you listening?' and they were supposed to respond: 'I'm listening!' The climax of this relationship was reached in *Gas Masks* which began with a character 'purifying' the air of the gasworks with a spray, and ended with the real night shift workers coming on duty. Obviously this is a deliberate subversion of the illusion. Its purpose is to focus the audience's attention elsewhere: on the public and social issues beyond the world of the drama.

The attractions imported from the circus served the same ends, by forcing the spectator to admire the performer as performer. Alexandrov's famous walk on the tightrope above the heads of the audience in *Wise Man* symbolised the dangers of returning to Bolshevik Russia for a White émigré, but it was exciting because of the inherent danger that the performer would fall off the tightrope. This is a specifically theatrical attraction because the danger is live, here and now. The same is true of the other acrobatic or gymnastic 'attractions', like the entry of the Komsomol youths in *Gas Masks*, vaulting over the workbenches, not to mention the extensive clowning.

Clowns like George and his mother in *Wise Man* (the mother being the red-wigged buffoon of the circus) are attractions in themselves, but often the techniques of clowning were adapted by Eisenstein to form other attractions. In *The Mexican*, for instance, there was an episode involving the fight audience when an alluring dancer began making eyes at a priest, who was watching in company with his wife. He began to respond, thereby attracting his wife's attention, whereupon she flew at the dancer and began beating her about the head with her umbrella. The husband rushed after, and dragged his infuriated spouse away to the loud guffaws of the gleeful

Figure 30 Gas Masks (1924), staged in a gas works, ended with the real night shift workers coming on duty.

stage spectators: a perfect example of an attraction, a self-contained unit, with characters who never reappear, in an action which adds nothing to the 'story' but, placed as it is between rounds of the boxing match, makes its own implicit comment on that fight. This little episode was itself implicitly commented on in the next pause between rounds when a Japanese docker offended a dignified elderly lady by his support for the unfancied outsider, and was attacked by her.

In *Can You Hear Me, Moscow?*, Marga, the Count's mistress, provides a more explicitly venal kind of attraction. 'Tie my boot-laces,' she suddenly cries when not enough attention is being paid to her:

> *Everybody throws themselves at her feet; the Count, wheezing, at last gets down on his knees with difficulty.*
> VOICES: What legs! Like marble! She's a goddess!
> POUND: In a New York music hall she could make a fortune.
> MARGA (*squealing and laughing*): Don't tickle! Whose are those whiskers? Count, stand up! . . . etc.[8]

Actually, Eisenstein directed the episode so that while the Count was doing up the laces on Marga's high boot, she placed her other boot on his neck in the pose of a big game hunter with a 'trophy'. It is the unexpectedness of the episode, and also perhaps its irrelevance in plot terms – in Meyerhold's phrase, its 'retarding' quality – which makes it so striking.

Another of Eisenstein's favourite devices for the creation of attractions is parody, often of a highly unexpected kind: the film of Glumov's diary parodies contemporary thrillers, for example, while Glumov's desire to hang himself a little later leads him to ascend on a rope to the ceiling in a parody of the Ascension. The entry of the aristocrats in the final scene of *Can You Hear Me, Moscow?* takes parody into political satire, while the entry of the aunt in *Wise Man* satirises bourgeois pretensions and parodies the circus to make its own distinctive attraction: the three suitors whom Mamayeva wishes to console turn (at a mention in the dialogue of 'a horse') into a horse and rider, and Mamayeva cracks her whip to make it prance as if in a ring.

Still other attractions provide the political message: out of a chaos of darkness, screaming and confusion after the boxing match in *The Mexican*, spotlights pick out the triumphant figure of Revolution, arising out of the mêlée. In *Gas Masks*, the anti-religious message is dramatised in a clown 'turn', when Vaska enters with an icon, pursued by a group of Valkyrie-like icon-wielding women, who set about him with their holy placards! In a few moments, the icons are smashed to firewood. The New Economic Policy is similarly mocked in *Wise Man* in a comic fight between Glumov and Golutvin, which ends with Glumov pulling a sign reading NEP out of Golutvin's pocket, which prompts a quick song-and-dance routine from the pair. The class war is caricatured rather more bitterly in *Can You Hear Me,*

Moscow? in the scene where Marga meets Kurt. 'Look at this dishy specimen', she says. 'What a chest, what a pair of eyes.' He disdains her, but she persists, inviting him to kiss her leg. 'Why not? They say my legs are very beautiful. Don't they tickle your fancy?'[9] She lifts her skirt higher. Kurt spits at her. She flies into a rage, attacking him and striking him with her whip until she is dragged away.

The show develops through such symbolic and melodramatic attractions. Other examples include the unmasking and murder of Stumm, the informer; [10] the pulling down of the builders' scaffolding at the end of Act Two; the unveiling of the massive portrait of Lenin in Act Three; and the apparently fortuitous placing of a hammer across a sickle in the play within the play. Here, typically, part of the success of the action resides in the fact that it *interrupts* another action: the pompous poetic commentary on the pageant concerns the Christianisation of the 'savages':

> MARGA: What delightful poetry!
> BISHOP: Very instructive.
> (*In the crowd of savages ready for the struggle, as if accidentally, the hammer and the sickle are crossed, one over the other.*)
> VOICES: The hammer and sickle! Look, the hammer and sickle!
>   It's November the Seventh!
>   Remember Moscow![11]

The interruption reveals the Marxist kernel of the situation: that in the oppression of the 'savages' there is the potential for revolution. This is precisely what is meant by each attraction containing its own 'point'.

But rarely are matters as simple as that. Much more usually, it is the relationship between the attractions, however varied they may be, that contains the meaning; that is, the meaning is in the montage, which then demands what Brecht was to call 'complex seeing': the different attractions set up a series of reverberations which are constantly modified in unexpected ways. In the interlude between Acts One and Two of *The Mexican*, Eisenstein devised a sequence of attractions which illustrate this clearly. Fairy lights light up the proscenium arch, the revolutionary leaders come forward and begin haranguing the audience about the evils of capitalism, especially as it manifests itself in Mexico. Destroying the stage illusion, they appeal to the spectators not to forget the plight of the real Mexico in their excitement about constructing socialism in the RSFSR. The speech ends with a policeman arresting the speaker as an agitator, bringing the spectator back into the fiction. Two clowns rush out, and knock down the policeman. The revolutionary escapes hastily through the auditorium, with the policeman in hot pursuit. The clowns remain. They now begin a cross-talk act with pointed references to contemporary features of life in the young Soviet state. They are interrupted by the appearance of two young women hanging on the arms of the impresario of the boxing match. The clowns watch amazed as they charm free tickets for the match from him and then con a lascivious passer-by into buying them at a hugely inflated price. The policeman returns, and his suspicions are alerted by the young women's heavy come-hithers. Is that a whiff of speculation he smells? Somehow, the clowns get involved again, the buyer of the tickets is dragged away, there is a noisy and acrobatically stunning chase on stage and in the auditorium, in the middle of which the director (or an actor playing the director!) appears and shouts at them to get to their places, the second act is beginning. They rush away, the house lights go down and the next act commences.

It is breathless, fast, funny and above all full of variety and surprises. There is a political speech, which works both within and outside the context of the play, an arrest, a chase, clowns making satirical comments, a cheeky piece of swindling, the use of sex to get one's own way, a theatrical chase and a highly unorthodox interruption to end the sequence. There is no precise 'meaning'; rather, the devices employed prod the audience into sitting up, rubbing their eyes and looking again, and perhaps, hopefully, into making connections between the various kinds of action presented. In *The Mexican*, the montage is a bit of a jumble, though what Eisenstein is aiming for is clear enough. In *Wise Man*, it was less a jumble than a riot. The method was considerably disciplined and tightened in *Can You Hear Me, Moscow?*, in which a much less overtly eccentric drama was presented in such a way as to focus on the political themes, at the expense of traditional characterisation and psychology. And in *Gas Masks*, the method was theatrically more or less consolidated.

By the time of *Gas Masks*, the theatre was, from Eisenstein's point of view, a limitation – hence his wish to present a play in a factory – largely because the method as he had developed it now required a greater potential for 'collisions' between the attractions. This the theatre could not provide, for after any striking moment the actors had to move on and reassemble for the next striking moment. Film provided much greater scope, for instance, to cut from a frowning face, to a cream separator, to a smiling face. Theatre cannot do this, but must work to a different rhythm.

Nevertheless, Eisenstein's achievement was extraordinary. He had developed a series of interlocking components which together comprised not so much a style as a new dramatic form – epic theatre (which, by the way, Aristotle had said was a contradiction in terms). It was an 'action construction' in the sense that meaning was in the action, not in reflections on the action (the boxing match, not the reactions to the boxing match). Its method was grotesque, that is, it allowed utterly dissimilar events, or styles or emotions, to occur in quick and apparently random succession, with absolutely no heed to dramatic unity or decorum. It proceeded by means of attractions, individual episodes, complete in themselves, which caught the spectator's attention and contained their own point. They were bound together by the montage, which provides the apparently disparate elements with a new kind of unity, one which relates to the world beyond the play. To revert to the terminology of the Formalists, montage 'makes strange' reality and organises the work's material in new and surprising ways so as to capture the spectator's imagination.

This was the first consciously defined form of epic theatre, a form more usually associated with Brecht. Thus, where Eisenstein talks of 'attractions' to describe moments like Marga's attack on Kurt, Brecht speaks of 'gestus' when referring, for example, to moments like Garga's attack on Shlink; Eisenstein's 'montage' bears a striking similarity to Brecht's 'interruptions'; and while the Formalists talk of 'making strange', Brecht uses the term '*Verfremdungseffekt*' or 'alienation'. The key concepts are virtually the same, but Brecht almost certainly got them from the Russians, ultimately from Eisenstein. This is not to imply any sort of simplistic handing over of a series of pre-packed instructions for the making of a play, nor is it to deny or belittle Brecht's own huge contribution to the creation and development of twentieth-century epic theatre. But the process needs to be located in the network of writers and theatre practitioners who were responsible for the working out of these creative methods and ideas, and the flow is generally from the Russians to the Germans, or more specifically, from Eisenstein to Brecht.

One central figure in this flow is Sergei Tretyakov, who did not go with Eisenstein into films, though after his stage career was blocked by the censors he did compose a number of screenplays: in 1928 he scripted *Eliso* for Nikolai Shengelaya, which was, according to Jay Leyda, 'a triumph'; in 1930 he worked out the scenario for *Salt for Svanetia* for Mikhail Kalatozov which Leyda calls a 'masterpiece' and 'the most powerful documentary film I've ever seen';[12] and in 1931 he wrote the screenplay for *Song About Heroes*, directed by Joris Ivens and with music by Hanns Eisler, about building the new industrial complex of Magnitogorsk. All that was after he had written other stage plays, most famously *Roar, China!* for the Meyerhold State Theatre, widely seen and acclaimed when the company took it abroad in their repertoire on tour in 1930; and *I Want a Baby*, which was instantly banned and, despite rewrites, has, to the best of my knowledge, never been staged. Yet it is a superb play, built up through a montage of disparate scenes, and almost the only leftist epic drama which deals specifically with the problems of human sexuality. It is perhaps significant that Brecht spent some time trying to make a German version of it. The banning of *I Want a Baby*, Tretyakov's dramatic masterpiece, seems to have turned him away from original play creation. Apart from his documentary film scripts, his only other dramatic work seems to have consisted of translations into Russian of several plays by Brecht, versions the author highly approved of, and insisted were used even in the frozen

Figure 31
Eisenstein with
his close
collaborator
Sergei Tretyakov
and the Chinese
actor Mei-Lan-fan
in 1935.

post-war Stalinist era when Tretyakov's name was utterly unmentionable. He was shot as an 'enemy of the people' in 1939.

Tretyakov's most interesting contribution to the development of the theory of theatrical montage came in the areas of playwrighting and stage speech. In 1923, after his experience with *Wise Man*, he wrote *Earth Rampant*, an adaptation of *Night* by the French Communist and pacifist, Marcel Martinet. In place of the lyrically decorative original, Tretyakov created a script which was sharply episodic, an 'action construction' which turned on the incidents of the story: in other words, where Martinet's play focused on the reactions to the events, Tretyakov's focuses on the events themselves. The individual episodes are 'marked by cinema-like captions with the aim of creating agit-collisions', Tretyakov commented, slogans and comments were projected on to screens. 'The largely figurative poetic phraseology was simplified', he added, and 'the re-formed action complied with the principles of montage.'[13]

The programme for this production at the Meyerhold Theatre stated that the 'montage of the action' was by Meyerhold, the 'montage of the text' by Tretyakov. In effect, this meant that Tretyakov had worked with the actors on the problems of speaking the text. He himself defined the problem as being 'to teach the actor-worker not to converse and not to declaim, but to speak'. This he attempted to do by shifting the emphasis away from the melodic elements in speech, the vowels, on to the 'articulatory-onomatopoeic (the consonants)', and away from 'conversational intonation (usually unreal anyway, since real conversation accumulates verbal rubbish as well as all sorts of drawings in of breath, hiccoughs, clearings of the throat and other messy noises)' on to 'rhythmical configurations' which were 'crystallised from examples of common phraseology'. Speech then took on the quality of 'verbal gesture' and the actor's task was to create a 'vocal mask' analogous to his 'set role'.[14] Once the actor has acquired this, he is equipped to 'jump' from expressive to utilitarian modes without strain. Thus, Tretyakov attempted to extend Eisenstein's theory of montage to text and speech, in effect to find a new way of writing plays and a new technique of acting.[15]

Tretyakov first met Brecht in Germany in 1930. In 1931 he returned to Germany to lecture on 'The Writer and the Socialist Village' and spent some time during his five months in the country with Brecht, who took him to Augsburg, his birthplace. Tretyakov's view of *Man Equals Man* in Brecht's 1931 production which he saw during his stay was that only Meyerhold's version of *The Magnanimous Cuckold* had made a deeper impression on him.[16] Brecht and he became friends and allies ('my teacher, tall and kindly', Brecht called him[17]) and equally targets for Lukács's polemics against unorthodoxy. Tretyakov published Brecht's *Epic Dramas* in Moscow in 1934, the same year that Brecht was telling an interviewer for the Swedish newspaper, *Ekstrabladet*, that 'in Russia there's one man who's working along the right lines, Tretyakov; a play like *Roar, China* shows him to have found quite new means of expression'.[18] The next year, Brecht stayed with Tretyakov in Moscow, where he was introduced to Viktor Shklovsky, the Formalist critic and film scenarist. '*Ostranenie*' was Shklovsky's term: it translates as '*Verfremdungseffekt*' or what has come to be known in English as the 'alienation effect'. As secretary of the international section of the Writers Union and committee member of the Society for Cultural Relations with Foreign Countries, Tretyakov was instrumental in arranging the performance programme of the visiting Chinese actor, Mei Lan-fan, at this time, and it was in his article written about Mei Lan-fan after watching him in Moscow, that Brecht first used Shklovsky's term and discussed the '*Verfremdungseffekt*': the essay is reproduced in Willett's *Brecht on Theatre* as 'Alienation Effects in Chinese Acting'.[19]

But, if Tretyakov is the closest and most obvious link between Eisenstein and Brecht, he is by no means the only one. For political-historical reasons, Germany and the Soviet Union were ostracised by the international community in the 1920s, and therefore took much notice of each other culturally. One couple involved in the traffic between the two countries were Bernhard Reich and Asja Lacis. Lacis studied acting with Kommissarzhevsky in Moscow, and then in 1920 at the State Film School, where she was when she appeared in Kuleshov's *On the Red Front*.

In 1922 she and Reich moved to Berlin, and in the following year Reich became director of the Munich Kammerspiele, where Brecht was due to mount *Edward II*. When Brecht met him and Asja Lacis he 'interrogated her. He was visibly interested in information about Soviet Russia and its cultural politics. This conversation was followed by many others.'[20] The 'cultural politics', of course, concerned Eisenstein and his relationship with the Proletkult, the development of Meyerhold's theatre and the progress of the infant Soviet film industry, particularly as it concerned Kuleshov, Eisenstein and others. Lacis became Brecht's assistant director on *Edward II*, and even played the part of the king's son. Not surprisingly in the light of Brecht and Lacis's 'many' conversations, 'the production contained the seeds of a new way of writing plays, and . . . a new technique of acting was revealed'.[21] These were based in the kind of theatre which Lacis had learned from the avant-garde in Moscow. Volker comments that this production 'became, as it were, the foundation stone of the Brechtian theatre'.[22] Reich explains at least part of the apparent originality:

German actors attach little importance to formal actions such as eating, drinking or fencing. They summarise them, simply indicate them casually. Brecht, however, demanded not only that they should be performed realistically and exactly, but that they should be skilful. He explained to the actors that such actions on the stage should give the audience pleasure.[23]

The technique, of course, is precisely that developed by Eisenstein for the boxing match in *The Mexican*, where he insisted that the fight be performed absolutely believably. This was in 1921, while Reich and Lacis were still in Moscow, and closely in touch with the circles Eisenstein and his company moved in.

In 1924, shortly after the *Edward II* production, Asja Lacis met the critic Walter Benjamin, who found her (as Brecht did) extremely attractive. She and Reich returned to Moscow in 1925, and Benjamin followed them there in 1926. On New Year's Eve, he met Meyerhold, having already been excited by his work, and was present at one famous 'dispute' about Meyerhold's production of *The Government Inspector*:

> Thousands collected in the huge hall to discuss Meyerhold's staging of [the play]. They followed the controversy with every fibre, interrupting, applauding, shouting, whistling. The Russian speakers fascinated Benjamin: he thought they were born tribunes. Among others, Mayakovsky, Meyerhold and Bely spoke.[24]

By 1928 Lacis was back in Berlin with the Soviet Trade Delegation responsible for film distribution. The following year she introduced Benjamin to Brecht, and a highly important connection was made: all Benjamin's shrewd comments on Brecht's theatre are informed by his 'fascination' with the Russian avant-garde theatre.

The list of mutual contacts between Eisenstein and Brecht could be prolonged considerably. There was, for instance, the musician Edmund Meisel, who composed the score for *The Battleship Potemkin* when it came to Berlin in 1926. He worked in the closest possible collaboration with Eisenstein to produce 'a new quality of sound structure . . . a unity of fused musical and visual images'.[25] At the same time Meisel was working almost equally closely with Brecht on *Man Equals Man*: Brecht 'sketched rough drafts of the songs that Edmund Meisel . . . actually composed'.[26] It was immediately after this that Brecht did his most potent work with music, in dramas such as *The Threepenny Opera*. Meisel went on to work extensively with Erwin Piscator, whose connections with the Moscow theatrical and cinema worlds are also well known. The chronicle could continue, but perhaps the point has been made.

Eisenstein met Brecht in Germany in 1929, and on the train to Moscow in 1932, when Eisenstein was, according to Brecht, 'ill'.[27] Both were also present at the same performance by Mei Lan-fan in Moscow in 1935. But by then, Eisenstein had left his theatre work far behind and Brecht was not in need of his personal support. Brecht certainly admired *The Battleship Potemkin* as much as anyone, and intended to invite Eisenstein to join his projected 'Diderot Society' in the later 1930s. But he never admitted to being influenced by Eisenstein in the development of his own concept of epic theatre, perhaps because he was unsure of just how great that debt might be. For Eisenstein's theatre work, which aimed to 'mould' the audience through a montage of attractions, should be seen as probably the earliest conscious demonstration of epic theatre in practice and his formulation as perhaps its first exposition.

Chapter 7

Eisenstein's Pushkin project

Håkan Lövgren

Looking at Eisenstein's career from the time of his Mexican–American adventure of 1931–2 to his last film, *Ivan the Terrible* in the 1940s, we find – with one ambiguous exception – a discouraging succession of planned, half-realised and completely aborted projects. Film projects were initiated, then abandoned for lack of official support; sometimes the shooting was started; and in one case several versions of the film were actually finished, only for the whole project to be abruptly cancelled. Set-backs and reversals of this sort came to play an ever greater role in Eisenstein's artistic life after the undoing of his Mexican film. Stalin's telegram to Upton Sinclair in November 1931, which declared that Eisenstein had lost his comrades' confidence and was regarded as a traitor who had deserted his country, effectively signalled the end of his American sojourn as well as the beginning of a period of hardship that unquestionably hastened his death. When Soviet representatives failed or refused to purchase the Mexican footage from Sinclair and have it sent to Moscow, the director lapsed into serious depression and had to be hospitalised in August 1933. To my mind, Eisenstein never really recovered from the loss of *Que Viva Mexico!*

Although he was not a man to complain about his own situation, these frustrations obviously had to find some outlet. Two drawings made on the same sheet in September 1939 graphically illustrate his state of mind.[1] The top one depicts a man blowing his head off with a gun, with the caption (in English) 'That's how I do feel'. The bottom one shows a mysterious one-eyed creature banging his head against the wall of a tower with the caption 'ALSO'. This last drawing recalls one of a ram-like rendition of Pushkin that Eisenstein made some time later in connection with his Pushkin project, *The Love of a Poet*.[2]

It was toward the end of the 1930s that Eisenstein's interest in Pushkin focused on the poet's biography, on his fate as an original artist at logger-heads with artistic traditions and, above all, on a collision course with representatives of the highest power in autocratic tsarist society. It is my conjecture in this chapter that Eisenstein's intense interest in Pushkin's biography – in the tragic inevitability of an artist's demise under oppression

– was in part prompted by parallels he drew between his own life and Pushkin's, based on his experiences in Stalin's Soviet Union. It was characteristic of those times that, in February 1937, Eisenstein had been forced to publish a disclaimer of rumours circulating in the Western Press that he had been arrested. He knew of course about the harassment of many of his colleagues – the arrest and disappearance of his mentor Vsevolod Meyerhold in June 1939 probably affected him the most deeply – and he no doubt thought that he might be next in line.

His career soon took an abrupt series of contradictory turns. On 23 November 1938, the obviously patriotic *Alexander Nevsky* opened in Moscow and Eisenstein thanked Stalin for his personal support for the film. In February 1939, he was awarded the Order of Lenin for the direction of *Nevsky*. In August of that same year, the film was completely withdrawn from the repertoire following the Molotov–Ribbentrop non-aggression pact. In December he was asked to direct Wagner's *Die Walküre* at the Bolshoi Theatre, also as a consequence of the pact. On 18 December 1940, he had to introduce a series of programmes on Radio Moscow directed at listeners in Nazi Germany. Eisenstein, a Jew, had to declare that the German–Soviet non-aggression pact was a solid basis for cultural co-operation between the two great peoples. Half a year later, when Germany attacked the Soviet Union, *Alexander Nevsky* was restored to the repertoire and Eisenstein made another broadcast, 'To fellow Jews of the world'.

I have tried to reconstruct and analyse the project that grew during this period out of Eisenstein's interest in the life of Pushkin, a colour film to be called *The Love of a Poet* (Lyubov' poeta).[3] The scenario is fragmented and incomplete, no doubt because it was worked out in several sketches and versions over an eighteen-month period. Although it did not come to fruition, Eisenstein seems never to have quite abandoned the idea. The script was to convey Pushkin's life through the use of colours which would not be naturalistically motivated, but rather based on leitmotivs that would also govern the musical score Prokofiev was to compose for the film. Colour was to be applied symbolically as an expression of Pushkin's situation and subjective perception of the world around him.

'Colour / in film / begins where it no longer corresponds to natural colouration', said Eisenstein in an interview shortly before his death in February 1948.[4] The idea of expressive, as opposed to natural, colour was basic to the storyboard script he prepared on 4 March 1940. This *mise-en-scène* contained seventy-five frames, fifty-seven of which showed the prostrate Tsar Boris in his famous monologue, 'I have attained the highest power', from Pushkin's ill-fated drama *Boris Godunov*. Eisenstein apparently planned a complete adaptation of Pushkin's play, but this detailed storyboard, with frames coloured in red and blue pencil, is all that remains of an initial idea that eventually moved in two directions: first, towards the script and synopsis for the Pushkin biography; and second, into the script for *Ivan the Terrible*. The colour sequence from this, his last film, is also the only realised example of what he had in mind when he spoke of colour in film.

Why did Eisenstein begin his adaptation with Boris's monologue, which is the seventh of the play's twenty-three scenes? We might find an answer in an article he wrote in February 1940, which discussed the genre of Soviet historical films.[5] In this he noted Pushkin's recommendation for a proper theme in tragedy: 'Man and the people. The fate of man and the fate of the people.' He went on to suggest a careful study of *Boris Godunov*, in particular the well-known monologue and the equally famous last scene, in which 'the people are silent'. These two scenes are the best foundation for an attempt to characterise the soloist and choir, the 'highest power' and the people, and their relationship. Contravening Pushkin's advice and example, Soviet historical films had tended to show either the 'highest power' or the 'silent people'.

Eisenstein's version of Boris's monologue gives great emphasis to the individual psychological reality of the tsar's predicament. This is done through the framing of the shots, the topography of the set, hyperbolic acting and the application of colour, all of which later surfaced in *Ivan the Terrible*. The relationship between ruler and ruled, tsar and people and ultimately tsar and poet/artist (the poet as a kind of representative of the people), is made more dynamic in Eisenstein's script through the tsar's *visible* and *hyperbolic* reactions to the accusations of the people, as though he had heard actual voices. Eisenstein has Boris plead before the Last Judgement fresco in the Uspensky Cathedral, and when the only answer is silence, he darts through the cathedral into the palace in a frenzied chase from one chamber to the next, only to find himself at a dead end in a small prayer room. From this climactic point of prayer, he rushes back the same way he came, crashing back through the cathedral, overturning candelabra and appropriately setting the whole place on fire before he sinks down in front of the horrible visions of the Last Judgements.

This nightmarish conception of Boris's emotions as he sums up his reign, from the glorious prospects outlined by the astrologers to the dismal isolation his own bad conscience has imposed upon him, is motivated by God rejecting Boris's wish to repent and be absolved from the people's accusations of having killed the true Tsar, Dimitri. I believe that the possibility of 'orchestrating' these elements of an individual psychological predicament – Boris being abandoned by God and responsible to the people only – was the initial reason for Eisenstein's choice of the seventh scene of *Boris Godunov*. This choice almost immediately led him towards Pushkin's biography, as is indicated by a comment on the first page of the script: 'NB. Much better for "Pushkin"'.

Pushkin's biography is structured as a number of overlapping triangular relationships, mostly involving an older and a younger man in rivalry over a woman. These relationships are for the most part based on themes from Pushkin's works: *Boris Godunov*, the verse narrative *The Gypsies* and other poems. I have used Roman Jakobson's idea of an emerging theme of destructive statues in Pushkin's poetry ('the myth of the destructive statue') in my analysis, since this seems to cohere with Eisenstein's notion of a 'gradual loss of colour', as Pushkin's life is gradually dehumanised.[6]

It is at the end of 1829, when Pushkin courted Natalia Goncharova, that the theme appears of statues representing old men who interfere disastrously with the lives of younger men. In Pushkin's work from this time the 'old husband, terrible husband' theme of *The Gypsies* – the work that provides the thematic starting point and leitmotiv of Eisenstein's 'First Outline' of the Pushkin project – regresses into something primitive and atavistic, into magical statues or *idols*, which inexplicably come alive to wreck havoc in the lives of these young men; a theme of development from youthful, dynamic passions toward mechanical, inexorable Fate.[7] Such was also the development Eisenstein outlined in his Pushkin biography: 'the poet's fate from the careless days in Odessa to the cold snow by Black Creek', the site of the duel that ended Pushkin's life.[8] What we see in Eisenstein's treatment is the evolution of a conspiracy to kill an artist.

THE LOVE OF A POET

Part I: *The Gypsies*: the theme of superstition, colour and the terrible husband

The Love of a Poet was Eisenstein's solution to the search for a suitable theme for a film in colour, 'where colour would not be used as colouration, but as an internally motivated dramaturgic factor'.[9]

> A *biography* of Pushkin in colour would result in the same vivid colour dramaturgy, the same motion of a colour spectrum in the key of the poet's developing life story as the one displayed in Gogol's output – not in his biography, but in the sequence of his *works*.[10]

The idea was inspired by Andrei Bely's monograph, *Gogol's Mastery*, which described how the spectrum of colour epithets in Gogol is increasingly 'depleted' to end with a range of only white, grey and black.[11] According to Bely, the reduction of colours followed a cyclical pattern that closely corresponded to the pattern of Gogol's psychological crises.[12]

The central conflict in Eisenstein's 'First Outline' is one of colour, the conflict between black and white in which traditional semantics is reversed: 'how nice that evil is not black but white', he writes to Tynyanov with obvious delight.[13] This first synopsis, dated two days after the Boris monologue, is a triptych with a prologue.

Prologue. Hannibal. The scene of a black among whites. One against all.
Like the nucleus of the scene that develops later (in Part III).
Pushkin alone against all of society and Nicholas I.[14]

Part I describes Pushkin's stay in Bessarabia and how his Don Juan tendencies develop. The point of departure is *The Gypsies* and the setting a shabby gypsy camp. We find Pushkin in the company of Aleko, the stranger-husband of the Gypsy Zemphira, the Old Man and Mariula, her mother who ran away with a younger Gypsy. Three basic themes are presented: (1) *Bes arapskii*, 'The Black Demon', Eisenstein's title for Pushkin's life in the South; (2) the Gypsy fortune-teller's warning to stay clear of a man in white; and (3) the composition of the romance 'Old husband, terrible husband'.

Eisenstein seems to have explored two variations of *The Gypsies'* plot. First he places Pushkin in the arms of Mariula, as a rival of the Old Man. In the second version, Pushkin plays the role of Zemphira's young Gypsy lover, who is killed by Aleko in the poem: 'Bessarabia. Tents. The Old Man wakes them up. Goodbye to Zemphira. Hasty departure; husband (with bear) returning. She meets husband with song, "Old husband, terrible husband". Pushkin grasps motive and escapes.'[15] By settling on the latter version, Eisenstein attaches Pushkin to a 'poetic myth' which predicts his fate to be killed, although that fate is postponed a number of times in the course of his Don Juan escapades (including the seduction of a Greek and a Turkish woman, of his superior's wife, Vorontsova, etc.). To underline the myth of *The Gypsies* and bring the theme of superstition and antithetical, fateful 'whiteness' into Pushkin's adventures, Eisenstein introduces an encounter with a Gypsy fortune-teller, who conveniently passes the old graveyard where Pushkin is hiding:

> The prediction: 'Beware of a man in white'. Pushkin laughs. In this series the motif is established. The motif is clothed in the words: 'Old husband, terrible husband. . . .' He rides across the steppe. (His white shirt is flying open. Close-fitting black pants.)[16]

The background colours of the steppe are toned down and diluted, Eisenstein suggests, as though painted with thin washes in the soft style of early nineteenth-century water colours.[17]

Part II: The Mikhailovskoye scene

Part II is set at Mikhailovskoye, Pushkin's estate. Here the theme of the devil is shifted from Pushkin's person ('The Black Demon') and expanded into a concept of Pushkin as the banished poet, haunted by real as well as imaginary devils and demons.

A blizzard rages, as in Pushkin's poem 'The Demons'. Here the saturated colours return to create a full spectrum of colour contrasts. Pushkin hears news of the Decembrist uprising at Senate Square and is horrified. Eisenstein writes:

> The poet perceived the image of the Tsar and tsar-murderer, Alexander, in Boris' face.
> The smouldering fire in the Mikhailovskoye fireplace flares up.
> It seems as if Tsar Nicholas stares at the poet from the fireplace (a quite permissible transition in film).
> The poet's hand is nervously drawing gallows on a piece of paper.
> Gallows, gallows, gallows.
> 'And maybe I . . . Even I . . .' – he nervously remembers the Decembrists.[18]

Another version of the scenario first presents the terrified Pushkin drawing gallows on a piece of paper.[19] There is a distant sound of church bells. His glance into the smouldering fire reveals the dim face of Tsar Nicholas. Pushkin violently throws the crumpled piece of paper into the fireplace. The flames flare up and turn into lit candles. The bells get louder and blend with the image of burning candles in the Uspensky Cathedral. Boris begins: 'I have attained. . . .' His face resembles that of Tsar Nicolas. Pushkin jumps up in anger, shouting at the fireplace: 'Yes, wretched he whose. . . .'

In Eisenstein's shooting script, when Boris finally falls in front of the fresco after the last lines of the monologue, there is a shot of a fire burning, another of a fireplace, and we see Pushkin hurl himself back into an armchair, away from the vision in the fire. 'Yes, wretched he whose conscience is not clear', is heard from an unknown source. The face of Nicholas appears in the fire; and a second shot shows Nicholas in front of his own fireplace 'with all the conceivable terror caused by an unclear conscience (when one is alone with oneself) reflected in his face. Or rather the horror caused by his fear of revenge.'[20]

The last version presents a more ambiguous state in which the idea of blame and guilt is transferred by association through cutting. The repeated cuts between shots of Pushkin and Nicholas in identical positions in front of a fireplace indicate that both suffer from an uneasy conscience through their association with the tormented Boris in front of the Last Judgement fresco, before a higher authority in the cathedral and before the people in the text of the monologue. Pushkin has a bad conscience because of his Decembrist connections and may still have to answer for his political views in the subsequent phase of reaction. History has turned Pushkin's *Boris Godunov*, whose monologue might have been conceived only weeks before the uprising, into something potentially dangerous to the poet himself.

Part III: Petersburg: the duel

In Part III Pushkin is ordered to leave Mikhailovskoye and he travels in a covered wagon to Petersburg. He appears at the theatre and the image of Boris recurs when Tsar Nicholas is seen sitting with a lady in a rear box entirely covered in red. The Tsar is dressed all in white ('beware of a man in white'), while the red of the box echoes the carpet and candles in the cathedral. Boris should be dressed in white as well, Eisenstein reflects.

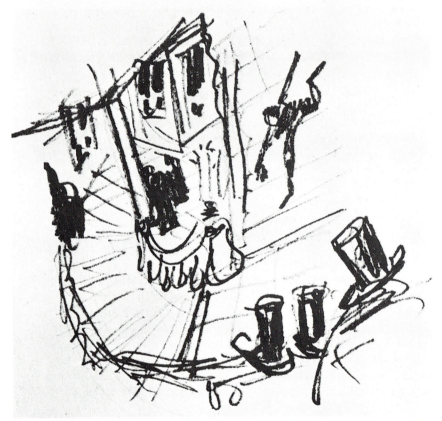

Figure 32 Sketch of a masquerade scene planned for the Pushkin film: the poet's flight from the ball in a whirlwind of movement and colour seen through the top-hats of bystanders.

With the image of Boris, Nicholas I and the theatre stage, a ballet or ball scene is introduced. The famous ballerina Istomina, from Pushkin's *Eugene Onegin*, dressed in violet and white, is juxtaposed with Natalia Goncharova, also in pale violet and white. Pushkin notices his wife-to-be at the theatre. Eisenstein writes:

The intoxication of love will end in marriage. The wedding (with Karamzina's blessing). Down to the last detail (there is no carriage, etc). The wedding ring falls. A bad omen. The first morning – she is not beside him. . . . He sees her in an adjoining room, by the window. And Nicholas passes by. A coincidence . . . or?[21]

Natalia is now presented as the pale violet and white doll who flirts with Boris and with the henchman Nicholas. She is becoming an instrument of death, a means of killing the poet. She becomes, as Marina Tsvetayeva wrote, 'that empty place toward which they are all drawn, around which all forces and passions clash'.[22]

Events begin to swirl in a gigantic vortex in which the 'devils' and 'demons' of Petersburg, characters and sites from literature associated with the city, Natalia, Pushkin's younger rival D'Anthès, Tsar Nicholas – all merge into something insubstantial. The themes of the ballet and ball return with the leitmotiv from 'The Demons'. Eisenstein describes a masquerade scene where colours shift from pitch-black to red in a kind of chromatic whirlwind.

First within one shot, then from shot to shot, then in a climax of smudged, out-of-focus shots (blood-red from the light of the candles) with a cut from one to the other; and then from a bright whirlwind to an absolutely black distorted shot. Pushkin runs out (to the Bronze Horseman). Everything around is an unclear hurricane. . . . A maddening whirlwind. (Devils in might and main). A whisper. At the very peak of the whirlwind a door is thrust open. Pushkin comes home.[23]

The theme of 'The Demons', superfluousness and exile, is appropriately transcended by the theme of doom, damnation and impending death. The whole action takes place in a nocturnal Petersburg and, while all colours begin to change, only black remains unaltered. Eisenstein makes the rhythm and fantastic character of the masquerade continue in Pushkin's sleigh ride to the site of the duel, Black Creek. Pushkin and his second meet all the familiar and indifferent faces, faces of people who ought to recognise the poet, but do not reveal that they do.

No one feels sorry for him.
And he is pleased.
He is on his way to a duel.
And he is very glad no-one interferes.
They pass a luxurious sleigh.
In it sits a fashionably dressed woman.
But the woman is near-sighted and does not recognise the curly-haired gentleman.

Although this curly-haired poet is her husband. [. . .]
A fleeting burst of cherry-red – it is the satin of Natalia's muff.
Natalia, the 'cross-eyed madonna'.
A dim grey tonality dominates now.
And the contrast of black and white.
Snow.[24] [. . .]

Meeting his rival.
The line Pushkin – D'Anthès – Nicholas.
The Bronze Horseman.
The disc of the moon in the blue-black darkness of the night.
Nicholas' bronze face.
'Just you wait!'
The theme of Othello.
The Gypsies once again. Not in the freedom of the South, but in a poor Gypsy apartment at Black Creek.
Morning pancakes.
The Gypsies sing Pushkin's own song from *The Gypsies* for him.
'Old husband, terrible husband . . .'
Just as they sang *byliny* to Ivan the Terrible in his old age, sang stories about him, about his taking Kazan.
Now the 'old husband' (although he is only thirty-seven), 'terrible husband' is Pushkin himself.
The order of cuckolds.[25]

The symbolism of the dominant colours, white, red and black, is simple, although the manner in which it is represented, the way themes and colours interweave, is quite intricate and technically sophisticated. The evil of white, the bloodstained guilt of red and the good of black: Boris Godunov dressed in white on the red carpets in the cathedral; Nicholas I in the theatre in a similar colour combination; the dancing couples at the masquerade suddenly looking like blood-red flames; Natalia's red muff and the red reflection striking her white hands through the red stained-glass window (a Lady Macbeth theme, of course) at Pushkin's home, after the mortally-wounded poet has been carried there; and finally, when all colours have been reduced to black, the poet himself, a black man, is visited by a lady all in black, Karamzina, the historian's wife. She watches him being lowered into the dark coffin, which is hurriedly taken away to the accompaniment of Prokofiev's Requiem into the black night.

THE LETTER TO TYNYANOV

In Eisenstein's synopsis, Pushkin is relentlessly driven to his own destruction by his uncompromising attitude towards his art and because of an early unspoken, but never forgotten, love for an older woman – his 'nameless love', as Yuri Tynyanov called it. In a letter intended for the critic, Eisenstein wrote about the Pushkin project: 'But – *mon Dieu*! – how to find a path for a compositional fairway in this ocean of adventures!'[26] The letter was written in 1943, while Eisenstein was filming *Ivan the Terrible* in Alma Ata, after he had read Tynyanov's novel *Pushkin* and an earlier article 'The Nameless Love', but was never sent due to Tynyanov's death.[27] Tynyanov's hypothesis was that Pushkin's entire life had been determined by his efforts to find an *Ersatz* for his youthful love, Yekaterina Andreyevna, wife of the writer and historian Nicholas Karamzin. Tynyanov believed he had found proof of this hypothesis in his own and others' analyses of the poet's correspondence and poetry, and in the fact that on his deathbed Pushkin calls first for Karamzina.[28] Eisenstein is enthusiastic:

> That's the theme. Of course! The clue to everything. . . . The immediate psychological credibility of your hypothesis is of course connected with the memory traces of the Freudian (*assez possible*) interpretation of 'Don Juanism' as a search for the one, the only one (there isn't a Don Juan in Pushkin's works 'for nothing').[29]

In an interview with Ilya Vaisfeld two days before he died, Eisenstein explained his own hypothesis about the reasons for Pushkin's tragic relations with women.[30] He maintained that the old man who prevents a young man from realising his dream is a theme that permeates Pushkin's work and has a strong autobiographical basis. Pushkin's frustrated love for Karamzin's wife is the motor behind his lifelong search for a woman to replace her, and the real explanation for his 'Don Juanism'. Eisenstein thought this also answered the mysterious question of why Pushkin fell in love with and married Natalia Goncharova. The frivolous and coquettish Natalia *somehow* reminded him of Karamzina – 'Natalia as a "formal" *Ersatz* for Karamzina'.[31]

Pushkin's relation to the twenty-year-older Karamzina has, in Tynyanov's characterisation, an obvious ring of the mother substitute. According to the Freudian account of the Oedipus complex, Karamzin then becomes a competing, threatening and potentially castrating father figure. Such father figures also played a decisive role in Pushkin's life and in his choice of artistic themes and symbols. As for Freud's explanation of 'Don Juanism', Eisenstein rejects this: 'No, Freud has nothing to say here. Pushkin's love had nothing to do with eroticism. This love becomes the tragedy of his life which marks his entire creation.'[32] Both Tynyanov and Eisenstein want to hold at bay the idea of Pushkin as a careless Don Juan.[33] Their 'de-eroticised' Pushkin may have less to do with reality than with a certain prudish wish to elevate the biographical to the same level as the artistic motives of a great poet.[34]

Figure 33 The critic and writer Yuri Tynyanov offered Eisenstein a persuasive interpretation of Pushkin's life as a search for his youthful 'nameless love'.

THE LIVING STATUES

The collapse of the Decembrist revolt resulted in political quarantine for Pushkin and a ban on publishing *Boris Godunov*. According to Jakobson, it was also the beginning of a gradual resignation that culminated in Pushkin's marriage to Natalia.[35] The poet became more and more convinced that the revolt had been premature and suicidal. His 'capitulation' was expressed in a letter to Zhukovsky in 1826: 'No matter what my political and religious views are, I intend to keep them for myself alone, and I do not intend to oppose madly the established order and necessity.'[36]

Towards the end of 1829, as Jakobson has shown, the 'myth of the destructive statue' emerges in Pushkin's poetry.[37] This finds expression in 'The Stone Guest' (1830), 'The Bronze Horseman' (1833) and 'The Golden Cockerel' (1834) and its appearance coincides with Pushkin's proposal to Natalia in 1829. Jakobson's three principles for the plot development in these poems are:

1 A man is weary, he settles down longing for rest, and this motif is intertwined with desire for a woman.
2 The statue, more precisely the being who is inseparably connected with the statue, has supernatural, unfathomable power over the desired woman.
3 After vain resistance, the man perishes through the intervention of the statue, which has miraculously set itself in motion, and the woman vanishes.[38]

The relationship implied in Eisenstein's scenario, the 'line of Pushkin – D'Anthès – Nicholas', 'The Bronze Horseman' and 'Nicholas' bronze features' is one of three men's rivalry over the same woman, Natalia. But this relationship of four is in fact triangular, since D'Anthès is only an agent of Tsar Nicholas in the conspiracy to eliminate the poet. Thus the inexorability of fate, the bronze features of Nicholas, come alive in D'Anthès, just as the statue of the Bronze Horseman comes alive to hound Eugene in Pushkin's poem. There is then a certain convergence of perspective between Jakobson's triangular scheme and Eisenstein's plotting of Pushkin's fate in Parts II and III of his scenario.

Eisenstein's image of Natalia also resembles a statue, a marble nymph like Dimitri's Marina in *Boris Godunov*. She is a symbol of 'whiteness', the colour of evil and destruction. But while Marina is ambitious and intriguing, Natalia is portrayed as a mindless and myopic doll, a treacherous tool used in Pushkin's destruction. In *The Love of a Poet* as a whole, the female and male roles remain largely constant in function, while their individual fates differ. They are all, men and women alike, unreliable, conniving, treacherous – apart from, of course, Karamzina and Pushkin. In Eisenstein's scenario, all the tsars and D'Anthès are evil people, dressed in

Figure 34 The destroyed third part of *Ivan* showed a prostrate Ivan before the Last Judgement, recalling the film's debt to Pushkin's *Boris Godunov*.

white, who are interchangeable: Boris becomes Nicholas, who in turn is likened to the Bronze Horseman, namely Tsar Peter, whose destructive role in Pushkin's poem is assumed by D'Anthès, the poet's killer.

Eisenstein's intention is to have Pushkin change roles with the triangular relationship of two men and one woman, to have him change position in the rivalry between a married older man and a young man over the married man's wife as his life comes to an end with the duel at Black Creek. In Part I of the scenario, Pushkin is temporarily saved from the fate of the young Gypsy in the poem, whose role he is playing. In Part III, he is overwhelmed by having to compete in two triangular relationships: both Tsar Nicholas and D'Anthès are rivals courting his wife Natalia. The younger D'Anthès seemingly wins and what remains is a triangle in which Pushkin suddenly has become the 'old husband'. He then understands that Fate has caught up with him, that the 'man in white' has finally arrived. The final sleigh-ride is presented as a confirmation of this fate by both the poet and the public he meets on the way.

The main dynamics of *The Love of a Poet* revolve around the slow inversion of life into death, of somebody into nobody, a poet's socially and politically induced resignation to fate. With it, Eisenstein wanted to use a new symbolic dimension of colour to decipher the social and psychological meaning of Pushkin's life and work in particular, and no doubt of artistic work under autocratic and repressive conditions in general. The fact that the destroyed third part of *Ivan the Terrible* included a prostrate Ivan in front of the the Last Judgement, before the Tsar of Heaven in the Uspensky Cathedral, shows how important this issue of power, guilt and responsibility continued to be in Eisenstein's work. The intervention of 'old men' in the lives of Pushkin and Eisenstein – Tsars Alexander and Nicholas in the former case, Stalin in the latter – led to the death of both artists. Pushkin from a bullet, Eisenstein more slowly from the decision to take his last unfinished project away from him.

EPILOGUE

When Eisenstein insisted on pursuing his proposal for Part II of *Ivan the Terrible*, he apparently understood that he could be signing his own death warrant.[39] The decision to persist must have been made some time during his simultaneous reading of Tynyanov's Pushkin works and further speculations on *The Love of a Poet*. On 2 February 1946, he finished editing the second part of *Ivan* and went to a reception and party in honour of the Stalin Prize winners later that evening. While dancing, he was struck by a severe heart attack and fell to the floor. He should have died, but miraculously survived, 48 years old. A fortune-teller in Hollywood had predicted that he would not die before his fiftieth birthday, but to Eisenstein what followed was a *post scriptum*, an extension to the life of an artist that in some sense was over. About three months after his release from hospital, the censors decided to shelve Part II of *Ivan*. It was never shown in Eisenstein's lifetime, just as *Boris Godunov* was never performed while Pushkin was alive. Eisenstein died between the 10th and 11th of February 1948, two weeks after his fiftieth birthday and, as Naum Kleiman has noted, 111 years and 11 hours after the death of Pushkin.[40] He was in the middle of preparing an article on colour in cinema and taking notes on the works of Pushkin and Gogol.

Chapter 8

Eisenstein and Shakespeare

N. M. Lary

Eisenstein's English-speaking audience views his last film project from a perspective dominated by the histories and tragedies of Shakespeare. Echoes of the plays abound in the two parts of *Ivan the Terrible* the Soviet film-maker was allowed to complete. Of course Eisenstein worked with a multiplicity of models; examples from many different artists were constantly finding application in his work. He noted with surprise the way something out of the great fund of works he had read and seen would come to mind at the very moment it could be useful to him. Other artists helped him – they also challenged him: Naum Kleiman has spoken about the sense of *contest* or *competition* in Eisenstein's relations with other artists.[1] While acknowledging the role of the many other artistic examples that continually interact in Eisenstein's work, we may focus on what Eisenstein learned from Shakespeare. And we are free to pass to the questions of how he measured himself against the playwright and how we ourselves measure Eisenstein against Shakespeare.

My undertaking here is a preliminary one, a clearing of the ground. I will review the history of Eisenstein's engagement with Shakespeare, consider some of the evidence that Eisenstein conceived his last film project as a tragedy and look at his late writings on Shakespeare to see how they bear on his use of Shakespeare in his creative work.

One difficulty may be mentioned at the outset. We are well advised to look for a typology of Elizabethan and Jacobean moments in the *Ivan* films but we cannot consider Eisenstein's relation to Shakespeare alone. We also need to remember the relevance of Marlowe, Ben Jonson and Webster (possibly his favourite 'Elizabethans').[2] He soon learned to see Shakespeare in relation to these other playwrights. He was helped in this by his friend, the scholar, critic and translator of Elizabethan and Jacobean plays, I. A. Aksyonov (who also wrote two studies of Eisenstein and one of Picasso), and by T. S. Eliot's *Sacred Wood*, which he read with close attention.[3]

Take Yevfrosinia's descent into madness at the end of Part II of the film as she clutches her dead son, mistakenly killed in place of Ivan as a conse-

Figure 35 Eisenstein sketched characters and a setting for Jonson's *Bartholomew Fair* in 1919.

quence of her wild scheming. Here Eisenstein gives us another great Jacobean mad scene. Or consider that critical juncture in Part I when Ivan is on his death bed: the last rites are being performed; the open Bible is held over him. The boyars stand around, waiting till their strong monarch is dead and they are free to resume divisive plotting against the state. Maybe Ivan is feigning illness; maybe he is really ill – we don't know. Compare this with a scene in Shakespeare, in *Henry IV*, Pt II: the King is brought into a place called the Jerusalem Chamber to die. His son, Prince Hal, is off hunting. It is a critical moment – without a responsible ruler the country will fall apart. The King sinks into a deep sleep, and Hal comes in, sees the crown lying on the bed, tries it on and goes out. Waking up and seeing that the crown is gone, the King imagines in a moment of panic that the crown has been stolen and already the country is being pulled apart. Crude striving for power, he thinks (with some reason), is all that governs men.

The analogies with the scene in *Ivan* are suggestive. But Ben Jonson's *Volpone* also bears on Eisenstein's work – the situation dominating the play is Volpone in bed, pretending to be on the point of death, in order to prey on the delusions of relatives and friends. Clearly, the analogies we see must be put in context. Rather than particular parallels we need a typology of moments.

EISENSTEIN ON SHAKESPEARE: THE RECORD

Eisenstein's most detailed notes relating to Shakespeare come from the year 1943 (right in the middle of his work on *Ivan* – and also the year of his very interesting comments on Dostoyevsky, which I have examined elsewhere). The history of his involvement with Shakespeare is, however, a long one. There were a number of stage designs for army theatres, which Jay Leyda and Zina Voynow list, noting that they may not have all been realized.[4] In 1917, there was *Hamlet*; in May and June 1920, *King John* (possibly not Shakespeare's). In the same year, there was *Henry IV* (Pt I? Pt II?), *Richard III*, and *Twelfth Night*. (And note too: in 1919, the set designs for *Bartholomew Fair* and *Volpone*.) From November 1921 to April 1922 he worked on Tikhonovich's production *Lady Macbeth*, finally put on as *Macbeth*. The sides of the stage were in grey, and tonal changes were produced through lighting and a background sky of black, gold and purple (a foreshadowing of Eisenstein's use of colour in Ivan?). A number of suggestive costume designs are connected with this production: the helmet of a Scottish warrior ('the faceless one'); Lady Macbeth's costume; and especially Macbeth's costume (his whole body disintegrating into black and red cones, barely holding together, with a helmet over his face giving him the appearance of an ominous bird). This production led to major conflicts with the director. It was impossible for Eisenstein to be restricted to the role of set- and costume-designer for another man's production: he had to be a total director.

Some drawings for *An American Tragedy* dated 26 September 1930, with the title *Exhumation*, refer to *Hamlet* (presumably the graveyard scene). On a sketch, dated 29 March 1931, of the murder of Polonius (for a stage production), he wrote: 'He pulls the curtain as in a sea of black silk.' In June 1931, in Tetlapayac, when the shooting of *Que Viva Mexico!* was interrupted by rain, Eisenstein produced 140 drawings connected (at some remove) with *Macbeth* – 'The Death of King Duncan' series. According to his biographer, Yon Barna, these were done 'very quickly, so as not to disturb the subconscious elements'.[5]

In his writings there are many scattered references to Shakespeare but the most important evidence relates to the time of his work on *Ivan the Terrible*. In 1943 – following his work on the script and the sets of the film – he devoted some writing specifically to Shakespeare, which was meant to enter into his big, proposed study, *Method*. In 1944 he made the two *Richard III* drawings, which are studies of evil (with a rather remote connection to the play). For present purposes I will ignore these drawings and also the many incidental references to Shakespeare. The 1943 writings are the ones that most repay examination. First, however, I want to take up a rather more general question – the evidence that the *Ivan* film project was a properly tragic one.

IVAN THE TERRIBLE AS A FILM TRAGEDY

Eisenstein situated his film in a world of Elizabethan drama. In *'Ivan the Terrible*: A Film About the Russian Renaissance' (1942) he characterised his hero as 'frightening and attractive, fascinating and terrifying, and – in the full sense of the word – tragic, owing to the inner struggle he unceasingly waged with himself, while struggling with the enemies of his country'.[6] Eisenstein's conception of the first all-Russian tsar was suited to shock audiences at home and abroad, first because of the 'decisive action, necessary cruelty, and occasional mercilessness of the man to whom history had entrusted the mission of creating one of the strongest and largest states of the world' and, secondly, because of the 'people of that Russian Renaissance of the 16th century never before seen on the screen in the whole sweep of passion for and interest in power'. Eisenstein stressed that Ivan's 'dark, unexpected, grim and frightful characteristics' were necessary for any statesman in

> a passionate and bloody epoch such as the sixteenth-century Renaissance – equally, without difference, in sun-drenched Italy or in England, which in the figure of Elizabeth was become Queen of the Seas, or in France or Spain or the Holy Roman Empire.

A common Machiavellian identity had to be brought out:

> Images of Russian feudal princes and boyars who are not inferior to a Cesare Borgia or a Malatesta will pass before the viewer; princes of the church whose imperiousness is worthy of the Roman Popes and who for political intrigues are the equals of Machiavelli or Loyola; and Russian women who are the match of Catherine de Medici and Bloody Mary.

Elsewhere Eisenstein expressed his general admiration for Elizabethan structure as 'exaggerated, passionate, overcharged, and in places far-fetched'.[7]

Initially, at any rate, Eisenstein also situated his film within, broadly speaking, a historical, Marxist project:

> The theme of autocracy is resolved in two aspects: One as Autocrat and One as alone. The former gives the theme of government power (progressive at that historical stage) – the political theme of the film. The other gives the personal, psychological theme of the film. Here lies the compositional unity of the personal and the social, the psychological and the political.[8]

The form of words allows one to see the story as the personal tragedy of a man who sought to develop Russia. This was the price to be paid for the making of Russia. In this view of the film, the historical – apologetic – categories are dominant.

In the course of work on the film Eisenstein changed to a more deeply tragic conception of the story – one that sees the limitations of the Marxist explanation of history (and of tragedy). In an unposted letter to Tynyanov in January 1944 Eisenstein writes of 'the tragic inevitability of autocracy and aloneness. . . . You yourself understand that this is just what in the very first instance they are trying to "replace" in the script and in the film.'[9] Now in the banquet scene in the colour sequence in Part II of the film – with its multiple deceptions, disguises, and even transvestism – the bounds of the merely personal tragedy are breached. We see the impossibility of the autocratic enterprise, the disintegration and corruption at the heart of autocracy. In Part III the theme of treachery was to be further explored – and in particular the impossibility of the adequate domination of another. Fyodor Basmanov, who in the dance scene, dressed up as a woman, offers himself to Ivan as a substitute wife, is a man who has abandoned his own father in order to become part of Ivan's 'iron ring' of oprichniks. Why then should Ivan believe in the loyalty of this shifty substitute son or wife? Already in the banquet scene in Part II there is a hint of Fyodor's future treachery (in Part III) as he jealously observes the apparent flirtation between Ivan and Vladimir.

The tragic dimensions of *Ivan the Terrible* became more apparent in the course of Eisenstein's work on it. Indeed there was a tragic dimension waiting to explode in all Eisenstein's film practice. His whole notion of the 'art of pathos' was closely allied to tragedy. The unfinished book *Direction* suggested that tragedy was the most pathetic art. In his introduction to the book he quoted Hegel:

> True originality in an artist and in a work of art consists of being penetrated and inspired by the underlying idea of a subject which is true in itself . . . true originality in art absorbs any accidental particularity.[10]

In art an idea became 'sensuous thought', so that it might be grasped through the feelings and emotions. Nature in art was not simply presented; it too was felt, everything being transformed into an expression of man's feelings. In a world of change, the most powerful art dealt with the experience of change. The most 'pathetic' art was an expression of a world of dialectical transformation.

For Eisenstein, tragedy – particularly Greek and Elizabethan – had come close to expressing the dialectical nature of the world. On occasion he used the two terms 'pathos' and 'tragedy' almost interchangeably. In pathetic art 'each manifestation of the structure had to reproduce the basic

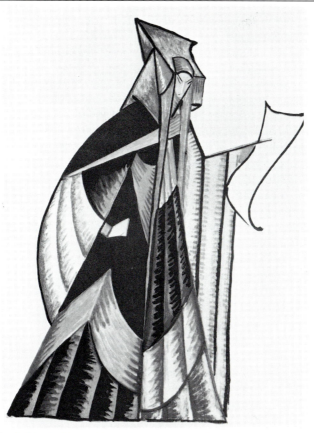

Figure 36 Lady Macbeth's costume from the Cubo-Futurist production that Eisenstein designed for Tikhonovich in 1921–2.

law according to which the imaged phenomenon, thing, or man was constructed'.[11] On a scale of ascending intensity, 'Gesture passed over into sound. Sound – into words. Speech – into measured prose. Prose – into poetry. The music of poetry – into song. Song – into music.' Light passed into colour.[12] In tragedy, as in the best, pathetic art, there were moments of 'ecstasy' or transition to an 'unforeseen' new quality. Tragedy relied on heightening – and ever intensifying – means of expression.

The ancient Greeks had been aware of these changes, but being unable to account for them in their cognitive schemes, assigned them to a 'deus ex machina'.[13] Since, in Eisenstein's aesthetics, the effect on the audience was central, he was not afraid to draw on Aristotle's notion of a cathartic experience. The effect of the moments of special intensity or ecstasy was 'passion raising the spectator above the level of ordinary experience'. It was an emotion beyond fear and pity, which could be produced by melodrama, where, however, they took the form of a feeling of nullity and futility.[14] Tragedy as a properly pathetic, ecstatic art left one with a 'feeling of relief and liberation at the highest point of tension of the drama, at a point moving to a new and unforeseen quality'.[15]

Tragedy was – or at any rate had been – the central pathetic art for another reason: it dealt with suffering, which was what 'pathos' originally meant. In tragedy suffering, too, underwent ecstatic transformation. And for Eisenstein, who remembered the cruelty he had sought to inflict in his early art of the cine-fist, his new film, conceived in the shadow of the Terror and made during the War, could offer vicarious suffering, leading to a cathartic experience of fear and pity, raw emotions which could not otherwise be admitted.

In Eisenstein's view of tragedy we recognise not only logical thought but also the kind of pre- or proto-logical thought explored by Mikhail Yampolsky and Arun Khopkar.[16] Tragedy embodied the conflicts of dialectical change: 'I think that historically each new shift seems to repeat the primary shift in an ever new qualitative aspect.'[17] Eisenstein stressed that Shakespeare was living in an age of major political and social change. That was the situation out of which Shakespeare was writing. It was also the kind of situation out of which Eisenstein was making his films. Now, in speaking about historical shifts which reflect earlier shifts, Eisenstein slides very quickly back to the stage of undifferentiated sensuous thought or exalted bliss underlying these shifts. The power of art is to release this undifferentiated sensuous thought – but at the same time this dreamlike state is also something that threatens art.

The intensification of pathetic means had other dangers. As Eisenstein noted, the living face might correspond to a duality or multiplicity of masks.[18] In later tragedy fixity of character gave way to inner conflict and change. Unity of character was threatened by dualism and fragmentation. Chaos threatened Eisenstein's tragic universe.

There was a tension in Eisenstein's work as he attempted to resolve certain conflicting ideas: firstly, the hope that the undifferentiated being of primal society would again be attained in a future socialist society, in which everyone – man and woman – would be equally recognized; secondly, the fear that art could not show the way to this future socialist society and would prove a regressive force leading to an enclosed dream-world; and thirdly, the fear, too, that there was no escape from evil in the world of the all-powerful tyrant (note that at the end of *Ivan* there is no good character waiting in the wings). On occasion Eisenstein resolves the tension through simple statements of faith in the great and glorious future. At other times he resorts to playful exploration of the concepts, an enjoyment of the contradictions that amounts to a refusal to be dominated by them.

EISENSTEIN'S LATE WRITINGS ON SHAKESPEARE

Playfulness appears in Eisenstein's late writings on Shakespeare. On the question of Ivan's possible relationship to Shakespeare's major tragic heroes, Eisenstein is tantalisingly reticent. There are some brief notes on Macbeth and Lear, to which I will return. There is a discussion of Hamlet, which for these purposes is not particularly useful: it is an intelligent examination of the limitations of T. S. Eliot's view of the motivation supplied for him.

He is at his most suggestive – and playful – in a discussion in 1943 of *Romeo and Juliet*. Provocatively he suggests that the germ of the story is this: 'Romeo – it is said – had much more definite intentions – and performed so brilliantly that Juliet was ready to commit any folly.' He stresses a different situation as the germ of the play – the social and political conflicts in the reign of Elizabeth and the question of succession. But for a work to attain greatness – a 'generalised general' has to appear through the 'particularised particular' of the situation. Eisenstein does not discuss the particular situations further but considers the general import of the tragedy – its magic attraction. Both the notion of repetition at a higher level of the spiral of history and the notion of penetration to the deepest level of protological, sensuous thought come into play. In *Romeo and Juliet* he sees a recurrence of the challenge to the institution of taboos and prescriptions governing marriages between groups or clans. In the historical shift from the feudal period to the Renaissance there is a repetition of a primal situation, which takes the form or *image* of a law or principle. 'The inevitable recurrence of the most general formula of relations is continually determined in its particular historical form by the fundamental principle which underlies the succession of historical forms and which governs the succession of epochs and structures.' But he does not develop this anthropology or psycho-anthropology, devoting instead considerable space to sensuous thought as a source of powerful artistic effect.

In a strange, very assertive move, as part of the argument that sensuous thought does underlie Shakespeare's play, Eisenstein takes Jacques Deval's play, *L'Age de Juliette* (1935) and examines the treatment of the myth in this work. In this version two petit-bourgeois families will not allow their children to marry because each of them needs to marry a richer person. And so the two young people go off to the Ritz, where they occupy a suite. And they take a bath – you see them splashing on stage. They disappear off stage, and when they return they have switched bathrobes (which are grey and white). According to Eisenstein, this exchange functions as more than just a sign that the two have made love; in the bath the two have returned to the state of undifferentiated primal being in which fish live, and which is connected with an early stage of our evolution (which is supposedly repeated in our development in the womb). They have supposedly rediscovered the bisexuality of our ontogenetic being. Deval, it appears, makes explicit something that is implicit in Shakespeare's play.

This is certainly entertaining (Eisenstein's account of Hamlet, based on a modified version of the Oedipus complex, which he relates to the origins of differentiated social existence, is interesting in relation to his struggle with Freud's ideas, but scarcely entertaining). There is a definite wilfulness of interpretation – certainly in relation to *Romeo and Juliet*. The interpretation seems to exist above all to allow Eisenstein to assert the presence of basic structures of thought and experience. In a wonderful development of this idea he switches to Leonardo's *The Last Supper* and sees the fingers of Judas and Christ mingling in the same cup as another symbol of sexual love. Judas' betrayal of Christ is an act of sexual jealousy. Here again is confirmation of man's basic bisexuality. And for this Eisenstein finds yet more confirmation in some writings of Stendhal and Christopher Marlowe.[19] The connections in Eisenstein's mind are richly fertile.

DIRECTIONS

From the point of view of Eisenstein's use of Shakespeare, it is disappointing that he did not write more on *Macbeth*, apart from some references to the image of borrowed clothes in this play (in the notes for *Method*). From all Shakespeare's tragedies, this study of power is surely the one that bears most directly on our understanding of *Ivan the Terrible*, rather than *Hamlet* or *Lear*, with their focus on the problem of self-knowledge. But in pursuing connections between the character Macbeth and the character Ivan, one would have to remember that Eisenstein specifically said that Ben Jonson's 'bichromality' of characterisation was of direct use to him in the conception of Ivan (although by the time we come to Ivan's inner disintegration in Part II we have surely gone beyond 'bichromality').[20]

His tantalising comments on the youthful *Romeo and Juliet* point in a direction that is certainly useful – towards the total image or metaphor of the work. One of the books he read with fascination was Caroline Spurgeon's large study, *Shakespeare's Imagery*, filling his copy with underlinings.[21] What drew him was Shakespeare's total metaphoric vision; and while Ben Jonson's visual metaphors appealed to him as film-maker, Eisenstein was finally a dramatic poet of film whose apprehension of the world transcended the visual. It is along the lines of connected metaphoric vision that Eisenstein's relationship to Shakespeare needs to be explored. One could take as a starting point Eisenstein's own reference to the image of borrowed clothes in the play, examine the images of disguise, deception and self-deception in *Macbeth*, and point to the total state of undifferentiated consciousness that is excited by these images of disguise and deception. One would also have to look at the understanding of evil shown in 'The Death of King Duncan' drawings. And one would have to consider

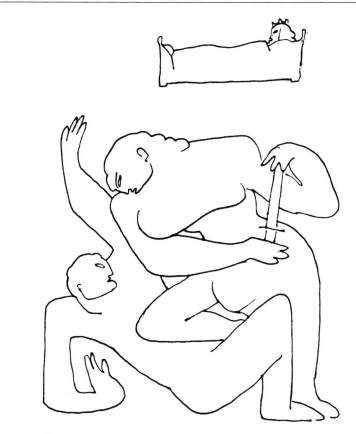

Figure 37 'The understanding of evil shown in the "Death of King Duncan" drawings.'

the shaping influence of Eisenstein's distinctive images of the All-Seeing Eye of God and of confession and regeneration.

But again Eisenstein's dialogues with other artists were never exclusive. François Albera has indicated how Eisenstein could suddenly pass from a dialogue with, say, Shklovsky to one with Malevich.[22] In at least two of Eisenstein's late notes about Shakespeare, that playwright's characteristic imagery is contrasted with the novelist, Dostoyevsky's. I will quote one of these notes:

> In *Lear* everything is woven together: the kingdom
>   is chopped up
>   a body is cut up
>   lacerating comparisons.
> In Dostoyevsky the psychological and the material or physical series do not penetrate one another but unfold alongside one another.[. . .]

The reader cries out within himself with excitement (just as the cherubim cry aloud in 'The Grand Inquisitor') for his task of inner collaboration as co-author amounts to 'unifying' the disconnected series of the author.[23]

In this note we see why Eisenstein was finally – or for a while – ready to move beyond Shakespeare. In Dostoyevsky he saw a way of returning to his old ambition of truly effective action on the spectator – by getting the spectator to act as co-creator and to connect parallel but separate series of physical and psychological images. In Dostoyevsky, I think, too, he saw a possible way of escaping from those powerful structures of undifferentiated being that threatened to plunge the artist into a dreamlike state of sensuous excitement and inaction – but that is a whole other question.

Chapter 9

Graphic flourish

Aspects of the art of *mise-en-scène*[1]

Arun Khopkar

> Carpenters and Brahmins must evolve a common language.
>
> Ritwik Ghatak[2]

THE FRAME

Eisenstein's unfinished work *Rezhissura* (Direction) occupies a unique place in his writings. Instead of an a posteriori analysis of his own work or that of other artists, this book offers something different. It is concerned with the minutest practical details and problems of *mise-en-scène* – the turning of the head, the raising of a hand, the size and shape of a window. But at the same time Sergei Mikhailovich is searching for solutions and means of solution – in different art-forms and sciences, in the diaries and letters of artists and scientists, and in his own experience. The breaks in the narrative (the line of solution) provide pleasure and increase our excitement. They give this book something of the form of a detective novel, a form which Eisenstein very much loved. But this whodunit has no simple, unique solution, since the deed is not done. We merely review different ways of doing it. It combines, so to speak, the crime with the psychology of crime, action with reflection. It is as if the imagination had left a fluorescent trail as it flitted from flower to flower.

And yet it remains the least-known of his writings. *Montage* and *Non-Indifferent Nature* and his writings on colour have been fully or partially translated into French, Italian, German and, finally, English. Given the split between film theory and practice today, this is scarcely surprising, but neither is it desirable.

What follows is not a summary of *Rezhissura*. It is an attempt to trace the various strands that form the concept of *mise-en-scène*. It is an establishing shot.

THE FROZEN AND TREMBLING CONTOUR OF
MISE-EN-SCÈNE

In their notes to the English translation of Nizhny's *Lessons with Eisenstein*, the editors define *mise-en-scène* thus:

> By this expression Eisenstein simply means what it means in the theatre, that is the arrangement of the actors on the stage . . . it has the limited meaning of: the determination of the details of action for stage purposes, including, primarily, the positioning of the actors at different places (or for different 'sections' of the action), their movement in the space determined by the set, the determination of the set to accommodate the action.[3]

Unfortunately, although this definition of *mise-en-scène* has the advantage of simplicity, it leaves out some of the most vital elements. It ignores the subjectivity of the director. The rest of Nizhny's otherwise useful book also gives us the impression that to every problem of *mise-en-scène* there is an ideal, absolute solution. The universe of a work of art, in particular a film, begins to resemble a Newtonian system where the space–time continuum is absolute. The 'logic' and 'laws' of composition seem to decide all the formal problems with an impersonal thoroughness. Even Leyda is uncomfortable about the tone of the book.[4]

Eisenstein's own definition of *mise-en-scène* is very open:

> What – posing the question in a concise way – is *mise-en-scène*? *Mise-en-scène* (in all stages of its development: gesture, mimicry, intonation) is the graphic projection of the character of an event. In its parts, as much as in their combination, it is a graphic flourish in space. It is like handwriting on paper, or the impression made by feet on a sandy path. It is so in all its plenitude and incompleteness. . . . Character appears through actions (in many cases these are determining aspects). Specific appearance of action is movement (here we include in 'action' words, voice etc). The path of movement is *mise-en-scène*.[5]

This definition contains all that the former covered, and much more. *Mise-en-scène* is supposed to project graphically the *character* of the event. This means that it should reveal something which is not on the surface. It involves turning an in-tension into an ex-tension.

The *graphic flourish* in space is like the mark of the director/painter. It involves much more than mere skill in the arrangement of the actors' movements and the determination of the set to accommodate the action. It reveals the director's personality and in particular his attitude towards the event.

The image of handwriting or footprints is carefully chosen. Sergei

Mikhailovich's interest in handwriting analysis is attested by that portion of his library preserved in the museum on Smolenskaya. Also, his adaptation with Tretyakov of the ideas of Rudolph Bode about expressive movement bears witness to this, as does his study of Ludwig Klages's work, to which I shall return later.

Eisenstein's writings on *mise-en-scène* indicate that it emerges as a synthesis of two tendencies: the graphic and the expressive. These are not mutually exclusive and in fact their fusion and interpenetration is the hallmark of great *mise-en-scène*. Their separation here is only for the purpose of analysis. I am taking the graphic as relating to geometry, number and proportion; and the expressive as relating to the organic. It is through their mutual tension that the contour of *mise-en-scène* comes alive.

LOCATING THE POLES: RITUALISTIC AND EXPRESSIVE

Mise-en-scène, as defined above, has to be located within a spectrum. At one (visible) end of this spectrum is ritual (the ultraviolet would be mathematics), while at the other lies the expressivity of our emotional lives (the infra-red would be the warm region of our unconscious and body-rhythms). Between these two poles, we have the entire range of the spectacular: festivals, theatre, puppets, mime, dance, circus, pre-theatre and the like. *Mise-en-scène* spans this entire range.

Ritual stands as the most consciously controlled event, with a predetermined form and purpose: even if it includes an unknown or chance element, the parameters of its operation are well-defined. So while there may be many variables – place (outdoor/indoor, dimension, natural/cultural setting), time (relationship with diurnal and annual cycles of the earth's time, the configuration of stars, weather, etc.), duration, participants, roles to be played, etc. – and each ritual will have its own code, one unified approach to the graphics of *mise-en-scène* may reveal common forms and structures underlying the specific codes. These would help us to generalise and abstract in our formulation of *mise-en-scène*.

The other line to be pursued is expressive movement. In Eisenstein this is not confined to the human world, but carries over into the animal kingdom and even the plant world. The dual nature of our investigations is not surprising. As Eisenstein noted:

The dialectic of works of art is built upon a most curious 'dual unity'. The affectivity of a work of art is built upon the fact that there takes place within it a dual process: an impetuous, progressive rise along the lines of the highest explicit steps of consciousness and a simultaneous penetration by means of the structure of the form into layers of profoundest sensual thinking. The polar separation of these two lines of flow creates that remarkable tension of unity of form and content which is characteristic of true art-works. Without this there are no true art-works. . . .

By allowing one or the other element to predominate, the art-work remains unfulfilled. A drive towards the thematic-logical side renders the work dry, logical, didactic. But over-emphasis on the side of sensual thinking, with insufficient account taken of the thematic logical tendency, this is equally fatal for the work: it is condemned to sensual chaos, elemental and raving. Only in the 'dually united' interpenetration of these tendencies resides the true tension-laden unity of form and content.[6]

The purpose of this chapter is to understand Eisenstein's concept of *mise-en-scène*, which the author feels would enable us to see the interrelationships between our own dance forms, painting, sculpture and theatre and would pave the way to a new synthesis in cinema. But before we apply Eisenstein in our own context, it is necessary to see him in his own. For this purpose, I have chosen to give first a brief account of the concept of *mise-en-scène* according to Kuleshov, Stanislavsky and Meyerhold. These were not only great contemporaries of Eisenstein, but influences and indeed exemplars of recurrent tendencies in the history of art.

KULESHOV: THE DEMANDS OF THE RECTANGLE AND THE RITUAL OF LABOUR

There is a beautiful description of the early years of Soviet cinema by Eisenstein:

In the early 1920s we all came to Soviet cinema as something not yet existent. We came upon no ready-built city, there were no squares, no streets laid out, not even little crooked lanes and blind alleys, such as we may find in the cinemetropolis of today. We came like bedouins or gold-seekers to a place with unimaginably great possibilities, only a small section of which has even now been developed.

We pitched our tents and dragged into camp our experiences in various fields. Private activities, accidental professions, unguessed skills, unsuspected eruditions – all were pooled and went into the building of something that had as yet no written traditions, no exact stylistic requirements nor even formulated demands.[7]

Recent research on the links between the pre-revolutionary cinema and the young Soviet cinema has shown that this *tabula rasa*–virgin land–goldrush picture is not to be taken literally. But it certainly captures something of the pioneering spirit of those days.

We find the same spirit reflected in Kuleshov. Reading him today, one finds his naïvety almost touching, but the singlemindedness of his 'experiments', the freshness of his approach and the tremendous impact he must have had on his colleagues can be felt even now. His path is well-known; and I only recapitulate some of the important points here.

Influenced by the systematising tendencies in many arts which had gathered force in the decade before 1917, Kuleshov wanted to find out what was unique to this new medium of cinema – wherein lay its power to move the viewer. Young Soviet film-makers had noticed what a great impact the American cinema had created: they studied these films and found that they had more camera set-ups and cuts than the Russian or European ones. This led to the proclamation of 'montage' as the main source of cinematic effectiveness, or the 'cinegenic' quality. The actual content of the individual shots was initially considered secondary to the effect that would be created from their various combinations. This led to the famous 'Kuleshov experiments'.[8]

Having succeeded in producing landscapes and persons that did not 'exist' and facial expressions that were not genuine, all by combining shots, Kuleshov soon ran into problems.

> When we began making our own films, constructed on this principle of montage, we were set upon with cries of: 'Have pity, you crazy futurists! You show films comprised of the smallest segments. In the eyes of the viewers the result is utter chaos. Segments jump after each other so quickly that it is thoroughly impossible to understand the action.' We listened to this and began to think what method we could adopt to combine shots so as to avoid these abrupt shifts and flashes.[9]

But Kuleshov realised that the problem was more than stylistic. What seemed to be a problem of film *continuity* was actually one of film *unity*. His solution was essentially Formalist. He felt that the key to filmic (visual) unity lay in the rectilinear shape of the screen, the element which was common to all shots. And this key was the 'Cartesianisation' of all visual elements.

The rectangle implied predominance of the rectilinear elements, in particular horizontals, verticals and diagonals. Straight lines were preferred to curves, geometric forms to natural ones and industrial rather than organic objects.

The principle was extended to acting and to *mise-en-scène*. 'We examined the movements of limbs as movements along three axes, along three basic directions' – actually the Cartesian co-ordinates.[10] The actor's training would henceforth be to break down his movements into units which would be articulated along the main lines of composition. The gesture must be 'digitised', which leads to a preference for certain kinds of gesture. Obviously he finds the movements of the skilled worker most photogenic – so productivity, work and efficiency take *mise-en-scène* into the geometrism and single-value system of ritual. Acting is finally reduced to a uniquely determined lexicon of gestures.

STANISLAVSKY: THE INVISIBILITY OF *MISE-EN-SCÈNE*

Stanislavsky occupies a curious place in the history of *mise-en-scène*. As an exponent of realism, he would seem the antithesis of Kuleshov on the one hand and Meyerhold on the other. He appears to have taken great pains to erase his handwriting from the *mise-en-scène*, to remove all trace of his presence at the scene of the action, so that it would look like a slice of life, an act of Nature without directorial intervention.

If the overriding design is to be kept invisible, then each part must appear to have the same degree of autonomy. Each actor must appear 'natural' – and the *mise-en-scène* will happen. Hence the concentration on the actor. The 'method' to be natural must be shared by everyone. Only then will the real hold together and have a design, even if this remains invisible.

But this 'maître des grands spectacles with the theatrical range of a Michelangelo' was not to be 'reduced to fiddling around with little bits of clockwork':

> In these ancient Hebrew and Armenian surroundings, the fanatics of the Moscow Art Theatre Third Studio are present to a man when Stanislavsky gives his lessons.
>
> 'No, authentic emotions! Let your voices resound! Walk theatrically! Suppleness! The eloquent gesture! Dance! Bow! Duel with rapiers! Rhythm! Rhythm! Rhythm! Rhythm!' – the insistent shouts of Stanislavsky resound.[11]

So the controlling factor, the flourish in space, was also a flourish in time. It is through rhythm that the actors' movements are mutually co-ordinated. 'Really this is the role of rhythm in what an actor creates. Rhythm belongs to the last steps of the line of generalisation of imagicity, which begins the transformation of a gesture into a metaphor.'[12] Thus rhythm, the most biological sensation, makes possible the highest level of generalisation. It is what distinguishes the *mise-en-scène* of the master from that of followers of 'the method'.

Eisenstein was an outspoken opponent of the Moscow Art Theatre in his youth, but he gave a detailed and considered analysis of Stanislavsky in the later works *Direction* and *Montage*. The relationship between the sense-memory and the construction of an image to motivate the actor had particular importance for him. In fact he compares Stanislavsky's method with the spiritual exercises of St Ignatius Loyola. His analysis of Stanislavsky is also important as an estimation of the *internal* approach to the problems of acting and creation of images in *mise-en-scène*.

In passing, it is interesting to note that Dnyaneshwar, the great Marathi poet who was a contemporary of Dante and who wrote a commentary on the *Bhagwatgeeta*, said in his introduction that he would make the suprasensuous sensuous for his readers. He carefully builds his images, choosing images from the five senses, and makes them clash to create an image which paints the beyond.

Eisenstein told his students that, although Stanislavsky and Meyerhold opposed each other theoretically and ideologically, in practice they realised the strong points of each other's work and absorbed it unconsciously, seeking not a compromise but a synthesis.[13] What he himself aimed at was not a synthesis of these two systems but their transcendence.

MEYERHOLD: THE MECHANICS OF ORGANICITY AND EXPRESSIVITY

Eisenstein wrote of Meyerhold:

Of all his principles, only one is productive. . . . [And] for this thesis I would be grateful to him till the end of my life, although that may not suffice. . . . The Alpha and Omega of the theoretical baggage of expressive movement, drawn from the exercises of biomechanics, is packed in its first thesis (and in the 16th, which is a direct corollary of the first):

1. The whole of biomechanics is based on the following: even if only the tip of the nose is active, then the whole body acts. If even the most insignificant organ functions, the whole body feels it.

16. Gesture is the result of the whole body working.

That's it. The rest in my studies of expressive movement is MINE.[14]

Meyerhold realised that the narrowly utilitarian gesture is economical and the expressive gesture is amplified. But it is necessary to find the right means of amplification.

I was lucky to view a short compilation of footage about biomechanics when I was in Moscow. It consisted of Meyerhold making a speech (although the film is silent), two exercises performed by his students and very brief excerpts from his production of Gogol's *The Inspector*. These fragments, even when projected at the wrong speed, still had a magic which – as someone fascinated by cats – I can best call 'feline'. When one figure was in shot, a single muscle moving produced a response throughout the whole body, penetrating into my body. When an ensemble moved, it had the unity of an organism: the result was more than the sum of its parts.

As I watched this film again and again, I understood why Sergei Mikhailovich had such tremendous respect for his unkind spiritual father. Through the imperfect projection, through the flickering shadows thrown

Figure 38 The portrait Meyerhold gave Eisenstein in 1936 was inscribed: 'I am proud of my student who has already become a master.'

on the wall of the cave-like hall, glued to my chair with my back towards the light, I became aware of the forces which moved me, as a flesh and blood spectacle must have moved Meyerhold's audiences. Forces that had the condensed power of thousands of years of spectacle.

Eisenstein learned a lot from Meyerhold. Take, for example, the movement of refusal. 'When you want to move in one direction, as a prelude you move (completely or partially) in the opposite direction. In the practice of scenic movement, it is called the movement of refusal.'[15]

This is not merely a theatrical trick. As an ancient device, popularised by Meyerhold, it contributed to Eisenstein's understanding of contradiction as a source of expressivity.

Meyerhold also changed the relationship between the spectacle and the spectator as his *mise-en-scène* surrounded the latter. In fact he took important steps towards what Eisenstein would later call the stereoscopic cinema, meaning the fulfilment of certain tendencies implicit in the history of spectacle. 'The image penetrates into the screen, carrying the spectator into depths he has never experienced . . . the image perceived three-dimensionally (it is a most spectacular effect) as if 'tumbling' from the screen into the auditorium.'[16]

EISENSTEIN: IMAGICITY, ORGANICITY AND THE NON-NEWTONIAN UNIVERSE

For Eisenstein the study of expressive movement begins with organisms which are almost immobile, namely plants. Consider the concept of 'tropism', defined as an involuntary orientation by an organism or one of its parts which involves turning and is accomplished by active movement that constitutes a positive or negative response to a source of stimulation (whether this is light, temperature or a chemical stimulus). The term is derived from the Latin *tropus*, which comes from the Greek *tropos*, meaning 'turn' or 'direction', and ultimately from the Sanskrit *trepate*, meaning 'to be ashamed'. In the Sanskrit origin we can see a metaphor, an implication of expressive movement.

The heliotropism of the sunflower has given rise to many myths and legends. The immobility of the body and the hypnotised mobility of the flower/head/eyes suggest a contradiction that becomes expressive. Walter Benjamin, writing in 1940, could not resist this metaphor: 'As flowers turn toward the sun, by dint of a secret heliotropism the past strives to turn toward that sun which is rising in the sky of history.'[17]

The association of light with knowledge, good, heaven and suchlike and of darkness with ignorance, evil, hell and the like is as old as memory and history can tell us. Considering its place in ritual and effect on our emotions, it is small wonder that light should play such an important role in *mise-en-scène* and that heliotropism has its place in the arsenal of expressive movements. Its opposite, apheliotropism, has the equivalent expressive value in absorbing light and seeking darkness.

Geotropism and apogeotropism are the tendencies of pulling towards and away from the earth. In terms of acting, they can indicate the heavy gesture borne down by its own weight, and the supporting, or the rising and floating gesture.

These are all reactions to external stimuli, but some of the most subtle forms of plant behaviours are nastic movements. These are movements of flat parts such as the leaf or budscale, which are oriented toward the plant rather than to an external source. They are brought about by disproportionate growth or increase of turgor in the tissues of one surface of a part, and typically involve a curling or beading outward or inward of the whole part in a direction away from the more active surface.

The curling of figures in Chola bronzes, the lotus opening gesture in Indian dance mudras (either representational or metaphoric), the graceful curves of our floral decorative motifs, all celebrate the expressivity of the movement motif. Lower organisms which exhibit forms of movement like taxis and kinesis need to be studied for their expressive potential and transformation into human gestures as well as to understand the phenomenon of expressive movement at all levels of life. As we trace the Descent (or Ascent) of Man, we find a complex relationship between the expression of emotions in animals and man.

Eisenstein's very first theoretical article proclaimed his interest in circus. The term 'attraction' in 'The Montage of Attractions' refers to the circus; and his first important article on cinema, recently discovered and published in its entirety, is similarly entitled 'The Montage of Film Attractions'.[18] He retained this interest in circus until the end of his life. It fascinated him as a 'plotless' spectacle, in which each event was an attraction, an aggressive movement producing a certain shock. He saw it as a metaphor of Man's evolution, with the animals, acrobats and clowns all affecting and moving the spectator at a very deep level, regardless of age, sex or culture. He writes about it with great feeling:

> What causes people to throng to the circus every night all over the globe? [. . .]
>
> And each of us recalls, if not with his head and memory, then with the aural labyrinth and once bruised elbows and knees, that difficult period of childhood, when almost the sole content in the struggle for a place under the sun for all of us as a child was the problem of balance during the transition from a four-legged standing of a 'toddler' to the proud two-legged standing of a master of the universe. An echo of the child's personal biography, of the centuries past of his entire species and kind.[19]

The Strike contains many examples of his use of the expressivity of animals. Sometimes this use is primitive, representational, eccentric, as in the case of the police spies: Owl, Bulldog and Monkey. But he also uses it tragically with the rolling eye of the dying bull in the slaughter scene.

The association of animals with human beings to express certain qualities of the latter (or, for magical purposes, to acquire certain qualities of the former) goes back to pre-history. Language retains its traces in such expressions as 'lion-hearted', 'feline grace', 'preening' and many others. And Darwin's classic study, *The Expression of Emotions in Man and Animals* (1872), showing how many human gestures and expressions cannot be understood unless we see the connection through evolution with other species, was important for Eisenstein.

In fact *Ivan the Terrible* reveals more significant use of animal gesture and symbolism. Leyda reproduces a Hiroshige woodcut from *One Hundred Famous Places in Ido* showing a hawk swooping and notes the striking similarity between this image found in Eisenstein's scrapbook and the famous profile of Ivan in the foreground with a serpentine line of people stretching into the background.[20] The whole film is charged with the vitality of animal movement: elongated necks, flashing eyes, snakelike sinuousness, the swooping flight of birds of prey, as well as such specific objects as the swan-shaped banquet servers. These are not just relics of our evolutionary past but relate to the beasts we harbour within.

The arts of India are rich in examples where the expressivity of animals is used. Jataka tales and their depiction in painting, the Narasimha legend, Nagas and Yakshas are only a few examples. But some of the most interesting cases are found in traditional dance forms, either at the level of mimesis or as sophisticated metaphors. Dances like Kathakali, which depict the demonic and the godly with the same strength, use the animal gesture to reach a truly cosmic range of expression. Indian cinema too, when it stops tinkering with poor imitations of reality and aspires to unleash the same mythic forces which have shaped the other art-forms, will find rich treasure in these forms.

As can be seen from the remarks on circus already quoted, Eisenstein was interested in those aspects of human experience which are prior to consciousness and memory. He was particularly intrigued by what prenatal experience might contribute to art and his study of Degas's *Bathing Women* analyses what he calls the 'floating tendency' of the figures.[21] The stage of being free from the struggle for existence and enfolded in protective warmth is associated with the state of weightlessness. This perhaps leads to the conception in many cultures of heaven as a place devoid of material needs, free from all physical laws and populated by beings floating or flying freely. We may remember here Tarkovsky's *Solaris*, where both real and 'imaginary' characters float in a state of weightlessness and the imaginary becomes more real while reality becomes dreamlike. If heaven is also associated with light and the movement towards it with heliotropism, the opposite follows that 'lower evil species (often reptiles) are depicted as creatures of darkness'.[22] This may relate to our toddler stage, with the first experience of dependence on material reality.

Freud attributed flying in dreams to the tendency observed in children of deriving pleasure from games in which they are tossed around.

> Children are delighted by such experiences and never tire of asking to have them repeated, especially if there is something about them that causes a little fright or giddiness. . . . The delight taken by young children in games of this kind (as well as in swings and see-saws) is well-known; when they come to see acrobatic feats in a circus their memory of such games is revived.[23]

But why should they enjoy such games in the first place? Freud proposes an answer:

> Dr Paul Federn . . . has put forward the attractive theory that a good number of these flying dreams are dreams of erection; for the remarkable phenomenon of erection, around which the human imagination has constantly played, cannot fail to be impressive, involving as it does an apparent suspension of the laws of gravity. (Cf. in this connection the winged phalli of the ancients.)[24]

This seems to me to be a case of putting the cart before the horse, since clearly the pleasure in tossing and weightlessness would be *prior* to the pleasure from erection and could scarcely be the cause of it. Without going into the relative merits of each argument, let me remark that in his correspondence with Wilhelm Reich, Eisenstein complained about psychoanalysis not concerning itself with the process of construction of a work of art which gives it form, and dealing only with its symbolic stuff.[25]

Pre-natal experience is also very important for our understanding of convex and concave space. The world is initially experienced by the unborn child as concave: the mouth which is concave has not yet found the convex breast, but perhaps 'feels' the absent object. In his study of Rodin and Rilke, Eisenstein says

> it is a question of the mirror-unity of form and counter-form, of relief and counter-relief. In a general way of speaking, it would seem that the fact of the unity of the concave and convex form has made incarnate and materialised two modes of knowing the essence of the phenomenon, seizing it from without and knowing it from within. Certainly, in an ideal case, the two ways would fuse into one.[26]

Eisenstein uses the image of passage from the womb and rejection by the mother in the last part of *Ivan the Terrible*, when Vladimir goes to meet his death. In fear and trembling, the lonely Vladimir moves through the colourless passage (in which Eisenstein had asked his designer to remove

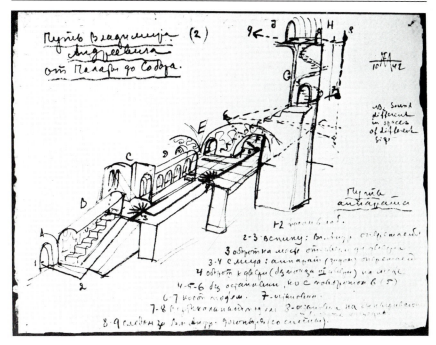

Figure 39 Ivan the Terrible. The passage from the womb and rejection by the mother structured Eisenstein's plan for a continuous ten-minute shot, in which Vladimir would leave the feast and meet his death in the cathedral.

all angularities), knowing of the dagger that awaits him at its end. Leyda gives the plan of the original *mise-en-scène* for this sequence which was conceived as a continuous ten-minute shot. In it, Eisenstein united the image of the birth trauma with the death of Vladimir. After the riot of colour in the (predominantly red) feast scene, Vladimir's face appears blue (evoking asphyxiation).[27]

The experience of birth is crucial for Eisenstein's concept of *mise-en-scène* because it marks the meeting of so many opposites: passivity and activity, darkness and light, concave and convex space, knowing from within and without, heliotropism and apheliotropism. It creates a unity of past experience with a vision of the ideal future, and could thus be related to the iconostasis of Russian Orthodoxy, where past, present and future meet, life and death touch each other, Heaven and Hell meet.[28]

Eisenstein saw intonation, mimicry, gesture and movement as successive stages of human expression, each preserving something from the previous one yet also adding something qualitatively different. He derived his theory of gesture from diverse sources, from Bode, Klages, Werner, Duchenne, Delsarte, Darwin and from Freud (especially his work on parapraxis). From his (and Tretyakov's) early translation and adaptation of Rudolph Bode, from his recently discovered early articles on montage, up to his analysis of an incident from Dostoyevsky's *The Idiot*, he shows a remarkable ability to synthesise diverse sources and give unity to his film practice.[29] He always qualified his a posteriori analysis by saying that creation is not a deductive process. But his most interesting writings take the form of dialogues (often with himself) while searching for a creative solution.

His writings on the formal principles of composition are certainly voluminous and crammed with references to various art-forms, epochs, cultures, disciplines. Is there a method in this mad erudition? If we go back to Eisenstein's definition of *mise-en-scène*, we find two key phrases: the 'character of an event' and 'graphic flourish'. Identifying the character of an event, I believe, led him to search for objective principles, which would have been outlined in his book *Method*, along with the specific studies of how pathos is 'constructed' in Dickens, Disney, Chaplin, *et al*.

But on the other side of this apparently absolute Newtonian universe was the knower, the artist, the creator, YO. Thus his book *My Art in Life* leads to the memoirs, to *YO! Ich Selbst*.[30] These memoirs are the 'other' of *Method*, where the creator reveals himself and the Absolute yields to the relativity of Eisenstein.[31]

Just as he brings his own subjectivity to the method of the creative process, subjectivity is a vital part of the recreative process which creates the final image in the spectator's mind.

Before the author's inward glance, coloured by his feelings, wanders an image which is the emotional embodiment of his theme. His task is to turn this image into two or three partial representations which by their unity and co-existence would conjure up for the reason and emotions of the spectator the same image that hovered before the author. . . . The spectator has to follow the same creative path which the author had to follow.

The practice of theory

Chapter 10

Eisenstein as theoretician
Preliminary considerations

Edoardo G. Grossi

> In Eisenstein we find a constant urge to operate in the interstices of different sciences, between linguistics and anthropology, between psychology and aesthetics, between the history of art and biology. This impulse might suggest a mistrust of the procedures of analysis but, on the contrary, it takes advantage of the relative weakness of the various paradigms to make the research more effective – and to obtain better results . . .
>
> The roles of scientist and scholar, wise man and pragmatist, are superimposed and merged: each appears just when the others seem to be asserting themselves.[1]

These very interesting reflections by Francesco Casetti help explain how, by taking stock of Eisenstein as a theoretician of cinema and also as a theoretician of art, we can discern his complexity as well as the importance of his multifaceted œuvre.[2]

There are innumerable starting points from which to reconstruct the Eisensteinian mosaic. Chronologically, the first is the six volumes of the *Selected Works*, published in Moscow between 1964 and 1971 and running to more than three thousand pages. These obviously contain writings of uneven quality, drawn from the different periods of Eisenstein's career. Alongside articles written for particular occasions, this edition includes such pillars of his thought as *Direction*, *Non-Indifferent Nature*, *Colour*, *On Stereoscopic Cinema*, *Memoirs*, as well as his reflections on montage dating from 1937–41, collected into the articles 'Montage 1937', 'Montage 1938' and 'Vertical Montage I, II, III'.

In the first part of an earlier article, I attempted a preliminary synthesis of the main translations of Eisenstein's writings, drawn from the *Selected Works* as published in France, Germany, Great Britain and the United States.[3] Apart from the writings that comprise *Direction*, this synthesis demonstrated that the great interest which Eisenstein aroused as a theoretician has only rarely been accompanied by deeper analysis or critical interpretation. Against this rich international panorama, the Italian reader has since 1981 found himself in a privileged position thanks to the series edited by Pietro Montani and published by Marsilio Editori.[4] This has given us a deeper sense of the immense work of theoretical research undertaken by Eisenstein over twenty years, which was by no means always closely linked to his better-known work as a director.

But, in spite of this great work, it seems that publication of the rest of Eisenstein's research, including all the manuscripts and thousands of pages of notes from his courses at the Institute of Cinematography in Moscow, is still a long way from completion.[5] To deal with the material held in the Eisenstein collection (*fond* 1923) of the Central State Archive for Literature and the Arts (TsGALI) would require a further six volumes, if not more.

This material includes the precious Diaries which Eisenstein kept without interruption from 1919 to 1948, amounting to seventy-three notebooks.[6] There are also the general research projects which he intended to develop but did not complete, such as the *Grundproblem* (Fundamental Problem) and *Method*; specific treatises on 'Zola and Cinema', 'El Greco and Cinema', 'Pushkin and Gogol', 'Pushkin and the Cinema' and 'Three Masters' (Griffith, Chaplin and Disney).[7] Among the projects and essays which remained in note or outline form are, for example, 'Pathos and Ecstasy', 'The Theory of Conflict', 'History of the Close-Up', 'On the Problem of Direction' and other material which, as was his custom, would have been inserted into the other more substantial works mentioned above.[8] Here we can also find his notes for a *History of Soviet Cinema* written in 1946–8 and, following on from this and from *Method*, the first draft of a study entitled *In Praise of the Cinema Newsreel* (paraphrasing Erasmus' *In Praise of Folly*), in which he attempted to analyse the beginnings of television.[9]

It is also worth mentioning here, among the still unpublished material, the researches described by Marie Seton in her biography of Eisenstein. Given the general character of her account and bearing in mind that Seton usually tried to make Eisenstein's work appear to follow from certain psychological or existential problems, critics have not attached too much importance to this source.[10] However, reading between the lines, we can deduce some important aspects of Eisenstein's thought, especially the 'anthropological' aspect of his research. We shall return to this later, but here are some of the most useful passages:

> He talked more and more of his plan to create a synthesis of knowledge for the development of film as an expressive medium. He hoped to realise this monumental task in a series of books, which he regarded as more important than any film he might make. Each was devoted to a different subject and its relation and application to the art of cinematography. Already he had extensive notes for some ten volumes. The first

volume, entitled *Direction*, he had commenced in Mexico, but though he had been working on it, the book remained unfinished at his death fourteen years later.

Another would be devoted to a study of psychology and film.[11] In this book he intended to draw extensively upon Freud, although Eisenstein had come to the conclusion that Freud's system had certain inherent limitations . . .

Another book was to be devoted to painting and what it could teach the cinematographer about the unity of form and content. The full realisation of the importance of composition in the enrichment of the film medium had come to Sergei Mikhailovich in Mexico, where composition had become one of his primary concerns. It was then he told me of his conviction that primary form – the triangle and the circle – revealed to man the 'mystery' of higher truths in symbolic form – the triangle: God, Man, and the Universe, and the circle: immortality.[12] [. . .]

In a fourth [book], he intended to examine the customs of people through the ages, analyse symbols and create a reservoir of research material for the film director. In connection with this book, he talked at length about the surviving customs of Greece and retraced the life of centuries to the age of myth, the age when it seemed to him there had existed a certain primal unity of all man's activities.[13] [. . .]

There was one book which he thought he would never write, though the notes for it existed on many pages of his books and on sheaves of paper. It was to cover the meaning of religious experience, of ecstasy and man's relation to his gods . . . For him there was a 'mystery', and the 'mystery' was finding the meaning of God and Christ.[14] The names evolved, the forms and symbols changed from place to place and epoch by epoch; but the 'mystery' remained.[15]

When we read these extracts, we can understand how Eisenstein's personality has become so much more complex and interesting since the publication of the six-volume *Selected Works*. The over-familiar image of the director of all those 'classics' of cinema history from *The Battleship Potemkin* to *Ivan the Terrible* has been gradually transformed into that of the author of equally celebrated critical and theoretical works.

In this prevailing trend of the last decade, it is the role of theoretician which has attracted most interest and is proving the indispensable way forward for almost all new Eisenstein research, whether on his films, his graphic output, his work in theatre or even on his writing.

Viktor Shklovsky, the founding father of Russian Formalism and author of an important biography of Eisenstein, had access only to the first four volumes of the *Selected Works* when he began to define this new image. With remarkable prescience, he wrote: 'I think that Eisenstein is the greatest theoretician of the Soviet period. He was an inspired director.[16]

Although he conceived his work on film, he was in fact a great philosopher.'[17] We could well adopt Shklovsky's claim, despite its typically laconic and 'compact' style, as a starting point for our own reflection on the study of Eisenstein as theoretician.

In hailing Eisenstein as a great Soviet theoretician, Shklovsky provides a key (which is rich in its potential even today) for reading Eisenstein's thought in its context, drawing out its full value in the context of twentieth-century Russian and Soviet culture. This emphasis is all the more important in view of the epithet 'genius' (accepted by both Shklovsky and Jakobson) and its corollary, 'a unique and irreplaceable figure', both of which encourage us to see Eisenstein as an isolated thinker. We have in mind here the studies by film critics, even the best of which, by Aumont and Andrew, take only a partial view of the links between Eisenstein and the main currents of twentieth-century thought.[18]

Eisenstein has most often been located within the great flowering of Russian art and its avant-garde,[19] alongside Meyerhold, Mayakovsky, Tretyakov, Vertov and Rodchenko, etc.[20] There can be no doubt that he does belong to this great artistic family and to the culture of the 'historical avant-gardes', at least in respect of questions of artistic creation and aesthetics. Within such a diffuse concept of contextualisation, there are a great many studies which seek to demonstrate the affinities and the differences that exist between Eisenstein and the other artists and movements of the avant-garde.[21] But this can only be a part of a more global reading of Eisenstein's work. In fact, amid the great number of problems he tackled during the 1930s and 1940s – and which recur in distinctive fashion in his films, from *Que Viva Mexico!* to *Bezhin Meadow* and *Ivan the Terrible* – the link with avant-garde culture gradually disappears.[22] One of the many examples which could be cited is his detailed study on 'the reasons for androgyny linked with the idea of bi-corporeality, which is born of the suppression of dual oppositions'. There were also the rituals which comprise 'the exchange and inversion of roles', especially by means of 'disguise' in all its forms.[23] In these studies, where he made use of certain ethnographic findings taken from Frazer, Eisenstein could not help but refute the less credible generalisations by which the British anthropologist, in his book *Aftermath*, had himself tried to systematise convincingly the great mass of material contained in *The Golden Bough*. Having reconsidered the rituals involving 'disguise', Eisenstein criticised Frazer in the following terms:

> In the interpretation of his collected evidence, Sir [James] Frazer speaks of the ritual of disguise as if it were a means of protection against . . . the evil eye or hostile forces. Even if this were true in some cases (which he refers to in another passage), as when a male warrior hides by donning a woman's clothes to escape the vengeance of the soul of the man

Figure 40 'An integral part of the Russian avant-garde.' Eisenstein with fellow members of the LEF group: Pasternak (*left*), Olga Tretyakova, Lili Brik and Mayakovsky.

or animal he has killed, in cases where there is an exchange, where the two protagonists remain alive and exchange only their roles, this interpretation is not convincing.[24]

This example, like the subjects of those books which remained at the project stage, *Method* and *Grundproblem*, shows that we need to situate Eisenstein in a much wider context than that of the 'historical avant-gardes', especially if we take into account all his theoretical speculation of the 1930s and 1940s.[25] This contextualisation in fact requires him to be located in the vast and diverse company of the Russian and Soviet scholars and theorists who have been lumped together as the 'Slav scientific tradition', 'which current has traversed the twentieth century between linguistics and culturology'.[26]

In an important study which traces the birth of Soviet semiotics and the theoretical paradigm that underpinned it, K. Eimermacher also sketches a general outline of this 'great scientific tradition' and unhesitatingly includes Eisenstein within it:

The Russian scientific tradition which was handed down from the 19th century (Potebnya, Baudouin de Courtenay, Veselovsky, etc) exercised a very direct influence on the linguistics and literary scientific work of the Moscow and Petersburg/Leningrad Schools, as well as on Russian Formalism (Bernstein, Bogatyryov, Durnovo, Jakobson, Yakubinsky, Yarkho, Larin, Polivanov, Propp, Reformatsky, Shcherba, Trubetskoy, Tynyanov, Ushakov, Vinogradov, Vinokur, Zhirmunsky). It produced, along with other external influences, several secondary orientations of a similar tendency in the science of religion and theory of art (Florensky), in the theory of literature and culture (Bakhtin, Medvedev and Voloshinov) and in aesthetics (Eisenstein).[27]

However it was above all the many studies produced by V. V. Ivanov, particularly in the 1970s, which established Eisenstein's place more precisely within the 'Slav tradition', among those other Soviet thinkers of the 1930s and 1940s who had so much in common while, as Ivanov is careful to note, also each having their own particularity.[28]

[We can find many common elements] in the most fruitful studies of the history of culture produced in our country during the 30s and 40s by such writers as M. M. Bakhtin, V. Propp, O. M. Freydenberg, L. S. Vygotsky, S. M. Eisenstein and others, whose work has only begun to occupy its deserved place in recent years, after its publication and translation.[29]

The contextualisation of Eisenstein in recent years has owed much to work done in linguistics and semiotics. This is why, from the start, such contextualisation, and in particular Ivanov's contribution, has come under fire from those who would deny any connection between Eisenstein's work and highly specialised semiotic research. A brief examination of several such objections will reveal one of the essential problems involved in reading Eisenstein critically: the fact that his thought developed not only in relation to the theory of cinema but also in the much wider field of the theory of art.

In a short article which appeared in 1979, J. P. Courtois criticised Ivanov's essays as an attempt to 'subordinate' the vigour of Eisenstein's theoretical system to the domination of 'early semiology'.[30] In our view, bearing in mind that the overall evaluation of Ivanov's vast research calls for a more structured criticism than mere accusations of 'subordination', it is quite possible to establish a relationship between Eisenstein's theoretical elaboration and semiotic research, as Ivanov does, especially if we recall that for Soviet semioticians

> the term 'semiotic' does not refer only to the abstract science of the universal properties of sign systems. It indicates instead a quite new scientific outlook which brings together what in other countries is studied in such separate disciplines as cultural (social, structural) anthropology, social psychology, historical ethnography, content analysis, poetics, art criticism, etc.[31]

This clarification by D. M. Segal gives us some inkling of the vast panorama which we will suggest here is a fundamental trait of Eisenstein's theoretical work and one that aligns him with the 'scientific' bent of the great Soviet semioticians.

Indeed it could be argued that Ivanov's theses and contextualisation of Eisenstein had the signal merit of considering his thought in its totality and of trying to find the first accurate interpretations, while certainly leaving scope for development and improvement on many points.[32]

At this point, it may be interesting to see in more detail how the approach outlined so far applies to specific aspects of Eisenstein's theoretical research. We shall take as an example the relatively homogeneous reflections on Walt Disney, dating from the 1940s, which are among the most important of his studies to be published recently.[33] These reflections show clearly with many examples how, even when tackling a subject which appears straightforwardly 'cinematic', he always sets himself more universal and elaborate questions about human artistic expression.

At the beginning of his work on Disney, Eisenstein states the theoretical goal of the essay:

> We shall try to enumerate the peculiarities and characteristic features which distinguish Disney's work. And we shall try to generalise these features. They will prove to be decisive features in any art form, but only in Disney are they presented in their very purest form.[34]

And several pages later he reveals the direction that his study will take: 'through his whole system of devices, themes and subjects, Disney constantly gives us prescriptions for folkloric, mythological, prelogical thought.'[35] This becomes clear as the essay develops into an extended study on themes found in Disney's work and more general reflections on the comic and on metaphor. For both of these he draws upon research in criminology (Wulffen), on the history of religions (Potter), on legal psychiatry, folklore (Kagarov), anthropology (Tylor and Lévy-Bruhl), historical poetics (Veselovsky) and child psychology (Kerschensteiner and Werner).[36]

The range of subjects raised by Eisenstein in this remarkable essay provides a perfect example of the main characteristics of his theoretical research during the 1930s and above all the 1940s. It is from this period of Eisenstein's maturity that the bulk of the research mentioned here dates, including the two great unfinished theoretical projects, *Method* and *Grundproblem*.[37] V. V. Ivanov has been able to read and study all of Eisenstein's unpublished work from these years and offers the following account of its concerns:

> In Eisenstein it is impossible to separate artistic creation from the fundamental problem of aesthetics.[38] And it was certainly not by chance that he tried to write two books about these two issues at the same time; so there are many ideas common to both *Method* and *Grundproblem*. The method of art (creation) is based upon the use of 'sensory' thought for its formal elements and draws upon strata of prelogical consciousness, which in art may mingle with ideas of modern logic.[39]

In analysing all the essays which would have comprised *Method* and *Grundproblem*, Ivanov leans towards such studies as 'Rilke II' in which Eisenstein deals with regressive forms of thought – especially the 'archaic nature of schizophrenic thought' as described by the psychologist A. Storch – and *Bali*, in which, while exploring the symbolism of the universal tree, he dwells upon the importance attached in Balinese rites to 'the sap (soul) of the tree in relation to the bark'.

In the Disney study and also in the essays related to *Method* and *Grundproblem*, as in several chapters of *Non-Indifferent Nature* and other writings of his maturity, Eisenstein is interested in the study of all forms of artistic and symbolic expression.[40] He pays particular attention, in relation to the 'fundamental problem', to forms of universal archetype linked with what he often termed 'the archaic strata of human psychology' which persist to the present day.[41] As G. P. Brunetta has noted, this particular cast of Eisenstein's thought is present in all his writings, from the most speculative to the most analytical:

> There is a constant orientation in his thought which leads it to seize

Figure 41 'Disney constantly gives us prescriptions for folkloric, mythological, prelogical thought', Eisenstein wrote in 1940–1, after meeting Walt Disney and his most famous creation in Hollywood in 1930.

analogies both superficial and profound (in relation to meaning and ideology) between literary, linguistic, musical and pictorial sign systems and strictly cinematic sign systems. The same principles of construction apply, he demonstrates, to certain novels, poetic and pictorial compositions and to certain films. These common elements correspond for Eisenstein to deep motivations whose origin is very ancient.[42]

The Disney essay provides a good example of this: in Disney's art the animation of inanimate forms and the 'animalisation' of human characters are for Eisenstein obvious signs of animism and totemism.

This direct relationship between cinematic and aesthetic thought, with frequent recourse to anthropological hypotheses, is equally apparent in Eisenstein's great 1937 treatise on montage, which has only recently been completely reconstructed by Naum Kleiman and published in translation for the first time.[43] At the heart of this work, Eisenstein proposes that prior to all forms of social relationship must be placed the ceremony during which the ancestor and the chief of the tribe 'were solemnly killed and eaten, according to a ritual which little by little was transformed into a symbol by the figure of Dionysos'.[44] Surveying all the transpositions which Eisenstein made of such ideas, F. Casetti considers this among the 'most enriching passages' of the book, recalling as it does Nietzsche's *Birth of Tragedy* and Freud's *Totem and Taboo*.

What seems to me most important in the essays like *On Disney*, and in the major studies like *Montage* and *Non-Indifferent Nature*, is the fact that Eisenstein succeeded in achieving sufficient mastery to make connections between some of the most interesting problems of this century in historical poetics, in anthropology and ethnography, including the study of folklore, and in linguistics and psychology (including psychophysiology, neuropsychology and psychoanalysis).[45] This breadth of view which distinguishes Eisenstein is also characteristic of the 'Slav scientific tradition': 'narrow specification is alien to the best traditions of our scholarship. Recall how very broad were the cultural horizons in the research of Potebnya and especially of Veselovsky.'[46]

Our thoughts can pause at this point. On the one hand, solid grounds have been found for inserting Eisenstein into the context of the 'Slav scientific tradition'. On the other, if we take precise note of the wide range of fields in which Eisenstein theorised, it will become clear which aspects of his theorisation remain to be further excavated and thus how further research into his thought should be developed. Only after such future studies will it be be possible to confirm Shklovsky's verdict: 'Eisenstein is the greatest theoretician of the Soviet period.'

Translated from the French by Ian Christie

Chapter 11

The essential bone structure
Mimesis in Eisenstein

Mikhail Yampolsky

I

Usually film theory acknowledges iconic quality, similarity and photographic quality as ontological features of cinema. Cinema emerges in this context as a mimetic art imitating reality. Eisenstein provides a very rare example of a radical denial of the usual notion of cinematic mimesis.

He devoted the speech he gave to the Congress of Independent Film-Makers at La Sarraz in 1929 to the problem of imitation, which he called 'the key to the mastery of form'.[1] He distinguished two types of imitation. He compared the first – the magic type – to cannibalism and utterly rejected it 'because magic imitation copies form'.[2] The embodiment of this kind of imitation was the mirror. Eisenstein contrasted this first type with a second – imitation of principle. 'Anyone who sees Aristotle as an imitator of the form of objects misunderstands him', he declared and added, 'The age of form is drawing to a close. We are penetrating matter. We are penetrating behind appearance into the principle of appearance. In doing so we are mastering it.'

This statement contained the two complementary hypotheses that were fundamental to the whole of Eisenstein's subsequent aesthetic: (1) the need for culture to pass beyond the 'stage of form', of the external appearance of objects and therefore primarily of 'mirror-image' mimesis; and (2) the stress on imitation of the principle behind objects. This latter formulation was rather enigmatic. What exactly was this principle (or, as Eisenstein liked to say, this 'order of things')? How could it be revealed? Where was it concealed? In the same speech Eisenstein proclaimed it to be the result of analysis ('Symbolism in myth is giving way to analysis of/in principle'). But what kind of analysis was it whose result had to be imitated?

Eisenstein's speech in La Sarraz coincided with his enhanced interest in protological forms of thought which later played an increasingly important part in his theorising. In his research Eisenstein turned to the group of linguists, psychologists and ethnographers who had posed anew the old problem of the origin of language and thought. Walter Benjamin called the 'theory' of these scholars (Bühler, Cassirer, Marr, Vygotsky, Lévy-Bruhl, Piaget, etc. – these were all very relevant names for Eisenstein) 'mimetic in the broadest sense of the word' because, according to the majority of these scholars, language derived from some primeval action that was imitative in character.[3]

It was essential to find in this mimetic action at the undifferentiated stage of thought a reflection not merely of external form but also of primeval generalisation (*obobschenie*) or 'principle', to use Eisenstein's terminology. In the books he had collected that dealt with the problems of 'protologic' he consistently underlined the places where the quasi-intellectual character of primitive mimesis was mentioned.[4]

Reading Emile Durkheim, Eisenstein's attention was drawn to the passage where the French sociologist had analysed the abstract geometric depiction of totems among the Australian aborigines:

the Australian is so strongly inclined to depict his totem, not because he wants to have in front of him a portrait that constantly renews the sensation, but quite simply because he feels the need to *represent the idea* that he depicts through a material sign.[5]

Andrew Lang, whom Eisenstein was also reading, devoted considerable attention to the problem of imitation and concluded, '"Savage realism" is the result of a desire to represent an object as it is known to be, and not as it appears.'[6]

But how is an idea or principle instilled into archaic representation? Eisenstein was hypnotised by the passage in Lévy-Bruhl's *Primitive Mentality* where he talks about Frank Cushing's work 'Manual Concepts':[7] 'To speak with your hands is to some extent *literally to think with your hands*. The most important signs of these "manual concepts" must therefore be evident in the sound expression of the thought.'[8] But, we add, if this is true of the sound expression, it will naturally be true to an even greater extent of the depiction of the thought. In Jack Lindsay's book, *A Short History of Culture*, Eisenstein underlined the passage: 'out of the harmoniously adopted movements of the body are mental patterns evolved.'[9] The grapheme that fixes the gesture or movement as the generator of the 'manual concept' is the *line*. Because of this Eisenstein attributed a very special significance to the line. By drawing a line, or 'running his eye' over it, to a surprising degree man got to the heart of the matter, to its sense. Eisenstein wrote: 'it is quite natural to "think" in a de-intellectualised way: running your eye over the contours of objects is an early form of rock drawing and is closely linked . . . to the cave paintings which are linear!'[10]

Eisenstein came to his own kind of pangraphism by discovering in all the infinite variety of the world a meaningful line beneath the visible surface.

Line was revealed in music as melody, in theatre staging (*mise-en-scène*) as the movement of the actors, in literary subject-matter (*syuzhet*) as plot (*fabula*), in rhythm as invariant schema, and so on. 'Line is movement. . . . Melody is like a line of chords, like volumes of sound pierced and strung together. The plot intrigue and subject matter are here like contour and spatial relationship.'[11] Elsewhere he wrote:

> we must learn to grasp the movement of a particular musical passage and we must take the trace of this movement – that is its line or form – as the basis for the plastic composition that should correspond to that particular music.[12]

The line and schema were seen by Eisenstein as the *obobshchayushchii osmyslitel'*, the factors that gave a phenomenon its meaning in context. He observed that they represented 'relationships in the most generalised way. The generalisation thus remains so great that it becomes what we call abstraction.'[13] Even the meaning of such abstruse things as ancient Chinese numerical concepts could be understood if we were to 'translate them into geometric outlines' and 'represent them graphically'.[14]

The line and schema had the ability to combine the abstract character of geometry and mathematics (the sphere of pure ideas) with emotional visibility (*naglyadnost'*). In the final analysis Eisenstein frequently conceived the very idea of 'image', which was so central to his theory, as a graphic schema. In his draft essay, 'The Three Whales', he talked about the three basic elements that underlay a visual text:

1 The depiction.
2 The generalised image.
3 The repetition.

In its pure form the first is naturalism, the second a geometric schema and the third an ornament.[15]

As we can see, the image was here directly equated with a geometric schema which was also the basis of the Eisensteinian theory of metonymy (the famous *pars pro toto*), because 'one facet (N.B. facet = line!) *here stands for the whole*'.[16]

The linear nature of the 'image' allowed Eisenstein to elaborate the concept of the general equivalence of different phenomena on the basis of the similarity between their internal schemas. It was this concept, based on the psychology of synaesthesia and essential for the construction of the theory of montage, that linked together not the surface appearances but the inner 'graphemes' of objects. Characteristically Eisenstein wrote, in response to criticisms by Hanns Eisler and Theodor Adorno of the theory of 'vertical montage', which linked sound and image:

> Eisler thinks that there is no common denominator between the pair:

galoshes and drum (even though a linear connection is possible, for instance). . . . Image is transformed into gesture: gesture underlies both. Then you can construct whatever counterpoints you want.[17]

The connection between galoshes and drum was possible because they were joined not by their surface appearances but by their images, the linear patterns that organised their gestures. A model for this general equivalence, based on Eisenstein's schema, is provided by Hitchcock's *Spellbound* in which an abstract 'pattern of black lines crossing a white surface' permitted us to establish an equivalence of meaning between a fork, a robe, a blanket and so on.[18]

The mimesis of form acted as a block to this panequivalence of objects, while in this context mimesis of principle opened up unlimited opportunities. Eisenstein quoted Guyau: 'Image is in effect the repetition of the same idea in another form and another context.'[19] Form changes. Idea, principle, image remain the same.

II

Needless to say, the reduction of 'principle' to a linear contour (a process that is at least contentious) raised doubts in the mind of Eisenstein himself. He admitted that he was 'disturbed' by 'a coincidence between the highest abstraction (the generalisation of the image) and the most primitive element, the line'.[20] He was able to avoid a regression to the archaic stage by resorting to the saving grace of using the dialectic and conclusions like the following: 'In content these lines are polar opposites: in appearance, in form they are identical.'[21] In this context appearance was subjected to a secondary criticism: it hinted too strongly at the vulnerability of logical processes. Eisenstein saw line simultaneously as a purveyor of protoconcepts and as the highest form of contemporary abstraction. This 'dialectic' was heavily dependent on Wilhelm Worringer's *Abstraktion und Einfühlung* (Abstraction and Empathy), published in 1908, which resolved a similar problem in a similar fashion:

> The most perfectly logical style, the style of the highest abstraction, of the strictest exclusion of life, is characteristic of peoples at a primitive cultural stage. There must therefore be a causal link between primitive culture and the highest, purest and most logical art form.[22]

It was from this perspective that Eisenstein persistently tried to separate the protological from the highly abstract element in line. He analysed the so-called 'rock-drawing complex' and tried to determine the boundary between the mechanical copying of a silhouette and contour as abstraction.[23] He viewed ornament as a synthesis of the protological (repetition) and the 'intellectual' (geometrism).[24] But none of these attempts to separate the high from the low was particularly convincing. Although he declared that the revelation of a 'principle' was the result of analysis, in practice it was achieved through imitation or mimesis. In order for the eye to 'think' in contour you have to *repeat* the movement traced by the hand. In order to comprehend the essence of Cushing's 'manual concept' you have to 'restore your hands to their original functions, forcing them to do everything that they did in prehistoric times'.[25] *To imitate a principle is to master it.* But all that gave a particular status to the science of analysis. Mastering the essence of a principle acquired the character of sympathetic magic. In this situation the artist took on the mantle of a magician, a shaman, a clairvoyant, while the 'principle', the idea, was transformed into a mystery, an enigma which had to be solved.

This theme was most fully developed by Eisenstein in his article, 'On the Detective Story':

> What is the essential difference between a 'puzzle' and a 'clue'? The difference lies in the fact that a clue provides the name of an object as a formula, while a puzzle presents that same object in the form of an image woven from a certain number of its attributes. . . . Anyone who has been initiated into its great mysteries can as an 'initiate' master to the same extent both the vocabulary of ideas and the vocabulary of images, both the language of logic and the language of emotions. The extent to which he grasps both as they approach unity and mutual penetration is proof of the degree to which the 'initiate' already has command of perfect dialectical thought. . . . He who can solve the puzzles . . . will know the very secret of the movement and existence of natural phenomena. . . . The wise man and the priest must be sure to learn to 'read' this ancient former language of image and feeling and not just to master the younger language of logic![26]

The detective performed exactly the same magic process: he was another hypostasis of someone who had been 'initiated into the secrets'. 'What of the detective story?' Eisenstein remarked. 'The theme that pervades the genre is the transition from image and appearance to reality based on understanding. . . . The same form – a simple puzzle – is the kernel of the detective story.'[27]

The artist was just like the magician and the detective:

> The artist works in the field of form in exactly the same way but he solves his puzzle in the directly opposite way. For the artist the clue is the 'given' fact, a thesis expressed in logical terms, and his job is to turn it into . . . a 'puzzle', that is to transpose it into the form of an image.[28]

This inversion of the process in the case of the artist (from thesis-schema to form) seemed destined to translate contemporary art from the sphere of the purely protological to a more rational sphere. But elsewhere, commenting on his work on *Alexander Nevsky*, Eisenstein recognised the ineffectiveness of this inverted process:

> It is hardest of all to 'invent' an image when the 'demand' for it is strictly formulated before the 'formula stage'. Here is the formula you need: make an image from it. The most natural and valuable way for the process to go is quite different.[29]

In other words the 'puzzle' had always to come first.

It is not surprising that Eisenstein projected the characteristics of the magician and the detective on to himself, attributing to himself a magic propensity to super-sight, the ability to perceive schemas, lines and principles through the visible surface. He wrote of the need for the special 'night vision', the eye of the 'pathfinder or his great-nephew Sherlock Holmes'.[30] 'I can see ahead with unusual clarity', he declared.[31] But this particular intellectual vision, because it was linked to the internal drawing of contour, was the actual genesis of conceptual thought: 'Even now when I write I am essentially almost "outlining" with my hand the contours of the patterns of what passes in front of me in an unending film of visual images and events.'[32] This was the reason for the unexpected criticism of normal vision, which was not connected with the tactile aspect of the protoconcept, that he developed in the chapter of his *Memoirs* entitled 'Museums at Night': 'Generally speaking, museums should be visited at night. Only at night . . . one can merge with what one sees and not just look at it.'[33] 'The bulb has only to blow . . . and you are completely at the mercy of dark hidden powers and forms of thought.'[34] Eisenstein, despite his passion for painting and the 'essentially visual nature' of his profession, chose a particular clairvoyant blindness reminiscent of poet prophets like Homer or Milton.

Eisenstein turned to the theme of night vision even before the *Memoirs* in an unpublished fragment from 1934. It is significant that, after discussing the mysticism of Swedenborg,[35] Eisenstein moved on by association to the idea of a multiplicity of worlds: 'Just imagine for a moment that the light goes out and the reality around you suddenly becomes a *Tastwelt* [a tactile world] of perceived reality.'[36] The world was divided into the world of the visible, the perceived, the heard and beyond them there was 'a multiplicity of worlds: the world of the real [*Handlungswelt*], the world of the imagination [*Vorstellungswelt*], the conceptual world [*Begriffswelt*]'.[37] In this multiplicity, the world of 'things in themselves' emerged, perceived through the veil of vision and appearance, and it was this world that the artist-clairvoyant also perceived through the magic dialectic. Once again in this mystical picture of world perception we find echoes of the old treatise of Worringer who had asserted:

> It is in primitive man that the instinct for the 'thing in itself' is at its most

Figure 42 'Generally speaking museums should be visited at night [when] one can merge with what one sees and not just look at it.' (*Memoirs*) The photograph of Eisenstein was taken by Tisse at the National Museum of Anthropology in Mexico City.

powerful. . . . It is only when the human spirit has travelled in the thousands of years of its development the whole road of rational discovery that the feeling for the 'thing in itself' reawakens as the final resignation of the conscious.[38]

Eisenstein could not help regarding his own consciousness as having existed for thousands of years. He perceived the world like a man who had lived forever.

III

The genesis of sense from gesture, movement, tactile quality, gave the text the character of a body. It was precisely for this reason that reading a text became a physiognomic activity, something that Eisenstein referred to more than once: 'We shall tirelessly train ourselves to sense keenly the physiognomy of one-eyed expression.'[39] According to Eisenstein's conception of the genesis of form, it was preceded by principle, schema and line, which were gradually overgrown with the body. Studying the experience of ecstasy, Eisenstein showed that the mystic dealt initially in things that were 'imageless' and 'objectless', in a 'completely abstract image' that then painstakingly ' "becomes objectified" in concrete objectivity',[40] and he pointed out that 'the imageless "beginning" is a set of laws . . . and the image of a concrete and objectified "personified" god is rapidly disclosed'.[41] He was talking about the almost physical discovery of the principle of flesh, the growth of the body according to the pattern: 'The formula, the concept, is embellished and developed on the basis of the material, it is transformed into an image, which is the form.'[42]

Eisenstein, as was his wont, applied this metaphor to the evolution of natural bodies, whose surface he saw as a static mould made from the movement of the body, just as the line is the shape of the mark left by movement.[43] In so far as the manifestation of the principle had, in Eisenstein's view, to repeat regressively the process whereby form took shape, it constituted essentially a 'decomposition' of the *body* of the text, a peeling away of the layers of body from the idea. It was natural therefore that Eisenstein should have a heightened interest in the leitmotiv of a body within a body, an envelope within an envelope, in what he called 'the kangaroo principle'.[44] He was interested in the Indian drawing in which the silhouette of an elephant encompassed the images of young girls,[45] or the enclosure of Napoleon's body in four coffins, each inside another,[46] and even in Surikov's painting *Menshikov in Beryozov* he detected the metaphorical structure of these repeating coffins.[47]

By removing the envelope you could get to the body, by preparing the body you could get to the heart. In 'The Psychology of Composition' Eisenstein developed in detail the metaphor of authorial self-analysis (to which he constantly subjected himself) as 'autopsy', as the dissection of a corpse. It is significant that to this end he analysed 'The Philosophy of Composition' by Edgar Allen Poe, a writer with whom he had much in common – the mythology of the perspicacious detective, the belief in physiognomic knowledge and so on. Eisenstein equated a detective story to a pathologist's investigation: 'The one conducts his analytical "autopsy" (revelation) in the forms of a literary analysis of the image he has himself created while the other uses analytical deductions of the detective kind.'[48] In the same context Eisenstein wrote of the transition from 'the examination of the "decomposition" of the body devoid of life . . . to the decomposition "for the purpose of analysis" of the body of a poem'.[49]

The analytical revelation of the body of a text supplemented a physiognomic reading. The ideal became a particular ability to see through the body to the graphic structure that organised it. I would call this the method of the *artistic X-ray* which highlights through the flesh the skeleton concealed inside it.

The metaphor of the skeleton, of the bone-structure, was to prove extremely important for Eisenstein's method of recognising a principle. The imitation of principle became the denial of the body in order to reveal the skeleton. It has to be said that this dark metaphor came to Eisenstein, at least in part, from those Symbolists who were involved in theosophy and anthroposophy. These recent mystical teachings were, like Eisenstein's theory, orientated towards a particular kind of evolutionism. Genetically preceding forms were preserved, according to Rudolf Steiner for instance, in the form of invisible astral bodies that were however revealed to the 'initiated'. The Theosophists were seriously involved in attempts to fix invisible geometric sketches of what Annie Besant called 'forms/thoughts' and in so doing they directly referred to the experience of X-rays.[50] Maximilian Voloshin, who was close to Anthroposophy, wrote an article with the significant title 'The Skeleton of Painting' in 1904 in which he stated: 'The artist must reduce the entire variegated world to a basic combination of angles and curves', that is, he had to remove from the flesh that was visible the skeleton that had been revealed inside it.[51] The same Voloshin read, for example, the paintings of K. F. Bogayevsky as palaeontological codes, seeing in them concealed prehistoric skeletons.[52] The Anthroposophist Andrei Bely in his *Petersburg*, which is suffused with the leitmotiv of the rejection of the corporeal and the journey to the astral, provided us with a description of the movement from formula to body that is very similar to Eisenstein's: 'Nikolai Apollonovich's logical premises furnished the bones; the syllogisms surrounding these bones were covered with stiff sinews; the content of his logical activity was overgrown with flesh and skin.'[53] Indeed, we note that the passage quoted ends with an episode for which the sequence of the gods in Eisenstein's *October* might be taken as a paraphrase. We are talking about the scene in which the head of an ancient primitive idol extrudes through the metamorphoses of the gods – Confucius, Buddha and Chronos.[54] The passage through accretions of flesh to the skeleton is analogous to the passage through appearance and the accretion of later deities to their schematic predecessor, and that is a thought process close to Eisenstein's. On the other hand, the development of abstraction from Theosophy was a path common to many artists at the turn of the century, including Kandinsky and Mondrian.

Eisenstein admitted, 'I have been attracted to bones and skeletons since childhood. This attraction is a kind of illness.'[55] He despised the emphasis in unskilled drawing on the corporeal because 'the finished drawing relies upon volume, shadow, half-shadow and reflex while a "taboo" is placed on the graphic skeleton and the line of the ribs'.[56] Eisenstein viewed with great suspicion paintings in which flesh was used to conceal the essential bone structure. He quoted the following passage on Chinese painting from Chiang Yee's *The Chinese Eye*:

> suddenly they may glance at the same water and rocks in a moment when the spirit is awake, and become conscious of having looked at naked 'Reality', free from the Shadow of Life. In that moment they will take up the brush and paint the 'bones', as it were, of this Real Form: small details are unnecessary.[57]

Eisenstein offered the following commentary on this passage: 'Here we encounter the word "bones". This linear skeleton, whose function is to embody the "Real Form", the "generalised essence of the phenomenon". '[58] There was a direct link here between the linear schema as a principle and the metaphor of the bones. Elsewhere Eisenstein, once again comparing a schema to a skeleton, was more specific: 'this "essential bone structure" may be swathed in all sorts of particular painterly devices.'[59] In a certain sense he was also reaffirming the independence of the bone-structure from the flesh that covered it.

Since for Eisenstein any hypothesis was finally proved by projecting it on to evolution, he developed this metaphor in an evolutionary way. He quoted from Emerson's account of Swedenborg's teaching (*Representative Men*) a fantastical passage in which the entire history of evolution from the serpent and the caterpillar to man himself is depicted as the history of adding to skeletons and rearranging them.[60] And in a note written in 1933 he enthusiastically revealed another fantastical evolutionary law of correspondence between a skeleton and a thought pattern: 'Self-imitation. (Hurrah!) Shouldn't I write about it as a process of developing the consciousness? Nerve tissue reproduces the skeleton etc. and thought reproduces action. It is the same in evolution.'[61] The nervous system as the purveyor of thought graphically repeated the pattern of the skeleton as the purveyor of action. In man there occurred an internal mirror-image mimesis of the schemas, structures and principles from which consciousness derived.

Eisenstein often wrote about the way in which schemas, lines and bone-structure shone through the body of a text. This magic X-ray was rooted in the particular mechanisms of Eisenstein's psyche. He recalled 'only one scene' from Frank Harris's memoirs, *My Life and Loves*: the story of the man who laughed 'and shook so much that the flesh "began to part from his bones"(!)'[62] The bones literally began to stick out through the flesh. In the passage in his *Memoirs* 'On Folklore' Eisenstein recalled that he had compared a certain Comrade E to 'a pink skeleton clad in a three-piece suit' and he recreated the psychology of the birth of this 'sinister image': 'First you picture a skull sticking out through a head, or the mask of a skull sticking out through the surface of a face.'[63] Even Eisenstein himself admitted that the image 'of the skull squeezing through the surface of the face' was a metaphor for his own conception of expressive movement, a model for the work of visual mime. This demonstrates why the physiognomic perception of the essential was so important in Eisenstein's method. The science of physiognomy counted bones through accumulated layers of flesh. But from that it was only one step to his concept of ecstasy, which may be understood as *exstasis* – the removal of the skeleton from the body, the principle from the text, the emergence of the body from itself, like 'the skull squeezing through the surface of the face'.[64]

The skeletal motif appeared in his films as well, in *Alexander Nevsky* and above all in *Que Viva Mexico!* In the scene of the 'Day of the Dead' in the Mexican film the 'essential bone structure' was transformed into an extended baroque metaphor. For Eisenstein the fact that the carnival death masks revealed real skulls was of decisive significance:

> Both the face like a skull and the skull like a face. . . . One living above the other. One concealed beneath the other. One living an independent life through the other. One in turn shining through the other. One and the other, repeating the physical schema of the process through the play of images of face and skull, of changing masks.[65]

The meaning in this constant play of physiognomies emerges through the flesh (mask) to become in its turn a mask. The essence of Eisenstein's concept of mimesis is concentrated in this image.

Research that concentrates attention on the montage stage of Eisenstein's semantic conception usually fails to link it properly with the *Grundproblematik*. However the montage stage of the creation of meaning in his conception would be unthinkable without the first stage of mimesis of 'principle', of the revelation of the schema, of the intellectual grapheme that fixes image and protoconcept. This initial stage of the creation of meaning depends on the intuitively magic physiognomic disclosure of the

Figure 43 The essence of Eisenstein's concept of mimesis is concentrated in the image of carnival death masks revealing real skulls beneath, from the 'Day of the Dead' sequence in *Que Viva Mexico!*

line which lies concealed within the body of the object (or text) – of the 'bone-structure'. Before the intellectual manipulation of the montage stage the artist passes through the 'corporeal' stage of creativity, which Eisenstein described as 'decomposition', an X-ray 'autopsy' of the visible, the flesh. Before we can begin to combine generalised image schemas, the 'all-important bone-structure', visible to the 'initiate', must 'elbow its way' through the face of the world around us.[66]

Translated from the Russian by Richard Taylor

Eisenstein and the theory of 'models'; or, How to distract the spectator's attention

Myriam Tsikounas

Eisenstein's silent films have often been described as 'mass films' or 'films without heroes'. In each narrative, however, a protagonist – played by a carefully selected non-professional actor – assumes more or less definitive individuality.[1]

Even in 1947, Eisenstein was still recalling the time lost in searching for 'types', in wearisome rehearsals and in make-up sessions required to 'hide the little mole-eyes of a Sebastopol boiler-man and transform him into the ship's doctor on the *Potemkin*'.[2] So why did he spend over seven years recruiting non-professionals, or parading members of his production crew like Maxim Strauch, Eduard Tisse and Grigori Alexandrov in front of the camera? What function was served by these novices who made only one appearance to illustrate the transition from the 'old' to the 'new'? Was their role identical in the films of commemoration and those of collectivisation, or was it subject to a dual evolution, both chronological and political?

In order to answer such questions, I shall attempt, after defining the features common to all these newcomers, to trace the itinerary that stretches from the dawn of the century (*The Strike*) to 1929 (*The General Line/The Old and The New*) and is signposted by two dates: 1905 (*Potemkin*) and 1917 (*October*).[3]

All four epics do in fact follow a similar pattern. In each, the first act sets the scene and even invites a charge of archaism. The 'model' *naturshchik* does not really put in an appearance until the second part. Then the action lingers upon him, immediately establishing him as both a semiotic and agential subject.[4] As a victim of injustice, the individual rebels and leaves his station to confront the old world. He may be mocked or killed, but none the less triggers a general mobilisation which reprogrammes the narrative. These emblematic figures – respectively a worker, sailor, a Bolshevik militant and a poor peasant woman – also share the characteristic of evolving alongside a counterpart who opposes, takes over, or aids in the fulfilment of their civilising mission.

THE WORKER IN *THE STRIKE*

The pretext for the strike, with which the second part of the film opens, is a false accusation. A worker, introduced in close-up, looks vainly – in a methodical alternation of seer/seen – for the micrometer which has just been stolen from him. He makes the audience a witness by means of a glance to camera. Two intertitles convey his thoughts – 'A micrometer costs 25 roubles' and 'Three weeks work for the Tsar' – and a third emphasises his quest: 'He goes to complain to the office.' There, in a series of action-reaction exchanges, the actor confronts the foreman and the manager. Accused five times of being a 'thief', he walks out, staring intently at the camera. The action leaves him to concentrate on the other actors, still glued to their machines. When we return to him, he has hanged himself but, in committing suicide, he has also acquired a name and transformed himself into a catalyst, calling on his workmates to repair the injustice by downing tools.[5] This summons has an immediate effect on the film's graphic style. The workers' bodies are fragmented into close-ups of legs running, angry faces, hands downing tools. Solidarity is expressed formally as the word is passed from one to another. Three extras, symbolising three generations, fold their arms in front of a wheel which stops turning. For the first time, actions succeed each other logically. The group retraces the victim's path and spreads through the factory with the cry: 'To the office, comrades'.

The corollary to this creation of a revolutionary space is that the 'old' loses its place. The bosses, briefly glimpsed, are wedged between the camera and a window (which they have to close, to avoid being stoned). But the crowd does not assume control of the narrative for long as we return to a system of opposing parallels in the next act.

While the workers hold an interminable meeting in a clearing, management is already preparing its response and, in the fourth part, the starving people are confined to their homes. At which point, enter 'the ragged proletariat' – their a priori opposite in every respect. The workers, who all appear alike, live with their families in a clearly defined district; while the motley elements of the 'lower depths' live alone, each in his underground barrel. Set design and editing, however, do their best to blur this contrast. The two camps, presented alternately, conspire in similar settings and boast exactly the same number of ringleaders. While four workers and a woman grouped near some casks formulate a plan, the 'King' summons four beggars and a whore from huge drums half-buried in the ground.

Above all, this underworld has its own individualised character who, throughout the narrative, derives his power from his metaphorical presence. First placed on screen by the police chief as he consults his file of informers, 'Owl' emerges from the book of mug-shots to hang up his hat and salute the audience. While spying, he hides among ropes which are

Figure 44 Workers' solidarity begins to appear in *The Strike* only after one of them has committed suicide.

progressively enlarged in a play upon perspective, or disappears into tombs and, in protean fashion, reappears metamorphosed into an eagle perched on a parapet. In the fifth act, this bird of prey takes control of the narrative. It is through his eyes that we discover the 'court of miracles' and when he photographs 'the dangerous ringleader' the action is set in motion. He develops the film 'that same day', sets a trap 'in the evening' for the worker, who falls into the ambush 'at night'. 'In the morning' he congratulates the police, who are beating up their prisoner and 'the following night' he gloats over his success, commenting 'They've had it'. After disappearing for a time, he returns to give the signal for repression to start. During the 'liquidation' he laughingly supervises the operation alongside the police chief.

The masses appear to be playing the central role in *The Strike*, but in fact it is just two individuals who manipulate the narrative. The first, established as a catalyst, encourages the emergence of a 'plural actor'; the second, his opposite, reins in this group and guides it towards its destiny – death. The strike fails not only because the old has not been undermined, but also because in this struggle, victims and executioners are counterparts, occupying the same place at the bottom of the social scale.

THE SAILOR IN *POTEMKIN*

The film offers an early identification: 'The sailors Matyushenko and Vakulinchuk'. These are introduced together and presented as twin.[6] They are first observed in parallel action in the sleeping quarters. The first, described as 'vigilant but blundering', strikes a cabin boy. The second, represented by an intertitle in huge letters, stirs up the crew and the montage indicates the efficacy of his speech. His every phrase (transcribed by a title) is followed by a shot of a sailor waking and agreeing with him. In the next section, the over-impulsive Matyushenko withdraws to the wings; Vakulinchuk monopolises the screen. 'In the morning' he criticises the food and urges the men to leave the mess. When Captain Golikov decides to put down the mutineers, the militant takes charge of operations and ensures victory by undermining the two tsarist symbols: the church and the army. His tactic becomes the subject of the whole second act.

As the episode starts, Admiral Gilyarovsky, framed to advantage (in low-angle close-ups against a white background), orders the quartermasters to execute the mutineers. Hesitating, the young sailors notice in reverse angle a priest 'descending from Heaven'. His appearance is stormy, with furrowed features haloed by a long white beard. As he holds out the crucifix and entreats, 'Lord, let the unruly submit', Gilyarovsky gives the order, under God's decree, to open fire on the tarpaulin which has been thrown over the mutineers. Time is stretched so that the various reactions may be recorded. Vakulinchuk lowers his head; the firing-squad takes aim;

Figure 45 The quarterdeck of the *Potemkin*: scene of the film's 'simple transfer of authority'.

the priest complacently toys with his cross. But the sailor lifts his head and sees a sequence of six detail shots (the ship's bows, tarpaulin, buoy, bugle, crucifix, firing-squad) symbolising the *Potemkin* and/or the 'old'. Vakulinchuk 'makes up his mind', which determines the precise timing of the outcome. The military command 'Fire!' is countered by 'Brothers! On whom are you firing?' The command 'Beware the Lord' is irreverently answered by 'Go to hell, fool!'

This last is enough to rout the foe. Suddenly filmed from behind in high-angle long shot, Gilyarovsky gesticulates on the bridge. The prelate no longer has his head in the clouds, but now emerges from the ground. He attempts the painful climb from the bowels of the ship. When Vakulinchuk strikes him, he resorts to nervous mannerisms – fearfully he peers out of one eye, then closes it again – and his cross buries itself in the deck like an axe. Demythologised, tsarism may now be capable of destruction. The sailors fraternise with the firing squad, arm themselves, throw the officers into the sea and ransack their cabins. Seemingly embarrassed, however, the narrative seeks a way to neutralise this wilful, self-appointed leader – the very embodiment of subjectivity and all those characteristics opposed to the idea of a vast social movement. It finds a solution. The act closes on a fade-out and reopens with a sacrifice. Vakulinchuk, shot (in the back) by Gilyarovsky, in turn falls overboard and it is on his face – smeared with impure blood and to be avenged – that the 'drama at sea' definitively closes.[7]

This *volte-face* enables the narrative to alter direction. 'The dead man who demands justice' becomes the key to the fate of the crew and the people of Odessa, summoned to unite in solidarity. The film changes gear. We turn from 'one cell in the battleship's organism to the whole ship as an organism; from a lone appeal for fraternisation to the ship's cry of "Brothers!"; from individual catering to collective revictualling by the yawls'.[8] This broadening out also affects the *Potemkin* itself. Hitherto the ship has remained a fixed space and only certain parts of it have been explored; now it is seen in its entirety. It becomes animate, establishing itself territorially, and is transformed into an actor asserting its name, 'Prince Tavrichesky' (Taurida).

Every effort is made to humanise it. We see it taking on supplies, cleaving the water, putting on a burst of speed, readying its guns and directing its lights, looming into camera like a face. The intertitles also help to anthropomorphise it. They indicate its position, 'The battleship is at anchor, it has mutinied'; recount its exploits, 'It replies to the army's atrocities'; name its adversary, 'The battleship against Destroyer No. 267'; stress its isolation, 'Alone against all'; and glory in its eventual triumph, 'The battleship proudly passes the fleet without a shot being fired'.

The sailor has released a collective force which takes up and amplifies the initial revolt. The same episode on the Odessa Steps is a counterpart to the tarpaulin. Once again tsarism looms from above (and from the field of a saint's statue and a church). Its presence is limited to a row of bayonets and giant Cossack shadows. The battleship responds equally abstractly. A single salvo blows up the Odessa Opera House, headquarters of the general staff. Ultimately, however, this 'figurative thrust' is contradicted by the diegetic action. We return suddenly to the *Potemkin* as a cockpit. Matyushenko, Vakulinchuk's 'double', is bringing the ship in; not only has he taken over the captain's cabin and assumed the authority to shout orders, he has also appropriated the 'old' equipment: optical instruments, telephones and maps.

The 'writing' (*écriture*) of *Potemkin* sets two worlds formally in opposition, but semantically it shows a simple transfer of authority and the perpetuation of ritual, suggesting areas of permeability.

THE STANDARD-BEARER IN *OCTOBER*

Like the worker and the sailor, the man carrying the banner who appears on the scene in the second act of *October*, during the 'July Days', is briefly established as both a semiotic and agential subject. Introduced by the title 'Saving the flag' and described as a 'Bolshevik', he also acts on an individual basis as he irrupts into the 'other scene'.[9] Cast in the role of a voyeur, he intrudes on the intimacy of an officer and his female companion, who are shown in three subjective shots. He thus undermines the old and pays with his life for his indiscretion. The bourgeois women, who have hitherto been merely spectators, now enter the action. For the first time their bodies are seen. Stamping feet break the shaft of the banner; and hands wield objects, no longer charming, but deadly as the umbrella-tips serve to pierce the young man's chest. Faces, now jarringly different, express a 'cannibalistic rage'.[10]

The camera loses its panoramic neutrality to stress the hysteria of those who shift the responsibility for their own confusion on to a third party. Furthermore, the displacement effected from the Bolshevik to his banner (torn to shreds by teeth) and then to the organ of his party (the copy of *Pravda* thrown into the water) reveals their lack of ideological purpose. Contrasted with this old-fashioned lynching of a militant, enlightened but possessed of an unhealthy subjectivity, is the death of two innocent emblematic victims: a woman and her horse.[11] This female extra, whose face remains hidden and who cannot be assigned to any particular camp by particularities of clothing, is killed on the dividing line between the spans of a bridge as these are raised. She thus rejoins the people on whose side she falls.

These three deaths reprogramme the narrative. The old world, however, continues to show its hand. At the end of the scene a minister pointlessly reissues the order (which has already been executed) to 'cut off the

Figure 46 The standard-bearer in the July Days episode of *October* who 'undermines the old and pays with his life for his indiscretion'.

workers' quarters from the centre'.[12] In the next section, an entire regiment is described as having gone over to the Bolsheviks, yet the Party headquarters is ransacked and its leaders are arrested in large numbers.

The 'July Days' give a starring role to the masses. However, if we consider the overall organisation of the film, this sequence, sandwiched between Lenin's arrival at the Finland Station and Kerensky's installation in the Winter Palace, also seeks to distract the spectator's attention and make him forget that historical change is effected by two figures alone.

The vanguard introduction of Lenin by a date title, 'The 3rd of April', immediately designates him as capable of changing the course of events. By graphic artifice, the letters 'HO' (but) which follow the titles 'Everything is as before' / 'Famine and war', change to 'OH' (he), 'Ulyanov', 'Lenin'. Like the statue of Alexander III which is dismantled/reassembled on 17 February, the actor is introduced in piecemeal fashion. We see his foot on a running-board, followed by an oblique shot of his body, cut off from the waist by a banner. His space, on the other hand, is constructed as the reverse of the Tsar's. The monarch was seated in an empty, over-exposed frame, whereas Lenin is standing at night in the middle of a dense crowd, whose immobility contrasts with the raging elements of wind and light. Behind him stand not cupolas, but the precise time on a clock.

Kerensky's downbeat introduction could not be more different. Unlike the Bolshevik leader – hailed by the people shouting his name – the head of the Provisional Government is supported by no-one. It is the film which names him and enumerates his titles: 'Supreme Chief', 'military and naval', 'Prime Minister', 'etc. . . . etc. . . . etc.' He is presented whole. Seen from behind, he plunges into a corridor, then ascends an interminable staircase. Associated from the outset with statues of women, the actor is soon confined to female quarters. The narrative insistently stresses that Kerensky is occupying the apartment of his namesake, the empress Alexandra Fyodorovna. The two men are soon engaged in a system of parallels. While the latter surrenders himself to the luxury of the royal furnishings and tableware, the former asserts his metonymic force. Of the revolutionary in hiding, we see only the Finnish hut, then the disguise. The argument is clear. Kerensky has chosen the palace of the Romanovs as his residence, but he is unfit to replace the Father of Russia, whom only Lenin is capable of thwarting.

Here again, though, displacements come into play. Although Ulyanov, the bearer of a programme, sets himself in opposition to the old world right from his first intervention, by the end of the film, standing on the rostrum, 'he draws his strength from his inscription within an institutional form [unless it be] the strength of the institution which henceforth subsumes the man.'[13]

THE PEASANT WOMAN BETWEEN *THE OLD AND THE NEW*

The peasant Marfa Lapkina is also introduced in the second act by two intertitles which name her and list her meagre chattels. Like her predecessors, she has an undeniable agential efficacy. As soon as she appears on the scene, the narrative stops marking time and starts to make rapid progress. Having left 'in the spring' to beg a horse from the kulaks, the woman returns empty-handed 'in the summer', and proceeds to harangue the villagers. The proposed co-operative is established with the help of two technicians from the city, who are introduced identically – in frontal close-up – after a title has noted their occupations. 'The Secretary' promptly disappears from the diegesis, while 'the Agronomist' supports the heroine in her civilising mission.

At first Marfa seems to be helping the Agronomist, making people forget that the actual decision was authoritarian. The act closes with a fade-out on the man declaring the kolkhoz constituted, despite the negative vote of the poor peasants, the '*bednyaks*'; but a kind of appendix reopens on the woman seated beside the only three sympathisers and closes with an iris on her smiling face. This schema is reversed during the second mission: learning how to use a cream separator. Marfa's spontaneity, her 'sensual, almost animal joy' is checked by the Agronomist, who cuts the miracle short by addressing a laconic 'I congratulate you' to the new members, doffing his cap in salute.[14]

When it becomes necessary to combat resurgences of the 'old' in the 'new', the two protagonists are once again placed in parallel. They enter the dairy in similar manner and both face the same task. Each must convince the peasants to return their hastily withdrawn profits and confront (in shot/reaction shot) the most stubborn of the *muzhiki*. Marfa slaps an old man and raises the real problem: money. She lectures them: 'The co-operative's money must not be spent', 'It would be wasted to no purpose', 'Give back the money'. The peasant, deaf to what she is saying, throws her to the ground. Providentially, the Agronomist appears and, hammering with his fist on the table, rallies the irresolute by sketching out a pro-gramme: 'What about the pedigree bull?', 'What about improving the breed?' He stares at the stubborn co-operative member, who lowers his eyes and returns his share.

A transference has taken place. Marfa has proved ineffectual and would be no more than an illusory heroine, except that a sudden shift in the narrative restores her to the central role. Dozing by the box of money filled at such cost, she dreams that she is in a collective of the future and there finds 'the pedigree bull'. But in fact Marfa has forgotten the object of her original quest – agriculture – in order to adopt a second goal dictated by the Agronomist, that of breeding livestock. Moreover this promised land of milk and honey is predicated on a lack: it is peopled only by women. The

sleeper awakes 'in the autumn' and realises that the agricultural im-
plements have still not been delivered.

The Agronomist joins her one last time and persuades her to go to town
to get a tractor. Having set this goal, he withdraws to the wings and his
place is taken by the waiting secretary, who accompanies Marfa to the
ministry. The two characters share the same point of view. Simultaneously
they see the portrait of Lenin and an official already in frame. But the man
acts alone and, when he proposes to 'lay down' a 'general / line', Marfa, as
at the beginning, staves off violence by enthusiastically concluding,
'Thanks to the workers'. Their buttressing job over, the two aides finally
leave, delegating their role as catalyst to the now-civilised heroine.
Returning to the village, Marfa hurries to the assistance of the tractor
driver who is repairing the defective engine. The spectator, whose attention has been distracted throughout, does not notice that in order to reach
this dénouement the protagonist has renounced first cultivation and then
livestock to devote herself to machinery. He also does not see that the
Agronomist, who assures the continuation of work on the land, has been
supplanted by the Secretary, an embodiment of industrialisation.

Moreover, the two epilogues that Eisenstein offered are in fact irrecon-
cilable. In 1926, Marfa benefits from the action taken: she has begged for a
horse and is given a tractor. She climbs up and takes the place of the new
man to drive the newly-acquired vehicle and present herself to the
audience, who once again see in a series of recapitulatory close-ups the
various stages through which she has passed during the story. In 1929, on
the other hand, Marfa merely sits beside the tractor-driver, masking this
urban interference. She disappears immediately after, since we leave the
countryside for a Taylorised factory. To counter the absence of an agential
subject, the film-maker concludes, non-diagetically, with a series of titles
addressed directly to the audience.

We can now better understand why, despite the enormity of the work
involved, Eisenstein committed himself to using 'types'. In each film a
character embodying a will and a conscience is established and then
progressively challenged or put to death. The essential function of this
mirror image is to mask the narrative's real beneficiary, a double who pulls
all the strings, hiding behind the man (*The Strike*, *The Battleship Potemkin*,
October) who risks his life to challenge the 'old' on his behalf; a double
who reveals (and duplicates) himself to protect the woman (*The General
Line*) of whom he asks only that she mitigate the violence employed.

Translated from the French by Tom Milne

Chapter 13

Eisenstein and the theory of the photogram[1]

François Albera

I want to investigate an aspect of Eisenstein's theory that has been little discussed – not least because Eisenstein himself scarcely developed it in his writings – yet which relates to what he called in the 1937 essay 'Montage', the 'fundamental problem of cinema'.[2] This is the illusion of movement created by cinema, the 'movement effect' or, as it is now often termed, the 'phenomenon of apparent movement' (*phi*-effect).[3] Although this 'effect' is often invoked to explain the phenomenon of the impression of reality, Eisenstein referred to it in his definition of montage at the point where he was elaborating his theory of 'intellectual cinema'.

It was in a speech prepared for the 1929 Stuttgart 'Film und Photo' exhibition (and intended for publication in German in the catalogue) that he first raised the issue.[4] He mentioned it again briefly in a preface to Vladimir Nilsen's 1933 account of trick photography and at greater length in the second chapter of 'Montage', where he made fundamental changes to the original Stuttgart formulation.[5] In 1929 Eisenstein wrote: 'For here we seek to define the whole nature of the principle and spirit of the film from its technical (optical) basis.'[6] And what is this 'technical (optical) basis'? 'We know that the phenomenon of movement in the film resides in the fact that two motionless images of a moving body following one another in juxtaposition blend into each other after sequential showing in movement.'

The significance of this reference to the technical-optical foundation of cinema lies in its recognition of the photogram, which is neither designated as such, nor by any other technical term, but simply as an 'immobility' (*Unbeweglichkeit*). A secondary relevance is the mode of articulation between these technological unities alongside the *mechanical* process propelled by the machinery of cinema.

> Two shot immobilities next to each other result in the arising of a concept of movement.
> Is this accurate? Pictorially – phraseologically, yes.
> But mechanically the process is otherwise.

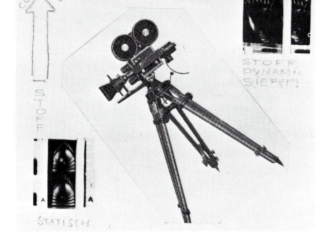

Figure 47 A Constructivist collage, made by Eisenstein for his 1929 essay 'A Dialectical Approach to Film Form', which asserts the primacy of the frame.

For in fact each sequential element is shot, not *next to* the other, but *on top of* the other.

For: the movement-percept (feeling) arises in the process of the superimposition on the received impression of the first position of an object of the becoming-visible new position of the object.

The still images do not succeed or follow one another in order to fuse, mix or dissolve in motion; they are *superimposed*, as in printing (*Eindruck*, or 'impression', is the term used in engraving). The choice of this term allows us to establish Eisenstein's most basic conception of montage, dating from the period of his 1923 manifesto 'The Montage of Attractions', when he was thinking in terms of photo-montage (and referring to Rodchenko and Grosz).[7]

This is why, after a description of the base phenomenon in terms not of the frame sequence but of the superimposition of frames, he can challenge Kuleshov's and Pudovkin's conception of a montage chain with his montage collision: 'According to my opinion, however, Montage is not an idea recounted by pieces following each other, *but an idea that arises in the collision of two pieces* independent of one another.' This sentence and the idea it expresses are well known; they had already appeared in Eisenstein's

1929 article 'Beyond the Shot'.[8] But again it is worth noting his precise formulation in the Stuttgart text, specifically (a) the importance attached to the 'piece' or element (*Stück*) and to the independence from one another of the *kadr* or *Bildausschnitte* as photograms (the English manuscript actually bears an autograph insertion after 'independent': 'even opposite');[9] and (b) the convergence between their mode of articulation and that which prevails in the system of language, via reference to the Japanese or Chinese hieroglyph.

'Beyond the Shot' is dominated by questions about the relationship of representation. The problem of the referent – how 'the combination of two "representable" objects achieves the representation of something that cannot be graphically represented' – is the origin of a problematic which will later come to dominate Eisenstein's thought, namely the distinction between representation and the 'global image' (*izobrazhenie* and *obraz*), and will eventually 'cap' the theory of ecstasy.[10]

'Stuttgart' states only that 'two independent ideographical signs ('Shots'), placed in juxtaposition, explode to a new concept.' Thus Eisenstein locates the minimal space of filmic articulation between frames, rather than between shots. Two frames which follow each other in super-imposition can differ minimally (A1 + A2 + A3 . . .), to a greater degree (A1 + A15), or can be totally disjunctive (A + B or Z). In the first case, movement will seem continuous; in the others it will be increasingly intellectualised, to the point of becoming a purely filmic movement, as in the example of the young peasant at the end of *October* who jumps with joy on the Tsar's throne. Here there is 'movement' in the form of a violent displacement of the subject from one side of the frame to the other without any transition.

To define the frame sequence as a sequence of successive phases of real movement, broken down into stills and reconstituted by projection, is thus to describe only one case and to capitulate to the dogma of continuity, to the flux of 'Life' that Bergson's philosophy celebrated.[11] The claims of conflict, discontinuity, omission and heterogeneity all challenge a Bergsonism which was evident in the first writings on cinema by Viktor Shklovsky. The consequences of these theoretical positions for Eisenstein's cinematic practice are largely to be found in the experimental sections of *October* (which were inserted during the second phase of its editing, after the first presentation during the 1927 anniversary) and in *The General Line*. They can be summarised as follows:

1 An emphasis on static objects: the material object (*veshch'*), which was central to the discourse of the Constructivist and Productivist avant-garde, tends to occupy the place of the object of perception (*predmet*), hence such ready-made images as emblems, illustrations, icons. As early as his 'Montage of Film Attractions' (1924), Eisenstein distinguished

theatre's concern with what is *made* from cinema's reliance on *conventional images* (photographs).[12]

2   (a) Attention to the cinematic mechanism – the row of regular units that constitute the film strip – leads to frequent self-referentiality: revelations of the process by means of slow and fast motion, repetition, temporal and spatial mismatches, and

    (b) the privilege accorded to the creation of any movement other than that of illusionist ambiguity, which is deemed naturalistic. The animation of inanimate objects – like the famous rampant stone lions and the plaster Bonaparte – but, more disturbingly, the tendency to make a movement or gesture something *filmic* rather than *filmed*. In addition to the peasant boy on his throne, *October* includes the example of the firing machine-gun created by the rapid juxtaposition of very brief still shots, reduced almost to single frames, of the gunner and his gun. The collision of frames whose plastic components – composition, geometric structure (which Mikhail Yampolsky has also noted in this volume), luminosity, etc. – these all produce a concept of 'firing' which exists nowhere else on film.[13]

    The Cossack's sabre slash in *The Battleship Potemkin* already pointed in this direction, but that could be explained by a technique of elision, of less intended to produce more (like Mallarmé's 'paint not the thing but the effect it produces'), or of a mental image being prompted.[14]

3 Paying attention to those instances of transition where the basic unities diverge and thus make possible recognition of the intervals which perception normally effaces and mechanical succession hides. Dziga Vertov wrote in his first manifesto 'We. A Version of a Manifesto' that 'intervals (transitions from one movement to the next) and not movements themselves constitute the material (elements of the art of movement)'.[15] But it is only in 'Stuttgart' that Eisenstein refers to intervals and gives them a place in the dialectic of film ('the place of the "explosion" is that of the concept', he writes).

4 Regarding the intertitle as having a shot 'value' (in Saussure's terminology).[16]

These four points qualify Eisenstein's hostility towards the *retinal* (as attacked by Duchamp also) and shed considerable light on his conception of an intellectual cinema whose later elaborations would tend in directions which remained secondary in 'Stuttgart'.[17]

Two circumstances can perhaps explain his taking up a position on this occasion which insists on a material definition of the medium and on the 'stripping bare' of the process. On the one hand, Eisenstein was here addressing members of the international avant-garde, and especially proponents of the 'pure cinema' whom he had previously lampooned in 'Béla Forgets the Scissors', but would now be depending upon during his

European tour, both at La Sarraz and in Paris.[18] On the other hand, he had also recently signed the founding manifesto of the last Constructivist group to appear in that decade, the 'October' group (1928–31), in which he and Esfir Shub were the only film-makers alongside the Vesnin brothers, Gan, Rodchenko, Klutsis, Ginzburg *et al.*[19] With its aim of giving form (*oformlenie*) to everyday life (*byt*), this group proposed a new design approach in all fields from architecture to the manufacture of utensils, and called for the dissolution of artistic institutions. His definition of art must therefore avoid the pitfalls of both the right (RAPP, vulgar naturalism) and the left (*Novyi Lef*, the 'fetishism of the material'). And finally, after the publication of Malevich's only two texts on cinema in 1925, Eisenstein could not but want to respond to the fundamental charge which the 'Pope' of Suprematism had levelled against both Vertov and himself: namely of having brought a new technology to the aid of perpetuating the old exhausted tradition of easel painting, even of resurrecting the 'Wanderers'![20]

At a time when, according to Marie Seton, he freely admitted to feeling constrained within cinema ('too primitive a medium for me', he had said to Hans Richter), and when he was working on projects like *Das Kapital* and *The Glass House* with an ambition which was without equal in the film-making of the period, everything would have encouraged him to believe that he was in fact going beyond cinema, as Malevich had transcended painting, forsaking the 'shaggy brush' for the 'sharp-pointed pen'.[21]

At any rate, this lecture cannot easily be accommodated within a unitary, continuous view of Eisenstein's thought, especially in view of the reworking which it undergoes in 'Montage'. The four points already noted show that it has very special epistemological implications which must now be explored further.

It belongs, as we have seen, to a tradition of enquiry into the nature of cinema inaugurated by Shklovsky, which starts from the medium's essential *dis*continuity. Also apparent is the influence of those Constructivist designers and photo-montageurs who worked only with 'found' images and 'ready-made' objects, giving these meaning through their reuse in constructions – an approach which the theory of attractions formalised for the cinema. Note that this position excludes, first, any problematic of the referent (either the partial or total image of the real); and second, any belief in the prior determination of the work by its material, which is understood as inert (nature as passivity). It operates in terms of the Suprematist challenge to create non-figurative images in the cinema.

The examples of non-diegetic, purely filmic or *zaum* construction in *October* reveal how much Eisenstein was influenced by such European avant-garde films as he had been able to see – particularly by *Ballet mécanique* and *Entr'acte* – and also how his project for a 'de-anecdotalised' cinema was prompted by the 'film without a story' of which Shklovsky had spoken.[22]

Figure 48 Léger's *Ballet mécanique* (1924) was one of the non-narrative avant-garde films that influenced Eisenstein's approach to *October*.

In this respect, the discovery announced at Oxford by Yuri Tsivian of an editing plan or script of *October* which amounts to a first version of the film is highly revealing.[23] Naum Kleiman has already analysed the 'interior monologue' that leads Vakulinchuk to shout 'Brothers!' in *The Battleship Potemkin*.[24] Here the filmic phrase that serves a similar function for the Bolshevik sailor in the Tsarina's bedroom sequence is constructed out of the debris of a narrative, by compressing and reordering its elements. Between the metaphors of the 'genital eggs' at the heart of an episode which is relatively coherent in narrative terms and the filmic phrase which deconstructs the political and religious statues of the 'holy' royal family to produce the concept of 'sterility', there appears a space which is perhaps that of Symbolism. And it is precisely this that stimulates what we may term, following Lacan, the Eisensteinian 'imaginary', to the level of construction which takes it into the 'symbolic'.[25] The reduction of the content to objects which are articulated according to a logic of conflict-deconstruction (the '*polonaise* of the gods' and the sailor's monologue) amounts to a kind of iconic purification, while those metaphoric sequences – like the raising of the bridges in the first part of the film – effectively dam up meaning: they emphasise without explaining.[26]

It is undeniable that Eisenstein's thought and practice alternated throughout the 1920s between two positions and that the 'shift' identified by David Bordwell was less a matter of actual transition (around 1930) than a continuing ambivalence.[27] We have already seen how an identical or similar phrase may function differently in the contemporary texts 'Stuttgart' and 'Beyond the Shot'. Now it is time to identify the source of this contradiction – obviously not something that Eisenstein himself recognised – which I believe lies in the opposition between the theory of 'attractions' – as decisive a discovery for cinema as that of collage for painting – and the theory of *pars pro toto*. Depending on whether he was citing a phenomenon to analyse a piece of film or vice versa, Eisenstein could take either point of view. *Pars pro toto* presupposes a unity of the whole, drawing on the Hegelian notion of difference or otherness as only an aspect of the totality which is anticipated in each of its parts, while attraction implies heterogeneity. 'Stuttgart' marked the culmination of Eisenstein's 'attractions' tendency and, although it remained unpublished at the time, he referred to it in a letter to Bryher and MacPherson as 'one of the most serious and basic in what I think about cinema'.[28] Returning to this text to integrate it into *Montage*, he 'hid' it beneath the now dominant theories of *pars pro toto* and *obraz*.

The second chapter of *Montage* deals with the base phenomena of cinema, movement and photography, and here he wrote of 'a series of still photographs representing different phases of one and the same movement', which are termed 'photograms' (*kadriki*, or 'little frames'). 'Stuttgart', it will be recalled, only spoke of 'stills' which enabled objects to be tackled, while here they have become the 'phases' of a movement. This is why, later, the distinction between *izobrazhenie* (representation) and *obraz* (total image) can be applied to the base phenomenon: the photograms are representations (inessential though visible), while movement is the *obraz*, the essential image (although 'mental' rather than visible). Representations will not occupy much space because they *fuse* (a term which had previously been spurned) in the animated image. Hence Eisenstein's hostility towards Futurism, at least as exemplified by Balla, to whom he again attributed an imaginary 'man with eight legs' (sometimes six), which 'gives only an impression of movement: this purely logical and mental game can only "lay bare the process" and thus ruin the "delicate deceit" which could have, with greater subtlety, created illusion.'[29] Hence also the now major interest – it was still secondary in 'Stuttgart' – in the painting of Tintoretto, in Daumier's drawings and in Serov, all of whom he believes inscribe movement in their forms without destroying its integrity.[30]

Painting and literature (a passage from Tolstoy) as *antecedents* serve to relativise the novelty of instantaneous photography and of cinema: 'mankind did not have to wait for the invention of the camera in order to seize a frozen moment from a dynamic process.'[31]

This reaffirmation of unity and continuity can be linked with the debate which Shklovsky began in *Literature and Cinema* .[32] Somewhat strangely, Shklovsky took up Bergson's views on movement, on the 'vital impulse' (*élan vital*) and the error of discontinuity that human consciousness commits when it dissects and freezes the movement of life. In *Creative Evolution* (1907) Bergson referred to 'the cinematographic mechanism of thought and the mechanistic illusion', in order to condemn this kind of thought for its inability to enter the flow or flux.[33] He accused it of taking 'snapshots' and of placing itself outside things so as to recreate them artificially, instead of merging with their inner development.

'The world of art is the world of continuity', according to Shklovsky; so if 'cinema is the offspring of the discontinuous world', it cannot belong to art and human ingenuity has created in its own image a new non-intuitive world.[34]

It was certainly the mechanical, the *Urphänomenon des Films*, which encouraged Shklovsky to deduce from this characteristic of cinema that it could not deal with pure movement, but only with movement-as-sign or movement-as-act (Bergson contrasted 'action' with 'act' and 'duration' with the 'moment'). Shklovsky's position was in fact rather ambiguous and he did not debate any of Bergson's assertions (which Gaston Bachelard would do in his *L'Intuition de l'instant* of 1932). He took from Bergson however the assurance that cinema could not possibly claim to 'capture' real life when he returned to the 'base phenomenon' in 1925 to condemn the Cine-Eyes. 'Cinema is the most abstract of the arts', he claimed in opposition to Vertov's factualism; and in this respect, Shklovsky remained always the most willing to 'hear' Eisenstein's ideas.[35]

Eisenstein's own position in relation to 'Bergsonism', both overtly and latently, was rather different, since he actually embraced all the negative points raised by the philosopher in respect of cinema or 'cinematographic' thought. Instead of denying the original sin of cinema, he wanted to display it: hence Kerensky's 'eternal' ascent of the same staircase. In his otherwise straightforward critique of *October*, Adrian Piotrovsky rather curiously qualifies this as a 'metaphor'.[36] But it is no such thing! We have here a proposition on the nature of film which seeks to dispel both the diegetic illusion of a Kerensky rising to full power and the purely optical illusion of a continuous rising movement, reinstating instead the 'lived' experience of duration. The staircase, by virtue of its regular divisions, equidistant steps and unidirectionality, offers a kind of analogue of the film strip, with its material base and structure of successive photograms. Acceptance of the mechanical character of the *phi*-effect and recognition of the intervals between frames and of the resulting discontinuity of movement, amounts to a 'stripping bare' of the process (indeed of 'the bride' by 'her bachelors').[37] This sequence has been insufficiently studied in relation to Duchamp's *Nude Descending a Staircase* or Léger's washerwoman, who climbs the same staircase nine times in *Ballet mécanique* and thus brings cinema back to what Eisenstein regarded as its true forerunner, namely the circular discs of Plateau's 'Phénakistoscope' and W. G. Horner's 'Zoëtrope'.[38]

For Bergson the interval was a neutral moment wherein is created an intermediate image derived from what came before and anticipating the next in line. In theorising the relationship between one photogram and another, Eisenstein was helped out of his impasse by the principle of the 'stop' (*Ausschnitt*) which he found in Tynyanov's *The Problem of Verse Language*, where the unity was termed *Abschnitt*, referring to a site of dynamisation, a movement not additional but multiplying.[39] Indeed movement in cinema is 'some kind of cut' + abstract time (of the apparatus) and is thus a 'false movement': Kerensky and his staircase exemplify this in relation to the illusory freedom to film movement. But, as soon as relationships are constructed which take account of the space between frames, the way out of the blind alley becomes clear. Yet Eisenstein distanced himself as much from any thought about the reproduction of movement as from Bergson's inner intuition: it is externality that is needed in respect of the object. The object, nature, is inert and passive (being-there) and it must be dynamised from outside (by an initiative conscious of its goal).

Finally, we may wonder what posterity has made of Eisenstein's sketch for a theory of the photogram. At the end of the 1920s, Charles Dekeukeleire carried this idea to its most extreme conclusion in his aston-

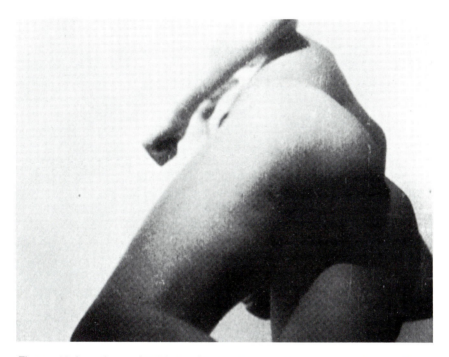

Figure 49 Impatience (1928) by Charles Dekeukeleire: a radical example of 'frame-based' cinema contemporary with Eisenstein's own experiments.

ishing work, especially the film *Impatience* (Belgium, 1928).[40] This leaves to the spectator's imagination whether or not a 'story' is constituted from four series of apparently diverse elements which are never correlated within the image, other than by juxtaposition and hence superimposition. The elements are a motorcycle, a woman who is sometimes naked and elsewhere dressed in leather, landscape and abstract imagery. These could be brought together intellectually by the sentence 'A woman rides a motorcycle through the countryside', but this would be absurdly re-ductive. The film's movement is mostly produced by filmic means, involv-ing collisions between frames, camera movements and very rapid cross-cutting.

Today, apart from such frame-based work as that of Sharits (based on blinking) or Kubelka (extreme fragmentation), mention should also be made of Werner Nekes's highly systematic work.[41] Nekes's theoretical and practical enquiry into what lies 'between the pictures' has retraced, in more radical fashion, some of Eisenstein's formative experiences.[42] In *Jüm-Jüm*, he created a woman swinging – a recurrent image in nineteenth-century optical toys and one also placed at the beginning of *Ballet mécanique*, in negative, by Léger – entirely by means of discrete single frames. And he has even realised the dream briefly entertained by Eisenstein of filming Joyce's *Ulysses*.

Translated from the French by Ian Christie

Chapter 14

The frame and montage in Eisenstein's 'later' aesthetics

Michael O'Pray

The name of Eisenstein is synonymous with the montage film method. Unfortunately this seems to act as a barrier to understanding the full richness and complexity of his writings and films. There is, in truth, much to call the conventional view of montage into question and encourage us to return more open-mindedly to Eisenstein's work. However, part of the problem is the neglect of his later writings, due, it seems, to the lack of support they give to the view of their author as political revolutionary film-maker *par excellence*. In fact, his later work, produced in the shadow of Stalinism, is treated with some suspicion, embodying as it does ideas and forms which do not rest easily beside the reasonably well-defined 'revolutionary' montage-based works. The upshot is that Eisenstein seems to divide too neatly into early and late, or montage and post-montage, or revolutionary and post-revolutionary. The lines of demarcation are many but inevitably cut across each other.

Eisenstein's work becomes more of a piece than is generally thought if we take seriously his own understanding of montage as a film construction necessarily involving a quite particular use of the film frame and its composition. This view undermines the idea of Eisenstein's later aesthetics being politically or aesthetically 'compromised' and, if true, the relationship proposed between shot and montage would apply to all montage film.

Eisenstein's later films, *Alexander Nevsky* and *Ivan the Terrible*, embraced historical and narrative tendencies, rejecting the montage method of *The Strike*, *Potemkin*, *October* and *The General Line*. The usual explanations for this transformation range from the effects of Stalinism and the broad tendency of Socialist Realism to Eisenstein's personal retreat from revolutionary to regressive artist. The identification of the historical subject-matter of the later films with ideological aspects of Soviet socialism at the time has of course been remarked upon, but the actual shift itself from the early montage-dominated theory to 'synthesisation' is very rarely discussed, let alone explained in any persuasive way.

Peter Wollen has suggested that Eisenstein's later writings were 'an attempt to shore up, scientifically and intellectually, an art increasingly preoccupied with emotional saturation, ecstasy, the synchronisation of the senses, myth and primitive thought'.[1] Noël Burch, on the other hand, sees the work of the 1930s and 1940s as a result of the conflict between Eisenstein's own aesthetic and the historical-political demands of the Stalin period. For Burch, the consequence is an 'entirely imaginary cinema . . . ensconced a thousand leagues from the dialectical and materialist cinema he had experimented with and theorised about from 1924 to 1929'.[2] In a more theoretical vein, David Bordwell traces the difference in terms of an Althusserian epistemological shift marking the different ontological and epistemological tendencies in Soviet philosophy, namely between the behaviourist Pavlovism of the early Constructivist and Formalist period and what may be termed the Hegelian idealism and syntheticism of the 1930s and 1940s.[3] In all three interpretations, the conclusion is the same: Eisenstein is judged to have moved away from a progressive or revolutionary theory and practice towards one which was less so, or, at worst, regressive and reactionary. What I want to propose here is a link, albeit in very general terms, between the early and later writings and films. A symptom of the problem is the fact that it is the very concept for which Eisenstein is famous – montage – which he continually reworks throughout his life.

To a large extent, the above criticisms rest upon a certain idea of the Russian revolution and its aftermath, namely the assumption that the revolution was lost under Stalin. Two fairly obvious points need to be made here. First, a revolutionary art can be judged so according to either its context (a relativist view) or its intrinsic form (an essentialist view).[4] Second, revolutions make sense only as events within what is otherwise 'stable'. That is to say, most revolutions are followed, politically at least, by periods of attempted consolidation and stabilisation. Revolution for its own sake and as a permanent state is an extreme position and rarely if ever achieved in practice. The criticisms in question also imply that there was a revolutionary art in the 1920s (probably true prima facie) and that such art remains essentially revolutionary even when the political context in which it exists has ceased to be.

Eisenstein lived through the revolution and its cultural impact in the 1920s to witness the attempts of the 1930s and 1940s to transform the economy, come to terms with the Russian past and defeat the threat of Western European fascism. In the same period, ideas of revolution were replaced in the Soviet Union by a nationalist ideology promoted by Stalin. Inevitably, opposition to Stalinism has been conflated with the negation of socialism itself. But criticism of Eisenstein for producing work under Stalin, and with the latter's support, seems narrowly idealistic, implying that Soviet communism is to be equated with any other form of dictatorship and that its art is inferior to both 'revolutionary' art and 'progressive' art produced in bourgeois society.[5] The issues here are prickly, to say the least, and judgements relating to the Stalin era are rarely detached and rational. Unavoidably, the morality of certain forms of social and political change besets most forms of analysis.

Eisenstein's later films did take on the character described above by Wollen. The two parts of *Ivan the Terrible* amount to a classic instance of the *Gesamtkunstwerk*, or 'total work of art', with an emphasis on the concepts of synchronisation of the senses, unity, excess and ecstasy. Their expressionist *mise-en-scène*, historical narrative as plot, compositional formalism, exaggerated acting style and what Eisenstein called 'vertical montage' are all features that demarcate these from the earlier films. Montage as the explosive perpetrator of meanings and as the means of constructing a cinematic language gives way to a different, seemingly more conservative, if not wholly conventional, form of editing. It is slower-paced, allowing development of action within the shot; and it rarely juxtaposes radically different images in metaphorical association. Such editing may, however, suggest a more complex notion of montage itself.

We must turn now to the shot considered in terms of its framing. There is a sense in which montage was originally called forth by a particular kind of framing, so meticulously composed that each shot could exist independently of any other. In these, the camera tends to be static and the image comprises a strong aesthetic structure which tolerates barely any unnecessary detail. The compositional precision and autonomy of individual shots lends them a photographic beauty quite distinct from the functionalism of, for example, Vertov's films.

Stanley Cavell takes Eisenstein's compositional formalism and 'saturation' of the frame as the determining factor for Eisensteinian montage.[6] The mode of shot framing and composition, Cavell argues, could not but result in the montage method, for there is no other means of merging or joining shots when the composition is so highly constructed and so aesthetically saturated. Cavell proposes that 'montage is necessary to film narrative only on the assumption that a certain species of frame is necessary'. Contrasting Dreyer's 'power with cinematic stillness, with the stasis of the frame' with Eisensteinian montage, Cavell is led into a fascinating discussion about how the frame, the shot's length and the discontinuity of shots might be determined by the mode of framing in much the same way that the size of the canvas is never arbitrary for a good painter, but is determined (and perhaps the determination works in both directions) by the compositional qualities of what the frame, so to speak, contains.

This view has at least the merit of breaking away from a purely intellectualist notion of montage. In other words, it sets out formal constraints and perhaps ultimately psychological ones, that are as determining of montage as are ideas about creating new meanings. Such an approach also suggests that Eisenstein's films are far from simply instantiations of a theory. It also seems to support the view that, whilst Eisenstein did radically qualify the 'explosion' view of montage in his later work, he seems never to have relinquished his commitment to the saturation of the frame. Cavell should be quoted more fully at this point, for his brief remarks on composition and montage include views which we will find echoed by Roland Barthes:

> one significance of Eisensteinian montage may lie fundamentally not in the juxtaposition and counterpoint of images but in the fact which precedes that juxtaposition or counterpoint, viz. that it demands, and is demanded by, individual images which are themselves static or which contain and may compound movements that are simple or simply cumulative. . . . If, say, the design of light and shadow made by certain frames of the Odessa steps is less significant than the fact that this design fills and simplifies the entire frame, then the sense conveyed may be that any pose of nature or society is arbitrary and subject to human change, that no event is humanly ungraspable, and that none can determine the meaning that human beings who can grasp it are free to place upon it.[7]

There are two points here. The first is a philosophical one about the conceptual relationship between montage and shot composition, when Cavell claims that primacy lies with the shot and not with montage. In other words, Eisenstein's fundamental commitment is to a type of shot and not to a means of concatenation of shots. Moreover, these two aspects are conceptually of a piece: the choice of one leads or is determined (and the choice of verb here is extremely important) by the other. Eisenstein understood this in some sense when he refused to allow the shot to be simply an element in montage, but spoke instead of it being a montage 'cell'. The biological vocabulary suggests that the connection he wanted was one of natural necessity, as in scientific law-likeness. At other times he spoke of the shot as the 'molecule' of montage. His desire to connect inseparably the shot and montage, refusing to allow them to be called elements, was an attempt to render them conceptual or theoretical terms. This reflects Eisenstein's embrace of dialectical materialism, characteristically using a physical science model as explanation in film theory. However, on Cavell's account, the link is a purely conceptual one and thus does not depend on the veracity of dialectical materialism; rather, it relies upon the idea of the static non-directional narrative quality of the Eisensteinian shot.

A second point arises from Cavell's observation that the overallness of the frame composition in the aesthetically saturated shot is crucial in how it imparts meaning. The shot's construction has an arbitrariness and thus an openness to interpretation of the real. It is on these grounds that Eisenstein's anti-realism is founded. And, paradoxically, the idea that reality is a social construction and as such indeterminable as meaning, rests on the highly determined construction of the shot and most importantly on the spectator's seeing it *as construction*. This amounts to an assertion of the historical nature of society. Interestingly, Eisenstein assessed montage in similar terms as late as 1948 when, in *Notes of a Film Director*, he defined it as the

> destruction of the indefinite and neutral, existing 'in itself', no matter whether it be an event or a phenomenon, and its reassembly in accordance with the idea dictated by attitude to this event or phenomenon, an attitude which, in turn, is determined by my ideology, my outlook, that is to say, our ideology, our outlook. . . . It is at that moment that a living dynamic image takes the place of passive reproduction.[8]

This too is Cavell's point.

In his important 1944 essay 'Dickens, Griffith and the Film Today', Eisenstein touched on the same issue when discussing Dovzhenko's film *The Earth*. He remarks that the failure of the sequence with the naked woman owes something to

> the oven, pots, towels, benches, tablecloths – all those details of everyday life, from which the woman's body could easily have been freed *by the framing of the shot* – so that *representational* naturalism would not interfere with the embodiment of the *conveyed metaphorical* task.[9]

Eisenstein returns time and time again to this idea of the frame. For him, as he reveals in these remarks on *The Earth*, the notion of framing is a necessary aspect of the notion of montage. It is intrinsic to Eisenstein's concept, in order for it to function as montage in the strict sense, that framing is subservient to a metaphoricism. And this is perhaps the essential difference between expressive editing and Eisensteinian montage.

In his essay 'Diderot, Brecht, Eisenstein', Barthes invokes the notion of the *tableau*. Diderot's aesthetic, he argues, rests upon the notion of the perfect theatrical play as being a 'succession of *tableaux*' each of which is a

> pure cut-out segment with clearly defined edges, irreversible and incorruptible; everything that surrounds it is banished into nothingness, remains unnamed, while everything that it admits within its field is promoted into essence, into light, into view.[10]

Moreover, for Barthes, Eisenstein's films are 'a contiguity of episodes, each one absolutely meaningful, aesthetically perfect'. These perfect frames become 'pregnant moments', according to Barthes, related to Brecht's 'social gesture'. Barthes asserts that 'the pregnant moment is just this presence of all the absences (memories, lessons, promises) to whose rhythm History becomes both intelligible and desirable'.[11]

The points made by Barthes are somewhat different from Cavell's, but they share the same source – reflection on the nature of the shot and what

Figure 50 A typical 'perfect frame' from *Ivan the Terrible* embodying the 'pregnant moment' that Barthes regarded as characteristic of Eisenstein.

that implies. For Barthes, as for Cavell, there seems little doubt that montage flows from the demands of the shot, which in turn is related to the social and artistic construction of a representation, and the revelation in such a method that it *is* a construction.

On such a view, Eisenstein's later aesthetic becomes less problematic, largely because it does not depend on the rather superficial view of montage implied by some of Eisenstein's critics. So we find, in *Ivan the Terrible* for instance, the aesthetic excess of the frame and the highly composed, almost 'decadent', sensibility reinforce the notion of the 'pregnant moment' or *tableau*. Often in *Ivan* the montage is not at the level of the editing, or sequence of actual cuts between shots in the film, but in the shifting composition that occurs within the same static frame, where each shift is held as an aesthetic moment. The result is an attempt to shift and transform the representations more subtly perhaps than in the earlier, more violent, montage method. Equally important, the frame saturation found in the earlier films is not to be found in the same form in *Ivan* and *Nevsky*, at least not in the 'overall' form suggested by Cavell. The framing, composition and shot duration of *Ivan* preclude the explosive montage method being used; nevertheless, according to Eisenstein, the method is still montage, albeit 'vertical montage'.

Finally, in the section entitled 'The Music of Landscape' in *Non-Indifferent Nature*, Eisenstein makes a series of remarks which would seem to support the view being put forward here. He begins by speaking of sound:

> The sphere of sound, of course, took upon itself the *rhythmicisation of the screen event* more easily and naturally, for under these conditions it was possible to achieve this even when the visual depiction itself was invariable and *static*!
>
> But this changing situation, as we said above, could not help but influence fundamentally the very principles by which 'linear' montage is constructed – that is, the combination of visual depictions of passages *within the actual visual components of the audiovisual construction.*
>
> The new position was expressed in the fact that under the new conditions the very *centre of support* of visual montage had to be moved to a new area and to new elements.
>
> This support, as we have shown before, was, although often excessively 'aestheticised', the *juncture between pieces*, that is, the element lying *outside* of the depiction.
>
> With the transition to audiovisual montage, the basic support of the montage of its visual components moves *into* the passage, *into the elements within the visual depiction itself.*
>
> And the basic centre of support is no longer the element between the shots, the juncture, but the element within the shot, the *accent within the*

piece, that is, the constructive support of the actual structure of visual depiction.[12]

Eisenstein is here referring to the shot and its internal construction: the 'visual depiction', as he calls it, 'the accent within the piece'. He cites the montage moment at the juncture, if we can call it that, between image and sound, so that the raw material of this dialectic is the shot as construction, plus the sound track. Attention is being drawn to montage understood in the vertical sense, where meaning is articulated in the interweaving of the shot's internal elements.

My intention has been to assert, in summary terms, the primacy of the shot in Eisenstein's theory. Whatever the changes in his conception of montage, there is a continued commitment in his writings to this notion of the shot and in many ways it provides the link between the early and the later aesthetics. There is nothing here that cannot be found in Eisenstein; all I have tried to do is to change the emphasis in our reading of his theory, against what is its more orthodox reading today.

The argument so far – or at least the attempt to set out the context or the elements for a future, more rigorous, argument – questions the view that there was a substantial break or difference between early and later Eisenstein (either in theory or in practice). This is not to say that there were no differences at all. Of course there were, but it now appears that these were shifts of emphasis rather than essence. Indeed in the final essays, particularly those on the synthesisation of the senses and pathos, Eisenstein seems to be moving towards the true centre of his aesthetic in a way that his early writings on montage did not. For it was always synchronisation – and here the difference with Brecht is crucial – that was at stake. His early montage theory was an attempt to establish a link between the cut-outs, the *tableaux*, the perfect aesthetic shots, and conjoin them within some overall idea or view. In synchronisation, that desire to provide each shot with the image that saturates each moment of the film, that gives the film its governing shape and idea is, in its embrace of aesthetic excess, a key not only to the later films but to the earlier ones as well.[13]

Notes

In these endnotes Eisenstein is usually referred to as E, while works cited frequently or by several authors are abbreviated in accordance with the list below. References to archival sources held in the Central State Archive of Literature and the Arts, Moscow (TsGALI) are given in the following standard form of three numbers: *fond*, followed by *opis'* and then *edinitsa khraneniya*.

Barna	Y. Barna, *Eisenstein* (London and Bloomington, Ind.: 1973).
Christie and Elliott	I. Christie and D. Elliott (eds), *Eisenstein at 90* (Oxford: 1988).
EAW	J. Leyda and Z. Voynow, *Eisenstein at Work* (New York: 1983).
ESW 1	S. M. Eisenstein, *Selected Works* (ed. and trans. R. Taylor) *Vol. 1: Writings 1922–34* (London and Bloomington, Ind.: 1988).
ESW 2	S. M. Eisenstein, *Selected Works* (ed. M. Glenny and R. Taylor, trans. M. Glenny) *Vol. 2: Towards A Theory of Montage* (London and Bloomington, Ind.: 1991).
FF	R. Taylor and I. Christie (eds), *The Film Factory: Russian and Soviet Cinema in Documents, 1896–1939* (London and Cambridge, Mass.: 1988).
Film Form	S. M. Eisenstein, *Film Form: Essays in Film Theory* (ed. and trans. J. Leyda) (New York: 1949).
IFF	R. Taylor and I. Christie (eds), *Inside the Film Factory: New Approaches to Russian and Soviet Cinema* (London and New York: 1991).
IP	S. M. Eisenstein, *Izbrannye proizvedeniya v shesti tomakh* (Selected Works in Six Volumes) (Moscow: 1964–71). The numeral indicates the volume number: e.g. *IP 1*.
Leyda	J. Leyda, *Kino: A History of the Russian and Soviet Film* (London: 1960).
Memories	*Immoral Memories: An Autobiography by S. M. Eisenstein* (trans. H. Marshall) (Boston, Massachusetts: 1983 and London: 1985).
NIN	S. M. Eisenstein, *Non-Indifferent Nature* (trans. H. Marshall) (New York: 1987).
Nizhny	V. Nizhny, *Lessons with Eisenstein* (ed. and trans. I. Montagu and J. Leyda) (London: 1962).
Seton	M. Seton, *Sergei M. Eisenstein: A Biography* (New York: 1960).

INTRODUCTION: REDISCOVERING EISENSTEIN

1 W. Blake, No. 67 of the Proverbs of Hell, from 'The Marriage of Heaven and Hell', *Poems and Prophecies* (London: 1991), p. 47. These lines were transcribed by E and are preserved, along with many other fragments from English literature, in the Eisenstein archive, Moscow.

2 In the regular *Sight and Sound* international critics' polls of 'top ten' films, *Potemkin* has come fourth in 1952, sixth in 1962 (when *Ivan the Terrible* also appeared in eighth place), third in 1972 and sixth in both 1982 and 1992. E however did not reach the directors' top ten until 1992. Both *Potemkin* and *Ivan the Terrible* came joint second (with five other films) in a Soviet critics' poll of 1987, *Nedelya* no. 44, 1987, p. 18; trans. R. Taylor, in J. Graffy and G. Hosking (eds), *Culture and the Media in the USSR Today* (London: 1989), pp. 73–7. Among recent film citations of the Odessa Steps are Zbigniew Rybczynski, *Steps* (1986) and Brian De Palma, *The Untouchables* (1987).

3 R. Roud (ed.), *Cinema: A Critical Dictionary* (London: 1980), p. 329.

4 Roud echoes the charge of 'a triumph of art over humanity' made by Robert Warshow in 1955; see 'Reviewing the Russian Movies', in *The Immediate Experience* (New York: 1970), p. 271. Walter Benjamin saw film as responsible for the decay of art's traditional 'aura', but perhaps underestimated how Soviet cinema created its own 'revolutionary aura' – a seeming authenticity unique to E's and some other canonic films of the 1920s. See 'The Work of Art in the Age of Mechanical Reproduction'' (1936), in H. Arendt (ed.), *Illuminations* (London: 1970), pp. 223ff.

5 L. Anderson, review of *ESW 1*, *Weekend Telegraph*, 19 March 1988, p. viii.

6 A. Solzhenitsyn, *One Day in the Life of Ivan Denisovich* (London: 1963), p. 95.

7 N. Mandelstam, *Hope Against Hope* (London: 1975), p. 296.

8 For example, A. Tarkovsky, *Sculpting in Time* (London: 1989, rev. edn), pp. 67, 114. See also, M. Turovskaya, *Tarkovsky: Cinema as Poetry* (London: 1989), pp. xix–xx.

9 See pp. 33–40 below. A conference on 'Film of the Totalitarian Epoch 1933–45', organised by Maya Turovskaya in Moscow, in July 1989, prompted vigorous debate about E's and other film-makers' 'complicity'.

10 Encouraged by the recent publication of a fuller text of E's and Cherkasov's interview with Stalin on 25 February 1947, *Moscow News* 32, 1988, pp. 8–9. See also, L. Kozlov, 'The Artist and the Shadow of Ivan', in R. Taylor and D. Spring (eds), *Stalinism and Soviet Cinema* (London: 1993).

11 See Carlo Pedretti's introduction to M. Cianchi, *Leonardo da Vinci's Machines* (Florence: 1988), pp. 5–7.

12 Among many admissions that practice did not follow theory, E wrote: 'when I myself am creating, I recall Goethe's remark, "grau ist die Theorie" [theory is grey], and I plunge headlong into creative spontaneity.' 'Poor Salieri!', *IP 3*, pp. 33–4. Blunt concludes his study of Leonardo's theory by observing that, especially in the drawings, 'material collected by the minute study of natural phenomena seems to have been transmuted by the imagination by an almost magical process of which Leonardo gives no account in his writings'. A. Blunt, *Artistic Theory in Italy 1450–1600* (Oxford: 1962), p. 38.

13 Letter to Maxim Strauch, 8–10 May 1931, trans. T. Taubes, *October* no. 14, Fall 1980, p. 56. A *kibitka* is a covered cart.

14 The 1935 All-Union Creative Conference of Workers in Soviet Cinema included a range of direct and oblique comments on E's concern with theory. Trauberg called for more, not less, theory 'of the right sort', while Kuleshov

defended himself by dismissing Yutkevich's remarks on E's erudition as envy. See *FF* pp. 349, 355. See also the 'official' post-war verdict of N. Lebedev: 'as an artist Eisenstein was ruined by his theories . . . original in form and false in content, the theory of Eisenstein did not move art forward.' *Ocherk istorii sovetskogo kino* (On the History of Soviet Cinema) (Moscow: 1947), pp. 161, 163.

15 The exhibition was organised by David Elliott and Ian Christie on behalf of the Museum of Modern Art Oxford, the British Film Institute and the Union of Cinematographers of the USSR. It was shown in Oxford in July–August 1988, at the Hayward Gallery, London, in September–December, and at the Cornerhouse, Manchester, in January 1989.

16 'Looking at one's own scholarly self' was E's title (in English) for one of his ironic self-portrait drawings, probably dating from around 1940.

17 The conference 'Eisenstein at 90', was held at Keble College, Oxford, in July 1988. One paper given at the conference does not appear here: Annette Michelson's 'Reading Eisenstein Reading *Ulysses*: Montage and the Claims of Subjectivity'.

18 See Ch. 3 below.

19 Both *The Strike* and Vertov's *Kino-Glaz* received gold medals at the Paris *Exposition* in October 1925, although it has been suggested that this was on the strength of their Constructivist posters rather than screenings. Gosfilmofond, the central Soviet archive for fiction (*khudozhestvennye*) films, was organised in 1948.

20 Dickinson recorded that '*Strike* . . . was never shown in Great Britain or America', T. Dickinson and C. de la Roche, *Soviet Cinema* (London: 1948), p. 24. *Strike* appears to have been first seen in Britain at the National Film Theatre in January 1958 and did not enter UK distribution until 1962.

21 Thompson, p. 56. The sale of the negative for hard currency has been confirmed by Naum Kleiman.

22 Ivor Montagu, in 'Notes on the *Potemkin* material at the National Film Archive', a typescript dated 18 December 1972, discussed the provenance of four prints of *Potemkin* and three published scripts. He refers to a 'quotation from Trotsky's book *1905*' following the title 'Act One' in the print derived from material originally imported by the Film Society in 1928–9. This was later replaced by a quotation from Lenin, which Montagu attributes to a 1930 Soviet sound version of which no further record is known.

23 Montagu confirms that E wanted the ship's flag stencil-coloured red, which effect was recreated for the 1987 London Film Festival presentation and included in a subsequent BBC TV transmission (albeit of a different version).

24 I. Montagu, *With Eisenstein in Hollywood* (Berlin, GDR: 1968), p. 143. See also Tsivian, p. 80 below.

25 *New York Times*, 10 October 1963, quoted in H. Marshall, *Masters of Soviet Cinema* (London: 1983), pp. 199–200.

26 *Kino*, 20 December 1927, quoted in Leyda, pp. 238–9.

27 Kleiman has indicated that Sidney Bernstein, originally associated with the London Film Society, had helped Alexandrov copy material only to be found, by this time, in the BFI 16mm print.

28 E's many visitors in Moscow during the editing of *October* included the artists Käthe Kollwitz and Diego Rivera, the American novelist Theodore Dreiser and the future New York MoMA curator Alfred Barr. He also started to read *Ulysses* in March 1929. His notes on *Capital* are dated from 12 October 1927 to 22 April 1928, and begin with the realisation that '*October* presents a new form of cinema, a collection of essays'. *Capital* was to be 'a film treatise'. 'Notes for

a Film of *Capital*', edited by N. Kleiman, were first published in *Iskusstvo kino*, January 1973, pp. 57–67; English translation in *October* no. 2, Summer 1976, pp. 3–26. On the compression of material filmed for *October*, see Tsivian, pp. 84–7 below.

29 See, for example, A. Piotrovsky, '*October* Must Be Re-Edited!' and T. Rotokov, 'Why is *October* Difficult?', *FF* pp. 216–17, 219–20; also V. Shklovsky, 'Eisenstein's *October*: Reasons for Failure', *Novyi Lef* no. 3, 1928; trans. D. Matias, *Screen* vol. 12, no. 4, pp. 88–90.

30 Ch. 5 below.

31 M. Seton, *Sergei M. Eisenstein: A Biography* (New York: 1960), p. 104.

32 Barna, p. 129.

33 Leyda, p. 262.

34 Ibid.

35 S. Khan-Magomedov, *Rodchenko: The Complete Work* (Cambridge, Mass.: 1987), p. 189.

36 Seton, p. 105.

37 Two slightly different accounts of this colouring have been given. Barna writes of 'inserting short lengths of film painted with abstract splashes of colour in the bull's wedding sequence' (p. 132). Montagu describes the effect of the sky at this point 'suffused wlth coloured fireworks' and goes on to describe an experiment on Hitchcock's *The Secret Agent* inspired by the example of hand-painting in *The General Line*, I. Montagu, *Film World* (Harmondsworth: 1964), p. 124.

38 In October 1928, E became director of a new Teaching and Research Workshop at the State Film School, GTK: see *ESW 1*, pp. 127–30. This period also saw the climax of the debate over sound and a series of major theoretical articles: 'Beyond the Shot', 'The Dramaturgy of Film Form' and 'The Fourth Dimension in Cinema', all written before E's departure for the West; *ESW 1*, pp. 138–94.

39 V. Shklovsky, *Eizenshtein* (Moscow: 1973), pp. 165–6.

40 Information from Naum Kleiman, who notes that Burov's design for *The General Line* influenced actual *Sovkhov* and *kolkhoz* architecture.

41 The documentary was directed by Stepanova; no further information available.

42 A copy of Kleiman's reconstructed version is now held by BFI Distribution and is available in the UK on Hendring Video.

43 See M. Hansen, *Babel and Babylon: Spectatorship in American Silent Film* (Cambridge, Mass.: 1991), Ch. 3, 'Chameleon and Catalyst: The Cinema as an Alternative Public Sphere', pp. 90–125.

44 A restoration of *New Babylon* in the mid-1980s by the Munich Filmmuseum is instructive here: when one of the surviving co-directors, Leonid Trauberg, saw it he complained that what had been 'restored' was precisely the material he and Kozintsev had removed in finalising the film for release! Current archival practice is moving away from combining *all* extant material towards the possibility of reconstructing different versions of the same film, as in a resto-ration of Dupont's *Moulin Rouge* (GB, 1928) currently under way at the National Film Archive in Britain.

45 'Step-printing' involves printing every second frame twice to 'stretch' a film originally intended to run more slowly than 24 frames per second, thus enabling a modern sound-track to be added. This results, however, in an apparent running speed of about 16 fps, which is too slow for all but a minority of pre-1928 films.

46 The BFI has shown *New Babylon* at a mixture of 20 and 24 fps (with

Trauberg's approval) and *October* at 22 fps. See K. Brownlow, 'Silent Films: What Was the Right Speed?', *Sight and Sound* vol. 49, no. 3, Summer 1980, pp. 164–7.

47 Recalled by E in *Memories*, p. 88.

48 Screenings of *Potemkin* and *October* organised by the BFI in 1987 and 1988, with Meisel's original music played by the Brabant Orchestra and Northern Sinfonia, both conducted by Alan Fearon, attracted large and appreciative audiences.

49 See texts in the BFI programme brochures for *Potemkin* and *October*; also a television documentary, *The Meisel Mystery*, produced in 1988 by Tyne-Tees Television.

50 T. Van Houten, 'Rhythm, Rhythm . . . Rhythm', *Potemkin* programme brochure (London: 1987), pp. 4–5.

51 See B. Eisenschitz, 'The Music of Time: From *Napoleon* to *New Babylon*', *Afterimage* 10, Autumn 1981, pp. 48–55; also BFI programme brochure for *New Babylon*, 1982.

52 See 'The Fourth Dimension in Cinema', *ESW 1*, p. 185.

53 In a letter to Moussinac dated 4 June 1929 : 'It is my obsession to add sound to *Old and New*. Have to do that abroad.' Quoted in *EAW*, p. 38. See also letters in the Montagu Collection on how this plan failed to materialise.

54 *EAW*, p. 38.

55 In his compilation *Eisenstein's Mexican Film: Episodes for Study* (1955), Leyda groups certain shots, such as the variant angles on an ancient statue, and suggests how E might have combined these as he had previously done.

56 'There are . . . rumours that E's personal copy of *Bezhin Meadow* was among the cans of film removed from his Potylikha apartment the morning after his death' (*EAW*, p. 151). Apart from such rumours – and the touching belief that 'everything' was somehow preserved in Soviet archives (banned material was more often privately preserved) – there seems to be no concrete reason for hope, although continuing archival discoveries must mean that this cannot be ruled out.

57 Ch. 2 below.

58 *Memories*, p. 226.

59 Shklovsky, *Eizenshtein*, p. 325 (Ger. edn); trans. in *EAW*, p. 100.

60 *EAW*, p. 101.

61 Seton, p. 441; *EAW*, p. 125.

62 *EAW*, p. 135; see also Kozlov, 'The Artist and the Shadow of Ivan'.

63 *EAW*, pp. 135–45.

64 *Glumov's Diary* (*c*. 112 metres) was reconstructed in 1977 from material held by the Soviet Documentary Film Archive at Krasnogorsk. It formed a part of one edition of *Kinopravda*, the series edited by Vertov, who had been Proletkult's supervisor for their first venture in film.

65 Ch. 7 below.

66 In his introduction to *Eisenstein: Two Films* (London: 1984), Leyda draws important and scrupulous distinctions between different kinds of published 'scenario', 'script' and 'shot list'. Yet the 'scripts' of *October* and *Nevsky* that follow obscure almost as many issues as they illuminate, due to the absence of comparative and variant material.

67 Montagu, 'Notes on *Potemkin* material', p. 8.

68 An English translation of *Ivan* appeared in *Life and Letters* in 1945–6. *Film Form* was also fully prepared before E's death, although not published until 1949.

69 According to N. Kleiman in a lecture at the National Film Theatre, London, September 1987.

70 The first volume of the *Selected Works* appeared in 1964, at the end of the Khrushchev 'Thaw', and the sixth in 1971.

71 Kleiman NFT lecture; see also I. Christie, 'Eisenstein at 90', *Sight and Sound* vol. 57, no. 3, Summer 1988, p. 186.

72 'Today I started to write my "Portrait of the Author as a Very Old Man" ', dated 24 December 1946 and quoted in *EAW*, p. 151.

73 Marshall's translation appeared in the USA in 1984 and in Britain in 1985. It is copyrighted 1983 and in his Acknowledgements Marshall says that it was in fact completed ten years earlier, 'but, alas, an English publisher held it up for all those years'. Apart from ignoring the intervening progress of Russian scholarship, Marshall's version randomly omits short passages of the 1964 Russian text throughout and, as in his adaptation of the Kleiman/Levina book on *Potemkin*, largely reproduces the original Soviet annotation without any acknowledgement or revision.

74 The French edition, under the general editorship of Jacques Aumont, appeared in six volumes between 1974 and 1985.

75 A translation of the revised Russian edition is due to be published by Seagull Books, Calcutta, and the BFI in 1993.

76 Occasional letters have been published in a variety of journals, including *Iskusstvo kino*, *Cahiers du cinéma* and *October*, but the majority remain in archives and personal collections. The most extensive selection yet to appear in book form is in the second of Leyda's Seagull series (see note 80 below). Diary material has been used by Leyda and, more recently, has appeared in the journal *Kinovedcheskie zapiski*.

77 See Ch. 4 below for sources of these texts.

78 Publication of the French edition was interrupted in the early 1980s, before a sixth volume appeared in 1985. The German edition, edited by Hans Joachim Schlegel, finished after only four volumes in 1983.

79 The Italian edition, edited by Pietro Montani, envisages eight volumes and follows approximately the pattern of major books that E envisaged, including *Montage*, *Method* and *Direction*. The British edition, edited by Richard Taylor, adopts a chronological approach for volumes one and three, with volume two collecting E's writings from different periods on montage.

80 The Seagull series, all edited by Leyda, includes: *On the Composition of the Short Fiction Scenario* (1984); *Eisenstein 2: A Premature Celebration of Eisenstein's Centenary* (1985); *Eisenstein on Disney* (1986); and *The Psychology of Composition* (1987), all published in Calcutta. The two collections edited by François Albera are: *Cinématisme. Peinture et cinéma* (Brussels: 1980) and, with N. Kleiman, *Eisenstein et le mouvement de l'art* (Paris: 1986).

81 Review of *ESW 1*, *The Economist*, 2–8 April 1988, p. 82.

82 Introduction to Barna, p. 8.

83 An example of such misconstruction: reviewing the Seagull series and *ESW 1*, Lindsay Anderson remarked: 'one cannot imagine this kind of stuff cutting much ice at the National Film School or at Robert Redford's Sundance Institute', *Sunday Telegraph*, 27 August 1989.

84 'Du cinéma en relief', in Albera and Kleiman, *Eisenstein et le mouvement de l'art*, pp. 97–158.

85 Ibid., p. 262.

86 Ch. 10 below.

87 Viktor Shklovsky (1893–1984), originally a leading 'Formalist' critic and

patron of the Serapion Brotherhood of writers; later film critic, scenarist and memoirist. Lev Vygotsky (1896–1934), pioneer Soviet psychologist who post-humously exerted a wide influence on education and psycholinguistics. Yuri Tynyanov (1894–1943), critic, literary theorist, novelist and scenarist. Mikhail Bakhtin (1895–1975), literary theorist and philosopher whose concepts of 'polyphony' and 'dialogism' have been influential in recent decades. Alexander Luria (1902–77), eminent psychologist and neurophysiologist, whose studies of *The Man With a Shattered World* and *The Mind of a Mnemonist* helped popularise neurological concepts of consciousness, memory and perception. E planned two courses on the psychology of art at Luria's request, in 1940 and 1947 (both in Leyda (ed.) *The Psychology of Composition*).

88 See Chs 6, 8, 11, 13, 14.
89 I. Christie, 'Musica plastica: versioni dell'ineffabile in Ejzenštejn' ('Plastic Music': Versions of the Ineffable in Eisenstein), in P. Montani (ed.), *Sergej Ejzenštejn: Oltre il cinema* (Venice: 1991), pp. 399–407.
90 *NIN*, pp. 219, 221.
91 See F. Albera, *Eisenstein et le constructivisme russe* (Lausanne: 1990), espe-cially Ch. III.8, 'Le psycho-ingénieur, le psycho-constructeur et la commande sociale', pp. 193–4.
92 A. Blunt, *Artistic Theory*, p. 37.
93 The chapter in E's memoirs entitled 'How I Learned to Draw' begins: 'Let me start with the fact that I never learned to draw. But this is how I draw and why', *Memories*, p. 39.
94 See, for example, *NIN*, pp. 185–90 (on Steinberg), pp. 266–8 (on Hogarth's *Analysis of Beauty*) and pp. 330–1 (on Hamlet's 'Do you see yonder cloud'); also Leyda (ed.), *Eisenstein on Disney*.
95 Josef von Sternberg (1894–1969), Austria-born director, best known for his lush eroticism and series of films starring Marlene Dietrich. Grigori Roshal (1899–1983) started his career with the Moscow Jewish Habimah theatre, but entered cinema in 1925, directing mainly musical and biographical films until 1965. E's 'automatic' drawings figured largely in the scandal of his departure from Mexico, when a batch of erotic works consigned to Upton Sinclair was opened by US Customs.
96 J. von Sternberg, *Fun in a Chinese Laundry* (London: 1966), p. 45; G. Roshal, 'Risunki S. M. Eizenshteina' (S. M. Eisenstein's Drawings), *Iz istorii kino 9* (Moscow: 1973), pp. 39–48.
97 See Yu. Pimenov (ed.) *S. Eizenshtein: Risunki* (Moscow: 1961) for repro-ductions of the childhood and other drawings; also N. Kleiman, 'Eisenstein's Graphic Work', in Christie and Elliott, pp. 11–17.
98 E sold topical cartoons to the *Petrogradskaya gazeta* and *Satirikon*. He recalled the circumstances and emotions vividly in 'First Drawings', *Memories*, pp. 51–5.
99 Seton, pp. 29–30.
100 Seton claims that E later said he planned to seek out Freud in Vienna. However, he volunteered for the Red Army in February 1918 and by 1919 had started amateur theatre work.
101 See Ch. 6 below.
102 D. Elliott, 'Taking a Line For a Walk', in Christie and Elliott, p. 20.
103 'How I learned to Draw', in *Memories*, pp. 42–5; see also R. Taylor's fuller translation in Christie and Elliott, pp. 50–7.
104 Kleiman, 'Eisenstein's Graphic Work', p. 14.
105 On some of the theoretical ideas about acting and physical expression current at the turn of the century, see M. Yampolsky, 'Kuleshov's Experiments and

the New Anthropology of the Actor', *IFF*, pp. 30–3. The definition of 'typage' is quoted by Kleiman from E's *Direction*.

106 Kleiman, 'Eisenstein's Graphic Work', p. 14.

107 The 'gods' sequence of *October* evokes a common graphic technique of illustrating the 'evolutionary gradient', here in reverse.

108 *The Glass House* seems to have been an architecturally inspired project, possibly influenced by contact with Burov on *The General Line*, which E revived in Hollywood after seeing an illustration of Frank Lloyd Wright's 'Glass Tower' project. See *EAW*, p. 44.

109 A small selection of E's theatre designs is included in Pimenov, *Risunki*, pp. 121–8.

110 *Memories*, pp. 44–5.

111 Seton, p. 195. The portrait is reproduced in I. Karetnikova and L. Steinmetz, *Mexico According to Eisenstein* (Albuquerque: 1991), p. ii.

112 Many of the titles of these are E's own and in English. Examples are reproduced in Seton, Pimenov, *Risunki* and Karetnikova and Steinmetz, *Mexico According to Eisenstein*.

113 Did E know the 'pataphysician' Alfred Jarry's 'The Crucifixion Considered As a Downhill Bicycle Race', which seems a possible inspiration for the Veronica series? Jarry casts Veronica as a press photographer. ('La Passion considérée comme course de côté', *Le Canard Sauvage*, 11–17 April 1903; reprinted in *Oeuvres complètes* (Paris: 1927), pp. 420–2.)

114 N. Leskov, 'Lady Macbeth of Mtsensk', in *Lady Macbeth of Mtsensk and Other Stories*, trans. D. McDuff (Harmondsworth: 1987). In Leskov's story (which also provided the libretto for Shostakovich's censored 1934 opera, later retitled *Katerina Izmailova*), the adulterous wife involves her lover in killing her husband.

115 There are similarities to the 'new classicism' of Léger and Picasso, as well as to Cocteau's playfully anachronistic drawings and designs.

116 On E's conception of ecstasy, see H. Lövgren, 'Trauma and Ecstasy: Aesthetic Compounds in Dr Eisenstein's Laboratory', in L. Kleberg and Lövgren (eds), *Eisenstein Revisited* (Stockholm: 1987), pp. 93–111; also J. Aumont, *Montage Eisenstein* (Paris: 1979), trans. L. Hildreth, C. Penley and A. Ross (Bloomington, Ind. and London: 1987), pp. 57–65.

117 Seton, pp. 234–5.

118 Part of Freud's controversial diagnosis of Leonardo as homosexual rested on an interpretation of the latter's childhood memory of a vulture striking him with its tail on the mouth (a phantasy of fellatio). However it transpires that the German translation of Leonardo used by Freud was defective: 'nibbio' is in fact the word for 'kite' instead of vulture. S. Freud, *Eine Kindheitserinnerung des Leonardo da Vinci* (A Childhood Memory of Leonardo da Vinci) (Vienna: 1910); trans. as *Leonardo* (Harmondsworth: 1963).

119 Ibid., p. 134.

120 See, for instance, T. Rayns, 'Submitting to Sodomy: Propositions and Rhetorical Questions about an English Film-Maker [Jarman]', *Afterimage* no. 12, Autumn 1985, p. 60; J. Babuscio, 'Before *Glasnost*: The Life and Times of Sergei Eisenstein', *Gay Times*, September 1988, pp. 28–31; also N. Almendros, 'Fortune and Men's Eyes', July–August 1991, pp. 58–61. A report in the Arts Diary of *The European*, 26–8 October 1990 , p. 13, attributed to Jeanne Vronskaya, claimed that an article in a forthcoming issue of *Kinovedcheskie zapiski* by Judit Glizer would reveal E to have had a long-standing relationship with the actor Cherkassov, as well as relationships with many actresses. The article, however, does not make these claims.

121 See Ch. 7 below.
122 Seton, p. 216.
123 *Memories*, p. 45.
124 Ibid., p. 50.
125 See Ch. 4 below, pp. 71–5.
126 Ibid., p. 73.
127 Ibid.
128 Leyda (ed.), *Eisenstein on Disney*, p. 69.
129 Ibid., p. 44.
130 Ibid., p. 2.
131 Ibid., p. 3.
132 Lövgren, 'Trauma and Ecstasy', p. 108.
133 Seton, p. 87.
134 Leyda (ed.), *Eisenstein on Disney*, p. 70.
135 'Foreword', *Memories*, pp. 1–7.
136 Reproduced in *EAW*, p. 110.
137 S. Eisenstein, 'The Embodiment of a Myth', in J. Leyda (ed. and trans.), *Film Essays and a Lecture* (Princeton, NJ: 1982), p. 85.
138 On the influence of Theosophy on Russian Symbolism, see R. C. Williams, *Artists in Revolution: Portraits of the Russian Avant-garde, 1905–1925* (London: 1978), pp. 94, 104–6. See also Tsivian on E's Symbolist inheritance, pp. 79–104 below.
139 Autobiographical note, written in 1939; trans. as *Notes of a Film Director* (New York: 1970), p. 61.
140 *NIN*, pp. 265ff. See also Yampolsky, Ch. 11 below.
141 'EX-TASIS' is reproduced in *NIN*, p. 155; 'Les Dons' were shown in 'Eisenstein: His Life and Work'.
142 The international conference 'Sergej Ejzenštejn. Oltre il Cinema: Le Figure, Le Forme, Il Senso dell'immagine', organised by Pietro Montani, was held in October 1990 in Venice, under the auspices of the Biennale di Venezia, Settore Cinema e Televisione (for details of published proceedings, see note 89).
143 While working on *Ivan* E wrote: 'The most important thing is to have the vision. The next is to grasp and hold it.' 'Notes from a Director's Laboratory', in *Film Form*, p. 261. The educational project 'Have the Vision' was organised by Oxford MoMA with Pegasus Theatre and Oxford Independent Video in July–August 1988.
144 Edmund Wilson adapted the motto given to Peter the Great in Pushkin's *The Bronze Horseman* on Petersburg as a 'window through to Europe' for his collection of essays on Russian culture, *A Window on Russia* (New York: 1972).
145 Theodore Dreiser, *Dreiser Looks at Russia* (New York: 1928); quoted in Seton, p. 103.
146 Jacques Aumont, *Montage Eisenstein* (Bloomington, Ind. and London: 1987), pp. 65–72. Aumont notes that Lenin's *Philosophical Notebooks* appeared in 1929 and the first Russian translation of Engels' *Dialectics of Nature* in 1935: both would strongly influence E's philosophy.
147 'The Psychology of Art', written in 1940, was first published in *Psikhologiya protsessov khudozhestvennogo tvorchestva*, ed. N. Kleiman and T. Drozhzhina (Leningrad: 1980). The quotation here is from A. Upchurch (ed. and trans.), *The Psychology of Composition* (Calcutta: 1987), p. 15.
148 Velimir Khlebnikov (1885–1922), pioneering Russian Modernist poet, proclaimed a powerful vision of future harmony and international union in his

writings from 1916 onwards. See *Collected Works of Velimir Khlebnikov*, ed. C. Douglas, trans. P. Schmidt (Cambridge, Mass. and London: 1987), part 4, 'Visions of the Future', pp. 320ff.

149 On the dispute between Lenin and the 'god-builders' Bogdanov, Lunacharsky *et al.*, see Williams, *Artists in Revolution*, Ch. 2, 'From Positivism to Collectivism: Lunacharsky and Proletarian Culture', pp. 23–58.

150 The ascetic and mystic Nikolai Fedorov (1828–1903), exponent of 'the philosophy of the common task' was an important influence on many Russian artists and philosophers of the Silver Age. See N. F. Fedorov, *What Was Man Created For?*, trans. E. Koutaissoff and M. Minto (Lausanne: 1990). See also I. Christie, 'Down to Earth: *Aelita* Relocated', in *IFF*, pp. 96–8.

151 Pushkin's historical drama *Boris Godunov*, set in Russia's 'time of troubles' around 1600, has attracted many differing interpretations, as well as posing problems of staging long considered insuperable. See also Ch. 7 below.

152 In a letter to Blake's biographer Alexander Gilchrist, quoted in Kathleen Raine's introduction to Blake, *Poems and Prophecies*, p. xi.

1 ARGUMENTS AND ANCESTORS

1 'Strekoza i muravei' (The Ant and the Grasshopper), *Lyudi odnogo fil'ma* (People of One Film), *IP 5*, pp. 480–93.

2 No further biographical information on Sukhotsky has so far come to light (Eds).

3 'The Problem of the Materialist Approach to Form', 1925, translated in *ESW 1*, p. 64.

4 E used this analogy on a number of occasions, notably in the article cited above, p. 62.

5 Vladimir M. Bekhterev (1857–1927), Russian neuropathologist and psychologist who developed a theory of reflexology.

6 Written in 1922 and translated in *ESW 1*, pp. 29–32.

7 For example, by Mira Meilakh in the third chapter of her *Izobrazitel'naya stilistika pozdnikh fil'mov Eizenshteina* (Figurative Stylistics in Eisenstein's Late Films) (Leningrad: 1971).

8 The Russian word *igra* can be translated either as 'acting' or 'play'.

9 E was given Tieck's *Puss in Boots* as a project assignment in late 1921.

10 A chapter of the Memoirs is entitled 'Mi Tu', after the name of the Litvinov's dog, which E interprets as 'Me too', *Memories*, pp. 223–4.

11 The reference is to Blok's poem 'The Scythians'.

12 Nikolai N. Evreinov (1879–1953) was a leading figure in Russian theatre before the Revolution, who directed and filmed a mass re-enactment of the October Revolution in Petrograd in 1920. He emigrated to France in 1925.

13 *The Exploits of Elaine* (1915) was an American adventure serial starring Pearl White which achieved worldwide popularity. Earlier, Louis Feuillade's five-part *Fantômas* (1913), based on the monthly mystery novels by Souvestre and Allain, had scored a great success throughout Europe and especially in Russia.

14 See Eisenstein, 'On the Detective Story', in *The Psychology of Composition* (Calcutta: 1987), which Alan Upchurch, as editor and translator, has provided with Fantômas illustrations, and the visual comparison between *Juve contre Fantômas* and *The Strike*.

15 It begins differently in the version published in Montagu, *With Eisenstein in Hollywood* (Berlin, GDR: 1968).

16 *Chapayev* (1934) was directed by Sergei and Georgy Vasiliev, who had studied with E at GTK. In it the White forces' 'psychological attack' against the Red partisans was conducted with parade-ground precision, recalling the troops' implacable descent of the Odessa Steps.

17 E undertook the production of Wagner's *Die Walküre* after the Nazi–Soviet Pact of August 1939. The première at the Bolshoi Theatre, Moscow, took place on 21 November 1940.

18 See Ch. 6 below.

19 The Herbert Marshall translation (*NIN*) is of an early compilation of this text, made for the Selected Works (*IP*).

20 These have not yet been published. However in October 1991, the USSR Film-makers' Union, as the body responsible for Eisenstein's legacy, enabled I. A. Aksenov's book *Sergei Eizenshtein: portret khudozhnika* (Sergei Eisenstein: Portrait of the Artist) to appear. It has been withdrawn from publication in 1935.

21 A draft constitution for an international Eisenstein Society, discussed at Oxford in 1988, was adopted by participants at the 1990 Venice conference. Its secretariat rests provisionally with François Albera at the University of Lausanne.

2 JAY LEYDA AND *BEZHIN MEADOW*

1 See the bibliography of Leyda's published writings compiled by John Hagan in *October* 11, Winter 1979, pp. 154–65. See also Annette Michelson's introduction to the same issue, which comments further on the historical significance of Leyda's work.

2 This paper results from research for a comprehensive exhibition of Leyda's photographic work held from 29 January to 27 February 1988, at Tisch School of the Arts, New York University, where Leyda taught from 1973 until his death. See the authors' catalogue for the exhibition: *Jay Leyda: A Life's Work* (New York: 1988).

3 For a useful historiographical overview, see: I. Christie's introduction to *FF*, pp. 1–17.

4 *EAW* includes a valuable summary of Leyda's *Bezhin Meadow* experience and reproduces a number of his production stills as illustrations.

5 Jay Leyda/Si-Lan Chen Papers, Tamiment Institute Library, New York University.

6 Leyda's short stories and poems were published in magazines such as *Blues: A Magazine of New Rhythms* no. 8, Spring 1930, pp. 3–4; *Pagany: A Native Quarterly* no. 3, July–September 1932, pp. 104–5, and no. 4, October 1932–March 1933, pp. 99–100.

7 Leyda's portraits (unattributed) may be found in *Arts Weekly: The News Magazine of the Arts*, 11 March–7 May, 1932.

8 J. Levy, *Memoir of an Art Gallery* (New York: 1977).

9 W. Alexander, *Film on the Left: American Documentary Film from 1931 to 1942* (Princeton: 1981), pp. 3–64; R. Campbell, *Cinema Strikes Back: Radical Filmmaking in the United States. 1930–1942* (Ann Arbor, Mich.: 1982), pp. 29–70.

10 Much of the biographical information in this essay derives from several interviews with Leyda conducted by the authors in 1986–7.

11 Jay Leyda Collection, Tisch School of the Arts, New York University.

12 Leyda Collection.

13 Leyda/Chen Papers.

14 Leyda edited a special Soviet issue, *New Theatre* no. 2, January 1935, as well as 'Soviet Theatre Speaks for Itself', in *Theatre Arts Monthly* no. 20, September 1936. Both issues contained articles by E.

15 Alexander, *Film on the Left*, pp. 50–2; Campbell, *Cinema Strikes Back*, pp. 56–8.

16 Leyda/Chen Papers.

17 Leyda/Chen Papers; letter from Ivens to Elena Pinto Simon, May 1988.

18 Letter from Leyda to E, January 1935, Leyda/Chen Papers.

19 See B. Amengual, *Que Viva Eisenstein!* (Paris: 1980), pp. 290–306. The circumstances surrounding the making and banning of *Bezhin Meadow* are the subject of the authors' *From the Storehouse of Creation* (Princeton: forthcoming).

20 See B. Shumyatsky, 'The Film *Bezhin Meadow*', *Pravda*, 19 March 1937; translated in *FF*, pp. 378–81. See also E's self-criticism, 'The Mistakes of *Bezhin Meadow*', reprinted in Seton, pp. 372–7.

21 Leyda, pp. 327–34.

22 J. Leyda, 'Eisenstein's *Bezhin Meadow*', *Sight and Sound* vol. 28, no. 2, Spring 1959, pp. 74–7.

23 Leyda/Chen Papers.

24 *Bezhin Meadow* took its title from and was based partly on Turgenev's story 'Bezhin Lea', one of the *Sketches from a Hunter's Album* collected in 1852. The story opens with a detailed description of the sky and light on a summer's day.

25 Leyda acted as an intermediary between Alfred Barr and Rodchenko, helping Barr to acquire material for the Museum of Modern Art. See letter from Barr to Leyda, 14 January 1936, Leyda/Chen Papers.

26 Levy, *Memoir of an Art Gallery*, Appendix.

27 Leyda's diary is used in the following: 'Eisenstein Directs the Russian Child', *World Film News and Television Progress* no. 1, April 1936, p. 27; 'Eisenstein's First Sound Film', unpublished MS (1936), Leyda Collection, NYU; Seton, pp. 354–7; Leyda, 'Eisenstein's *Bezhin Meadow*'; Leyda, *Kino*, pp. 327–34; *EAW*, pp. 84–95.

28 H. Klehr, *The Heyday of American Communism* (New York: 1984); I. Howe and L. Coser, *The American Communist Party: A Critical History* (New York: 1974).

29 A. W. Wald, *The New York Intellectuals: The Rise and Decline of the Anti-Stalinist Left from the 1930s to the 1980s* (Chapel Hill: 1987), pp. 101–255.

30 Reprinted as 'Soviet Cinema, 1930–1940, A History', in D. Macdonald, *On Movies* (New York: 1981), pp. 192–248.

31 Campbell, *Cinema Strikes Back*, pp. 193–235.

32 Letter from Leyda to Macdonald appeared in *Partisan Review*, no. 5, August–September 1938, p. 71.

33 S. Stern, 'Film Library Notes Build "CP Liberators" Myth', *New Leader*, 23 March 1940.

3 EISENSTEIN'S EARLY FILMS ABROAD

1 This chapter stems from ongoing research on a larger project dealing with European avant-garde cinema styles of the 1918–33 period; thus it presents only some preliminary conclusions on this topic.

2 A contemporary Soviet trade paper, *Kinogazeta*, published figures showing that – contrary to the myth – *Potemkin* was actually slightly more popular than the Douglas Fairbanks film, *Robin Hood*, at least in Moscow. See 'The Box-Office Decides', in H. Marshall (ed.), *The Battleship Potemkin* (New York: 1978), p. 101.

3 'Was die L. B. B. erzählt' (What L. B. B. Recounts), *Lichtbildbühne* vol. 15, no. 3, 29 July 1922, p. 21.

4 Ad, Wiking, *Lichtbildbühne* vol. 16, no. 3, 20 January 1922, p. 34; H. Fr., 'Der erste Russenfilm' (The First Russian Film), *Lichtbildbühne* vol. 16, no. 10, 10 March 1923, p. 17.

5 'Ein neuer russicher Kunstlerfilm' (A New Russian Art Film), *Lichtbildbühne* vol. 19, no. 32, 8 February 1926, p. 3; 'Aelita (Der Flug zum Mars)' (Aelita (The Flight to Mars)), *Lichtbildbühne* vol. 19, no. 49, 29 February 1926, p. 14; 'Der provinzielle Postmeister' (The Provincial Postmaster (see below n. 15)), *Lichtbildbühne* vol. 19, no. 85, 10 April 1926, p. 12.

6 Marshall, *Potemkin*, pp. 119–21.

7 '*Panzerkreuzer Potemkin*' (*The Battleship Potemkin*), *Lichtbildbühne* vol. 19, no. 118, 19 May 1926, p. 3.

8 J. Tarvel, 'Un film révolutionnaire a révolutionné Berlin', *Comœdia* no. 4904, 31 May 1926, p. 1.

9 *Jahrbuch der Filmindustrie* vol. 2, 1923–5 (Berlin: 1926), n. p.; A. Jason, 'Zahlen sehen uns an' (The Figures Show Us), *25 Jahre Kinematograph* (Berlin: 1931), p. 69.

10 'Provinzerfolge des *Potemkin*' (*Potemkin*'s Provincial Success), *Lichtbildbühne* vol. 19, no. 129, 1 June 1926, p. 3.

11 H. Fraenkel, 'Latest from Germany', *The Bioscope* no. 1030, 8 July 1926, p. 50.

12 J. Tarvel, 'Le film de l'année' (The Film of the Year), *Comœdia* no. 5346, 26 August 1927, p. 3.

13 Advertisement by Prometheus, *Lichtbildbühne* vol. 19, no. 211, 4 September 1926, p. 1.

14 '*Panzerkreuzer Potemkin* und seine Einnahmen' (*The Battleship Potemkin* and Its Receipts), *Lichtbildbühne* vol. 19, no. 157, 3 July 1926, p. 7. See also Marshall, *Potemkin* p. 104.

15 *The Station Master*'s enormous success abroad (where it was generally known as *The Postmaster*) may have been due partly to the fact that it was also one of the least objectionable Soviet films to foreign censors; it was frequently passed in countries that banned virtually all other Soviet films. It may also have gained prestige from being a Pushkin adaptation.

16 'Russlands Aussenhandel' (Russia's Foreign Trade), *Lichtbildbühne* vol. 20, no. 253, 22 October 1927, p. 14; 'Die Verbreitung des Sowjet-Films' (The Distribution of Soviet Film), *Lichtbildbühne* vol. 21, no. 115, 12 May 1928, p. 22.

17 A study of Soviet production published in *Lichtbildbühne* in late 1926 suggests a similar figure; it says that Sovkino's gross income from 1 March 1925 to 1 March 1926 was ten million roubles, of which about one million was profit. See 'Sieg der Qualität' (Victory for Quality), *Lichtbildbühne* vol. 19, no. 265, 6 November 1926, p. 36.

18 'Soviet Russia is Primitive in Theatres', *Variety* vol. 90, no. 13, 11 April 1928, p. 20.

19 'Sieg der Qualität', p. 36.

20 'Russischer Optimismus' (Russian Optimism), *Lichtbildbühne* vol. 20, no. 15, 18 January 1927, n. p.

21 A. Ivanowsky, 'La production en Russie soviétique', *Comœdia* no. 5127, 14 January 1927, p. 3.

22 'Die Russische Filmproduktion', *Lichtbildbühne* vol. 20, no. 160, 6 July 1927, n.p.

23 H. Fraenkel, 'First Parufamet Production', *The Bioscope* no. 1065, 10 March 1927, p. 36; 'Russian Films Flood Germany', *Variety* vol. 86, no. 10, 23

March 1927, p. 8; 'Campaign Against Russian Films', *New York Times*, 6 March 1927, sec. 2, p. 9.

24 Advertisement by Prometheus, *Film-Kurier* vol. 10, no. 102, 30 April 1928, n.p.

25 'Die Todesbarke' (*The Bay of Death*), *Lichtbildbühne* vol. 20, no. 94, 20 April 1927, n. p.

26 Letter [from Lt. Col. Frederick L. Herron?], Motion Picture Producers and Distributors Association (New York City) to William R. Castle, Jr (Chief of Western European Division, Dept. of State), dated 28 June 1926 (MPPDA files, NYC). My thanks to Richard Maltby and Ruth Vasey for this reference.

27 'Excellent Idea of Foreign Legion in "Beau Geste" – A Russian Film', *New York Times*, 5 September 1926, p. 1.

28 V. Petrić, 'Soviet Revolutionary Films in America (1926–35)', (unpublished Ph.D. dissertation, New York University, 1973), vol. 1, p. 37; ' "Potemkin" Set Dec. 4', *Moving Picture World* vol. 83, no. 5, 29 November 1926, p. 1.

29 S. Smith, ' "Potemkin" . . . the Unique Mob Picture', *Moving Picture World* vol. 83, no. 77, 11 December 1926, p. 420.

30 ' "Potemkin" 's New Manager', *Variety* vol. 85, no. 12, 5 January 1927, p. 12. This brief article is quoted here in its entirety.

31 'Emissary Sees Market For Our Films in Russia', *New York Times*, 19 December 1926, sec. 7, p. 7.

32 Petrić, 'Soviet Revolutionary Films in America', pp. 511, 513; 'Foreign Films in the United States', *Film Daily Year Book* no. 10, 1928, pp. 511–12.

33 'Technical Assistance Contract for the Soviet Cinema Industry', *Economic Review of the Soviet Union* vol. 5, no. 16–17, 1 September 1930, p. 359.

34 S. Gould, 'The Little Theatre Movement in the Cinema', *National Board of Review Magazine* vol. 1, no. 5, September–October 1926, p. 4.

35 ' "Potemkin" in Washington; Jazz Week, $17,500', *Variety* vol. 86, no. 13, 13 August 1927, p. 8.

36 'Red Hot Loop; Too Hot For Biz; "Glory" Did Best – Broke Record', *Variety* vol. 88, no. 10, 21 September 1927, p. 8.

37 'New and Old Films Whoop Up Broadway During Slow Week', *Variety* vol. 88, no. 11, 28 September 1927, p. 7.

38 'Heat and Holiday Jammed Up B'Way Film Houses – Six Specials Remain', *Variety* vol. 91, no. 13, 11 July 1928, p. 9; 'Silent "Racket" Beats Sounded "Warming Up" on Day and Date; "Street Angel" $366,000 in 3 Wks', *Variety* vol. 92, no. 4, 8 August 1928, p. 9.

39 R. Van Dyke, 'Paragraphs Pertaining to Players and Pictures', *Cinema Art* no. 7, July 1927, p. 42.

40 C. Stafford, 'Paragraphs Pertaining to Players and Pictures', *Cinema Art* no. 7, November 1927, p. 39.

41 'Ten Days That Shook the World', *Variety* vol. 93, no. 4, 7 November 1928, p. 24.

42 'Russian's Reception', *Variety* vol. 93, no. 7, 28 November 1928, p. 19.

43 '15 B'way Film Houses Did $1,100,000 During Two-Week Holiday Period', *Variety* vol. 93, no. 13, 9 January 1929, p. 7.

44 ' "Potemkin" Surprise, $10,000 in Balto.', *Variety* vol. 87, no. 6, 25 May 1927, p. 6.

45 'Kino von heute!' (Today's Cinema!), *Film-Kurier* vol. 10, no. 81, 3 April 1928, n. p.

46 See, for example, 'Mitteilungen des Volksverbandes für Filmkunst' (Reports of the People's League for Film Art), *Film und Volk* vol. 2, no. 6, July 1929, p. 16.

47 'Die Haager Ausstellung' (The Hague Exhibition), *Lichtildbühne* vol. 21, no. 107, 3 May 1928, p. 4.

48 'Russian Classics in 16mm', *Cinema Quarterly* vol. 2, no. 4, Summer 1934, p. 262; also *KINO News*, Winter 1935, n. p.
49 'Comment', *Film Art* vol. 1, no. 3, Spring 1934, p. 34; 'Comment', *Film Art* vol. 2, no. 6, Autumn 1935, p. 90.
50 R. Campbell, *Cinema Strikes Back: Radical Filmmaking in the United States 1930–1942* (Ann Arbor, Mich.: 1982), p. 45.

4 RECENT EISENSTEIN TEXTS

Introduction: Eisenstein at La Sarraz

1 Seton, pp. 128–30.
2 *ESW 1*, pp. 113–14; *FF*, pp. 234–5.
3 *ESW 1*, pp. 115–22, 138–50 and 181–94 respectively.
4 See pp. 184–8.
5 *ESW 1*, pp. 68–9 and 172.
6 *ESW 1*, pp. 179–80 and 193.
7 *ESW 1*, pp. 185–94.
8 *ESW 2*, pp. 371–99.

Imitation as mastery

1 First published as 'Nachahmung als Beherrschung', *Film und Fernsehen* (Berlin, GDR: 1988) vol. 1, pp. 34–7.
2 In the first draft: 'According to Aristotle, the essence of art.'
3 A mask of Uzume was one of the images in the sequence of different deities in *October*. In fact Uzume was not herself the sun goddess but the goddess whose dancing initially lured the sun goddess Amaterasu out of her dark cave.
4 This is in fact the *second* commandment, after 'Thou shalt have no other gods before me'. The full version in Exodus, 20, vv. 4–5 is: '4. Thou shalt not make unto thee any graven image, or any likeness *of any thing* that *is* in heaven above, or that *is* in the earth beneath or that *is* in the water under the earth: 5. Thou shalt not bow down thyself to them, nor serve them: for I the Lord thy God *am* a jealous God.'
5 In the first draft this paragraph read:

> Imitation is not the last word. We can imitate form or principle. In art we have until now imitated form. We are the cannibals. In cannibalism we have to deal with the literal meaning of words: "Man is what he eats." [see n. 6 below] He eats his own likeness in order to live. That is how it has remained with the animal – the pig.

6 There is a play on words in the original German: 'Der Mensch ist, was er isst.'
7 In the first draft this paragraph read: 'Saturn consumes his own children and that is a symbol of eternity and immortality.'
8 Eugen Steinach (1861–1944), Austrian physiologist and biologist, author of *Verjüngung durch experimentelle Neubelebung der älternden Pubertätsdrüse* (Rejuvenation through the Experimental Revivification of the Ageing Pubertal Gland) (Berlin: 1920). Vorontsov was a Russian doctor of medicine living in Paris who conducted similar experiments in rejuvenation.
9 Gilles de Retz (1400–40), French alchemist who killed around three hundred children in his search for gold and the elixir of life and was eventually hanged. He served as the model for Duke Bluebeard.

10 In the first draft: 'The whole progress of science follows the path from cannibalism, from mythic symbolism and story-telling to the principle of analysis.'

11 Liane Haid (1897–?), Austrian stage and screen actress.

12 The Swiss Charles Edouard Jeanneret, known as Le Corbusier (1887–1966), and the Germans Walter Gropius (1887–1969) and Bruno Taut (1880–1938) were among the leading European architects of the early twentieth century.

13 The reference is to Eduard Fuchs, *Das erotische Element in der Karikatur: Ein Beitrag zur Geschichte der öffentlichen Sittlichkeit* (The Erotic Element in Caricature: An Essay on the History of Public Morality) (Berlin: 1904).

14 *Madame Dubarry* (1919, dir. Ernst Lubitsch) and *Lady Hamilton* (1922, dir. Richard Oswald) were popular German films. Tom Mix (1880–1940) starred in a number of early Hollywood westerns.

15 A reference to the allusions in 'The Montage of Attractions', written in 1923 and translated in *ESW 1*, pp. 33–8.

16 In the first draft:

> Fiction film. With the actor as the object of imitation. Interpretation. Human fate. The importance, not of precedents, but of emotional ideological results. Man as means. That can however also be different. Man. Mass. Universe. The bridge is the imitation of rounded form. We touch it with our hands. Or with our eyes. We *repeat* form.

17 This particular book, in the planning stage in 1929, never came to fruition.

18 The German term *Sachlichkeit* could here refer to the *Neue Sachlichkeit* or New Objectivity movement of the 1920s.

19 Bartolomeo (also known as Varfolomei) Rastelli (1700–71) was the leading Baroque architect in eighteenth-century Russia. Among his most important buildings were the Winter Palace in St Petersburg and the palace at Tsarskoe Selo.

20 The 'film of fact' refers to Dziga Vertov's (1896–1954) characterisation of his own approach to cinema. '"Factual" play' is Vertov's description of E's approach, while 'play with facts' is E's own characterisation of his own work, a 'montage of visible events'.

Some personal reflections on taboo

1 First published as 'Neskol'ko lichnykh voobrazhenii o tabu' in 'Eizenshteinovskie chteniya' (Eisenstein readings), *Kinovedcheskie zapiski* no. 6 (Moscow: 1990), pp. 130–2.

5 EISENSTEIN AND RUSSIAN SYMBOLIST CULTURE: AN UNKNOWN SCRIPT OF *OCTOBER*

1 A. Piotrovskii, 'Oktyabr' dolzhen byt' peremontirovan!' (*October* Must Be Re-Edited!), *Zhizn' iskusstva* no. 13, 27 March 1928, p. 12; translated in *FF*, p. 216.

2 *IP 6*, pp. 65–86.

3 Ibid., p. 85.

4 *IP 4*, p. 726.

5 M.-C. Ropars-Wuilleumier, 'La Fonction de la métaphore dans *Octobre* d'Eisenstein', (The Function of Metaphor in Eisenstein's *October*) *Littérature* no. 11, 1973, p. 115.

6 A. Blok, *Sobranie sochinenii v shesti tomakh* (Collected Works in Six Volumes) (Leningrad: 1980–), vol. 3, p. 53.

7 Myriam Tsikounas has pointed out that Lenin's arrival at the Finland Station in *October* forms a discursive symmetry to the sequence of the falling monument. See p. 197.

8 The metaphor tempted a later critic to explain it psychoanalytically: D. Fernandez, *Eisenstein* (Paris: 1975), p. 168. There is no way to avoid psycho-analytical vocabulary when analysing E's films but it is doubtful whether it gives one real access to E's subconscious mind. E was well read in Freud and his followers and, if some of his sequences seem to demand a psychoanalytical reading, it is often because E wanted them to do so. He was also fond of providing details of his own life with a Freudian subtext, which has misled some simple-minded biographers. E's psychoanalysis is not so much a manifestation of the subconscious as a method of textual construction.

9 Blok, *Sobranie sochinennii v shesti tomakh*, p. 13.

10 *IP 1*, p. 309; translated in *Memories*, p. 77.

11 *IP 1*, p. 382; *Memories*, p. 130.

12 If we ignore as general a matrix as, for example, Gogol's *The Overcoat*, the symbol of empty clothes is quite new to Russian literature. In Blok's case it may be said to have a cinematic origin. The famous gag in early film (when one person literally beats another out of his clothes so that that person disappears and the clothes remain) was used by Chaplin (*The Tramp*) and André Deed (*Le Roi de boxe* and elsewhere). The gag first appeared in Méliès's *La Boîte à malice* and was extensively used in his films around the time when Blok wrote his play. Méliès grew tired of it in 1908 after *Le Conseil du Pipelet ou le tour à la foire*. Blok was a film addict and his overtly farcical *The Fairground Booth* would be the appropriate play for cinematic borrowings. If this is the case, the motif of empty suits would have made a complete circle from film to stage and back again to E's *October*.

13 Directional mismatches in this sequence are not meant to form the stylistically functional 'conflict' cuts that are characteristic of E's editing from *The Strike* to *The General Line*. As for eye-line mismatches, it is interesting to note that in the latest (sonorised) version of *October*, re-edited in 1967 by Alexandrov, we can trace an effort to 'correct' these by regluing them base to emulsion. This ruse is betrayed by an inscription on a sailor's hat, which is reversed by the procedure.

14 The objection may be made that location shooting in the Winter Palace might have obstructed access to the camera angles required by continuity editing. It is not generally known that many of the interior scenes in *October* were *not* shot on location. Special sets, including those for the Tsarina's bed-chamber, her prayer-room, wine cellars, the trunk-room and others, were built in a Leningrad film studio and real objects from the Winter Palace museum were brought to the studio to furnish the sets. See *Kino* (Leningrad), 28 June 1927.

15 B. Tomashevsky, 'Foolish Wives', *Zhizn' iskusstva* no. 10, 1924, p. 16.

16 Yu. Krasovskii, 'Kak sozdavalsya fil'm *Oktyabr'*' (How the Film *October* Was Made), in *Iz istorii kino 6* (Moscow: 1965), p. 47.

17 F. Albera, 'Stuttgart: Dramatique de la forme cinématographique: S. M. Eisenstein et le constructivisme russe' (Stuttgart: The Drama of Cinemato-graphic Form. S. M. Eisenstein and Russian Constructivism) (unpublished doctoral thesis); and F. Albera, *Eisenstein et le constructivisme russe* (Lausanne: 1990). See also Ch. 13 below.

18 The decapitation/castration metaphor was already latent in the morbid 'widow' name for the guillotine used in the days of the French Revolution. E was

fascinated by this name and by the mechanism itself. A passage in his memoirs referring to the period of Kerensky's rule in 1917 helps one also understand the opening sequence of *October* with its 'executed' monument:

> Kerensky was thundering against those who wanted to see a guillotine on Znamensky Square. (A policy that I considered a direct attack against me.) How many times, walking past the memorial to Alexander III, had I mentally measured 'the Widow' – the machine of Dr Guillotin – for its granite base? I wanted dreadfully to be a part of history! And what history could there be without the guillotine?
>
> (*IP 1*, p. 273; *Memories*, p. 51)

19 *Novyi Lef* no. 4, 1928, p. 31; translated in *FF*, p. 230.
20 'A Dialectic Approach to Film Form' in *Film Form*, p. 56; translated as 'The Dramaturgy of Film Form' in *ESW 1*, p. 174.
21 G. K. Chesterton, *The Man Who Was Thursday* (Harmondsworth: 1976), pp. 64–5.
22 A. Bely, *Petersburg* (Leningrad: 1981), p. 501.
23 D. Bordwell, *Narration in the Fiction Film* (London: 1985), p. 239.
24 S. Tret'yakov, *'Oktyabr' minus Bronenosets Potemkin'* (*October* Minus *The Battleship Potemkin*), *Sovetskoe kino* no. 2–3, 1928, p. 17; reprinted in *Iskusstvo kino* no. 11, November 1987, pp. 103–6.
25 *Novyi Lef* no. 4, 1928, p. 33; *FF*, p. 230.
26 *IP 6*, p. 428.
27 A. Suslov, *Zimnii dvorets 1754–1927: Istoricheskii ocherk* (The Winter Palace, 1754–1927: A Historical Essay) (Leningrad: 1928), p. 62.
28 N. Burch, 'Film's Institutional Mode of Representation and the Soviet Response', *October* no. 11, 1979, p. 90.
29 B. Arvatov, 'Teatral'naya parfyumeriya i levoe neprilichie' (Theatrical Perfumery and Left-Wing Indecency), *Zrelishcha* no. 31–2, 1923, p. 7. Meyerhold's production dated from 1923 but Terentiev's was staged in April 1927 and caused a public scandal. It would therefore have been freshest in Eisenstein's mind during the making of *October*.
30 L. Reisner, 'V Zimnem dvortse' (In the Winter Palace), *Novaya zhizn'*, 11 November 1917.
31 A. Pushkin, *Polnoe sobranie sochinenii* (Complete Collected Works), (Moscow: 1937–9), vol. 2, poem 227.
32 S. Eisenstein, 'Notes for a Film of *Capital*', in *October: The First Decade, 1976–1986* (Cambridge, Mass. and London: 1987), p. 128.
33 Ibid., p. 127.
34 Bely, *Petersburg*, p. 118. This passage has, perhaps not surprisingly, been glossed over in the published English translation by R. A. Maguire and J. E. Malmstad, *Petersburg* (Harmondsworth, 1983), where it should appear on p. 79.
35 Eisenstein, 'Notes for a film of *Capital*' p. 129.
36 The typescript is in the Eisenstein Museum in Moscow.
37 *A Susan Sontag Reader* (New York, 1982), p. 417.
38 S. Eizenshtein, 'Vse my rabotaem na odnu i tu zhe auditoriyu' (We Are All Working on the Same Audience) (ed. N. Kleiman and Yu. Tsivian), *Iskusstvo kino* no. 1, January 1988, p. 78.
39 This typescript is held in the Jānis Rainis Museum of Art and Literature in Riga (Eiz$^R_5^1$ inv. No. 180123). / / are Eisenstein's bracket signs; ( ) are mine.
40 This probably refers to the passage in the Winter Palace known as the Dark Corridor, rather than to just any dark corridor.

41 The typescript is defective at this point.
42 There are no script lines numbered 432–3.
43 Probably a reference to one of the Beauvais tapestries in the Winter Palace.
44 The cuff is here a metonym for Lenin. Earlier in the script the appearance of Lenin's cuff among the bayonets was evidently meant to signify the leading role of the intelligentsia in the Revolution. The omission of the shot from the final version of the film was probably due to the introduction of a more official political doctrine that avoided subjecting Lenin to any sociological analysis.
45 There is a similar line in another version of the script:

A gloomy person gets into his car and raises his collar / THE CHAIRMAN OF THE R. S. D. L. P. – CHKHEIDZE /

6   EISENSTEIN'S THEATRE WORK

1 *Film Form*, pp. 7, 8.
2 *Lef* no. 3, 1923, pp. 70–5; translated in *ESW 1*, pp. 33–8.
3 *Can You Hear Me, Moscow?* and *Gas Masks* are published in S. M. Tretyakov, *Slyshish', Moskva?!* (Moscow: 1966).
4 *IP 1*, p. 34.
5 Ibid.
6 From *Rabochaya gazeta*, 22 April 1923; quoted in Seton, pp. 62–3.
7 *Film Form*, p. 17.
8 Tretyakov, *Slyshish', Moskva?!* p. 10.
9 Ibid., p. 12.
10 *Stumm* is the German word for 'dumb'.
11 Ibid., p. 26.
12 Leyda, pp. 273, 293, 310.
13 S. Tretyakov, 'Tekst i rechmontazh' (Text and Speech Montage), *Zrelishcha*, no date; Central State Archive of Literature and Art (TsGALI), Moscow, 963/1/335, pp. 34–5.
14 Ibid.
15 See note 19 below.
16 H. Witt, *Brecht As They Knew Him* (London: 1974), p. 72.
17 B. Brecht, 'Is The People Infallible?', in *Poems* (London: 1976), p. 331.
18 J. Willett (ed.), *Brecht on Theatre* (London: 1973), p. 65.
19 Ibid., pp. 91–9.
20 Bernhard Reich, quoted in J. Fuegi, *Bertolt Brecht: Chaos According to Plan* (Cambridge: 1987), p. 22.
21 Ibid., p. 29.
22 K. Volker, *Brecht* (London: 1979), p. 72.
23 Witt, *Brecht As They Knew Him*, p. 41.
24 Asja Lacis, quoted in W. Benjamin, *Moscow Diary*, (Cambridge, Mass.: 1986), p. 145.
25 Barna, p. 109.
26 J. Willett, *The Theatre of Bertolt Brecht* (London: 1959), p. 126.
27 L. Kleberg and H. Lövgren (eds), *Eisenstein Revisited* (Stockholm: 1987), p. 63.

7   EISENSTEIN'S PUSHKIN PROJECT

1 The sheet is reproduced in *EAW*, p. 105.
2 See N. Kleiman, '. . . Nachnem s Pushkina', *Iskusstvo kino* no. 2, 1987, p. 65.

3 Primary sources for my discussion are the first published reconstruction 'The Colour Elaboration of the Film *The Love of a Poet*', *IP 3*, pp. 492–9; 'S. Eizenshtein's Shooting Script of a Scene from *Boris Godunov*', *Iskusstvo kino* no. 3, 1959, pp. 111–30; 'Pushkin's Colour Biography', which is a later, more complete and annotated reconstruction of E's handwritten notes, published in *Voprosy literatury* no. 10, 1971, pp. 186–92; and E's unposted letter to Yuri Tynyanov, in G. Pomerantseva (ed.), *Yuri Tynyanov, Pisatel i uchenyi* (Moscow: 1966), pp. 176–81. A complete presentation of the material relating to E's Pushkin project was promised (*IP 3*, p. 650) for the sixth volume of the selected works but did not appear in it.

4 I. Veissfeld [Vaisfeld], 'Mon dernier entretien avec Eisenstein', *Cahiers du cinéma* no. 208, January 1968, p. 21.

5 'Problema sovetskogo istoricheskogo filma', *IP 5*, pp. 110–29.

6 R. Jakobson, *Pushkin and his Sculptural Myth* (The Hague/Paris: 1975), pp. 1–45.

7 Ibid., p. 5.

8 *IP 3* p. 492.

9 Pomerantseva, p. 177.

10 *IP*, ibid.

11 A. Bely, *Masterstvo Gogolya* (Moscow: 1934).

12 Another writer with an interesting perspective on Pushkin and colour at this time was Marina Tsvetaeva. Her *My Pushkin*, published abroad in 1937, develops the symbolism of black and white in a way that is sometimes strikingly similar to E's (cf. *Voprosy literatury* no. 10, 1971, pp. 187–8). There is however no evidence that E ever came into contact with Tsvetaeva's essay.

13 Pomerantseva, p. 177.

14 *Voprosy literatury*, p. 188.

15 Ibid., p. 189.

16 Ibid.

17 Cf. Pomerantseva, p. 177.

18 *IP 3* p. 493.

19 *Voprosy literatury*, p. 190.

20 *Iskusstvo kino* no. 3, 1959, p. 130.

21 *Voprosy literatury*, ibid.

22 Quoted in *Voprosy literatury*, p. 187.

23 Ibid., p. 191.

24 *IP 3* pp. 494–5; *EAW*, p. 121.

25 *IP 3* p. 499.

26 Pomerantseva, p. 178.

27 Y. Tynyanov, *Pushkin i ego sovremenniki* (Moscow: 1969), pp. 209–33; the essay was first published in 1939.

28 For a more sober evaluation of this relationship, see Y. Lotman, *Aleksandr Sergeevich Pushkin* (Leningrad: 1983), p. 28.

29 Pomerantseva, p. 178. E then relates his observations of Chaplin's escapades in Hollywood, particularly his infatuation with Marion Davies, who 'belonged to the newspaper magnate Randolph Hearst'. E claims that Hearst represented the same kind of 'father figure' as Karamzin did in relation to Pushkin, and implies that such triangular relationships as Hearst/Davies/Chaplin and Karamzin/Karamzina/Pushkin exemplify a psychological schema prevalent in Pushkin's work.

30 Veissfeld, pp. 19–21.

31 Pomerantseva, p. 179.

32 Veissfeld, p. 19.

33 Tynyanov, p. 232.
34 We may also wonder if the same prudishness played a part in E's curious omission of several lines from Boris' monologue in the script. The 'cut', as E calls it, eliminates the following lines:

> . . . Is this not
> What happens when we're young?
> We fall in love and thirst for
> Love's pleasure, but as soon as we've appeased
> The hunger of the heart with momentary possession
> We cool, grow bored, and languish . . .
>
> > (C. Emerson, trans. *Boris Godunov*
> > (Bloomington: 1987), p. 113)

This expression of 'post-coital depression' would seem an adequate illustration of the disillusion suffered by the Pushkin of the 'nameless love' thesis. E nevertheless eliminates the lines and explains why:

> Not remembering the existence of these lines, I had *earlier* planned to make the length of the path through the empty cathedral correspond to the space between 'my' and 'in vain'. In such a path the melody of these lines is to be found, but I removed the words since they fall outside the direct acting *treatment* of the scene (if you like – a certain primitivisation is unavoidable in film).
>
> > (*Iskusstvo kino*, no. 3, 1959, p. 115)

E thus first forgets and then eliminates these lines in order to replace them with the actor's movement! Although it could be argued that the lines are inappropriate for the sacred setting E gives the monologue, the director's forgetting just these lines smacks of suppression, of an effort to adjust the image of Boris and, indirectly, of Pushkin to fit the romantic idea of the 'nameless love'.
35 Jakobson, p. 15.
36 Quoted in Jakobson, p. 14.
37 Ibid., p. 11.
38 Ibid., pp. 4–6.
39 H. Marshall, *Masters of the Soviet Cinema: Crippled Creative Biographies* (London: 1983), pp. 228–9.
40 *Iskusstvo kino* no. 2, 1987, p. 74.

8 EISENSTEIN AND SHAKESPEARE

1 See Ch. 1 above.
2 See, for instance, *IP 3*, p. 139 and *IP 5*, p. 405.
3 Aksenov's 1935 book on E has recently been published. See Ch. 1 n. 20 above.
4 In *EAW*, pp. 7–9.
5 Barna, p. 143.
6 *IP 1*, pp. 193–4.
7 *IP 4*, p. 610.
8 *IP 6*, p. 548.
9 Y. Tynyanov, *Sbornik* (Moscow: 1966), pp. 177–8.
10 *IP 6*, p. 16.
11 *IP 4*, p. 240.
12 *IP 4*, p. 234.
13 *IP 4*, pp. 260f.

14 *IP 4*, p. 231.
15 *IP 4*, p. 259.
16 See Chs 9 and 11 below.
17 From E's notes, out of which Naum Kleiman is reconstructing *Method*.
18 *IP 3*, p. 137.
19 In the same unpublished note from 1943 on *Romeo and Juliet*.
20 *IP 3*, p. 139.
21 Published in 1935.
22 See Ch. 13 below, p. 204.
23 Kindly supplied by Naum Kleiman.

9 GRAPHIC FLOURISH: ASPECTS OF THE ART OF *MISE-EN-SCÈNE*

1 Although *mise-en-scène* is generally rendered as 'direction' elsewhere in this book, it has been retained here since its etymology and associations are central to Khopkar's purpose [Eds].
2 Ritwik Ghatak (1925–75), radical Bengali film director.
3 Nizhny, p. 168.
4 Leyda noted: 'The only fault that I can find with Nizhny's usually wise transformations of stenogram into book is that E sounds here more like a lecturer than he did actually.' See also, p. 141.
5 *IP 2*, p. 338 (all translations by the author, unless otherwise stated).
6 *Film Form*, pp. 144–5.
7 Ibid., p. 3.
8 See M. Yampolsky, 'Kuleshov and the New Anthropology of the Actor', in R. Taylor and I. Christie (eds), *Inside the Film Factory: New Approaches to Russian and Soviet Cinema* (London and New York: 1991), pp. 31–50.
9 'Art of the Cinema', in R. Levaco (ed. and trans.), *Kuleshov on Film* (Berkeley, Calif.: 1974), p. 55.
10 Ibid., p. 56.
11 V. E. Meyerkhol'd, 'Odinochestvo Stanislavskogo' (The Solitude of Stanislavsky), *Vestnik teatra* no. 89–90, 1921, pp. 2–3; translated in E. Braun (ed. and trans.), *Meyerhold on Theatre* (London and New York: 1977), p. 179.
12 *IP 2*, p. 458.
13 *IP 4*, p. 751.
14 Ibid.
15 'Uber die Schwebetendenz' (The Floating Tendency), *Sovetskoe Iskusstvo* no. 11, 1985.
16 '*Kupal'shchitsy* Degasa' (Degas's *Les Baigneuses*), unpublished notes from E's diaries kindly made available to the author by Naum Kleiman.
17 'Theses on the Philosophy of History', in W. Benjamin, *Illuminations* (ed. H. Arendt and trans. H. Zorn) (New York: 1968), p. 257.
18 L. K. Kozlov and N. I. Kleiman (eds), *Iz tvorcheskogo naslediya S. M. Eizenshteina, Materialy i soobshcheniya* (From S. M. Eisenstein's Creative Legacy: Materials and Information) (Moscow: 1985), pp. 6–36; trans. in *ESW 1*, pp. 39–58.
19 *The Psychology of Composition* (Calcutta: 1987) p. 10.
20 *EAW*, p. 128.
21 'Uber die Schwebetendenz'; '*Kupal'shchitsy* Degasa'.
22 'Uber die Schwebetendenz'.
23 S. Freud, *The Interpretation of Dreams* (1899) (trans. J. Strachey) (Harmondsworth: 1976), pp. 516–17.

24 Ibid., p. 518.
25 *Schriften* vol. 4, p. 257.
26 S. M. Eisenstein, *Cinématisme: Peinture et cinéma* (ed. F. Albera) (Brussels: 1980), p. 249.
27 *EAW*, p. 131.
28 See A. Bird, *A History of Russian Painting* (Oxford: 1987), p. 19:

> From the end of the fourteenth century . . . we find in the Muscovite state a whole screen of icons extending high above the sanctuary doors and offering a kind of simple encyclopedia of Christian belief. . . . The iconostasis became a vital bridge between heaven and earth. [Eds]

29 *IP 4*, pp. 717–38; also in *Le Mouvement de l'art* (ed. F. Albera and N. Kleiman) (Paris: 1986), pp. 171–206.
30 Naum Kleiman and Valentina Korshunova, the editors of the German-language edition of E's memoirs, which is to date the most complete published version, suggest in their introduction the following derivation for the title:

> On 18 May 1946, when he was copying out a quotation from *Uncle Tom's Cabin* for his textbook on *Direction*, he found in passing a title for his 'life story' – 'Yo'.
> 'Yo' is the Spanish for 'I'. Perhaps the Spanish language gave an ironic distance to the book title and deprived it of its absolute egocentricity. There are certainly also underlying resonances of Eisenstein's longing for Mexico, where he had learnt a little Spanish. There was of course also an element of reminiscence: it must have made him think of Mayakovsky, of his poem 'I' and of his autobiographical sketch 'I Myself'.
>
> (S. M. Eisenstein, *YO! Ich selbst: Memoiren* (I Myself: Memoirs) (ed. N. Kleiman and W. Korschunowa) (Berlin, GDR and Vienna: 1984), vol. 1, p. 21)

31 Here I am indebted to Naum Kleiman for explaining the relationship between E's various proposed books. The notes to *IP 4*, pp. 741–9 and the introduction to *YO! Ich selbst*, vol. 1, pp. 15–25, also discuss these.

10 EISENSTEIN AS THEORETICIAN: PRELIMINARY CONSIDERATIONS

1 F. Casetti, 'L'immagine del montaggio' (Imagination and montage), in S. M. Eisenstein, *Teoria generale del montaggio* (Venice: 1985), p. xxv.
2 J. Aumont describes the necessity of reading the work and understanding E's character as 'structured on several levels' – an operation necessary to give 'force' and 'homogeneity' to research – even if it is often difficult to fix clear and precise boundaries between E's different 'practices'. See J. Aumont, *Montage Eisenstein* (Paris: 1979), trans. L. Hildreth, C. Penley and A. Ross (Bloomington, Ind. and London: 1987) pp. 9–12.
3 E. G. Grossi, 'Eisenstein e il progetto di *Regissura*', in *Studi Urbinati B 3* vol. 58, pp. 219–26.
4 *La natura non indifferente* (1981); *Il colore* (1982); *Teoria generale del montaggio* (1985); *La regia* (1989); *Memorie* (1990).
5 The most recent attempt to list all E's published writings is a bibliography of over 500 items compiled by B. Amengual and J. Aumont, appended to Amengual, *Que Viva Eisenstein!* (Lausanne: 1980), pp. 650–90. See also 'A Bibliography of Eisenstein's Writings' in Aumont, *Montage Eisenstein*, pp. 223–35.

6 Yu. Krasovskii, 'Kinematograficheskie materiali v TsGALI' (Cinema Materials in TsGALI), *Iz istorii kino* vol. 9 (Moscow: 1974), p. 177.

7 *Voprosy literatury* no. 1, 1968, pp. 98–103. See also the important collection of E's writings, ed. with a commentary by F. Albera, *Cinématisme, Peinture et cinéma*, pp. 15–144.

8 See N. Kleiman, 'Conversazione con P. M. De Santi', in the catalogue *Eisenstein/disegni* (Pesaro: 1981), p. 12. The first chapter of *On the Problem of Direction*, entitled 'Mise en jeu i mise en geste', was published in *IP 4*, pp. 717–38 (Italian translation in *Bianco e Nero* no. 7–8, 1971, pp. 90–108).

9 Information on 'In Praise of the Cinema Newsreel' supplied by Naum Kleiman in 1982.

10 Seton's interpretation of E's interest in Lewis Carroll and especially *Alice in Wonderland* is typical:

> the fascination of Carroll's work was for more personal reasons than his wonderful anatomical chart of the absurd, which had such great appeal for Eisenstein. In Carroll's use of psycho-physiological symbols – Alice's shrinkage in size and becoming awkwardly large – Sergei Mikhailovich found literary expression of the painfully acute psychic feelings which he experienced.
>
> (Seton, p. 292)

11 Some indication of themes that E intended to pursue in this book may be found in these articles: J. Aumont, 'Eisenstein avec Freud' (E with Freud), *Cahiers du cinéma* no. 226–7, 1971, pp. 68–74; V. V. Ivanov, 'Eisenstein et la linguistique structurale moderne' (E and Modern Structural Linguistics), *Cahiers du cinéma* no. 220–1, 1970, pp. 47–50; M. Vannucchi, 'Ideogramma, monologo e linguaggio interiore' (Ideogram, monologue and inner language), in *Il cinema di Eisenstein* (Rimini, Florence: 1975), pp. 189–237.

12 Seton, pp. 298–9.

13 Seton, p. 300. Some of V. V. Ivanov's articles on E clarify issues raised by Seton. E's speculation on 'the primary unity of all human activity' is dealt with by Ivanov in 'Doctor Faustus: "Il problema fondamentale" nella teoria dell'arte di S. M. Eisenstein' (Dr Faustus: 'The fundamental problem' of the theory of art in E), in *Strumenti critici* no. 42–3, 1980, p. 472:

> Starting from the study of exchange as a 'full social fact', ethnologists have concluded that there existed in antiquity an undifferentiated society, in which the exchange of social values and materials, reciprocal ritual relations and all the activities which are associated with the concept of art in modern society, were practically indistinguishable.
>
> Eisenstein reconstructed a sketch of this primordial society. The idea of an unstructured chorus in [his production of] the *Valkyrie*, which also appears in other works from the early period, is linked with the image of a unitary primitive society, in accordance with the principles of modern ethnology.

14 Again Ivanov usefully clarifies:

> [Some of E's research] dealt with the geometry of Mexican ritual: the places where Mexican Catholics genuflect toward saints are sites of ancient pagan rituals. These observations on the survival of pre-Columbian religion in modern Catholic practice anticipated by thirty years the most recent studies.
>
> ('Doctor Faustus', p. 473)

15 Seton, p. 301.

16 It is important to note that in 1967, at the very time Shklovsky was writing this,

Roman Jakobson had also reached much the same conclusion on E: '[in E's writings] there are ideas and passages which prove that Eisenstein was not only a genius as a film-maker but that he was also a great scientist, a theoretician and historian of cinema and of art.' A. Aprà and L. Faccini, 'Conversazione sul cinema con Roman Jakobson' (Conversation on Cinema with Roman Jakobson), in *Cinema e Film* no. 2, 1967, p. 158.

17 V. Shklovsky, 'Sur "La théorie de la prose"' (On 'The Theory of Prose'), in *Rassegna Sovietica* no. 1, 1971, p. 110.

18 J. Aumont, *Montage Eisenstein*; D. Andrew, *The Major Film Theories* (New York: 1976), pp. 42–75.

19 The bibliography is very large and we can only cite here the main works: A. M. Ripellino, *Majakovskij e il teatro russo d'avanguardia* (Turin: 1959); *Eisenstein Künstler der Revolution* (Berlin: 1960); *Cahiers du cinéma* no. 220–1, 1970, special issue, 'Russie: années vingt' (including a useful bibliography and chronology, pp. 114–9), also no. 226–7, 1971, special issue 'S. M. Eisenstein'; *Il cinema di Eisenstein* (Rimini, Florence: 1975). Crowning these and many other studies is B. Amengual, *Que Viva Eisenstein!* (see note 5).

20 The link between Meyerhold and other areas of E's research is undoubtedly the most important of all those mentioned so far. In addition to E's reflections on theatre of the period 1920–4, there are numerous passages in *Direction*, such as the consideration of *otkaz* [refusal] and the repeated theorisation of 'expressive movement'. These are discussed in: Grossi, 'Il concetto di efficienza nella riflessione di Eisenstein sul teatro' (The concept of efficiency in E's reflection on theatre), written for a seminar directed by J. Aumont, 1984–5 (unpublished).

21 See for example M. Le Bot, 'Serge Eisenstein, théoricien de l'art moderne' (S. E as theorist of modern art), in *Contre-champ* no. 2, 1962, pp. 13–16, also no. 5, 1963, pp. 53–64; F. Albera, 'Eisenstein et l'avant-garde russe' (E and the Russian avant-garde), in *Notes sur l'esthétique d'Eisenstein* (Lyon: 1973), pp. 21–77; A. Michelson, 'Scène de l'action, espace du mouvement: la crise de la représentation cinématographique' (Scene of Action, Space of Movement: the Crisis of Cinematic Representation), in *Une histoire du cinéma* (Paris: 1976), pp. 38–44.

22 See M. Tafuri, 'Piranesi, Eisenstein e la dialettica dell'avanguardia' (Piranesi, E and the dialectic of the avant-garde), in *Rassegna Sovietica* no. 1–2, 1972, pp. 175–84.

23 The reconstruction and interpretation of these studies by E were reported by V. V. Ivanov in two notable essays: 'Significato delle idee di M. M. Bachtin sul segno, l'atto di parole e il dialogo per la semiotica contemporanea' (The Significance for Contemporary Semiotics of M. M Bakhtin's Ideas on the Sign, the Speech Act and Dialogue), in: *Michail Bachtin: Semiotica, teoria della letteratura e marxismo* (Bari: 1977), pp. 67–104; 'The Semiotic Theory of Carnival as the Inversion of Bipolar Opposites', in *Carnival!* (Berlin: 1984), p. 11–35. Ivanov shows in these articles how the themes recur in *Que Viva Mexico!* and *Ivan the Terrible*.

24 This passage, from an unpublished chapter of *Method*, is quoted by Ivanov in 'The Semiotic Theory of Carnival', p. 13.

25 See I. Ambrogio, *Formalismo e avanguardia in Russia* (Formalism and the avant-garde in Russia) (Rome: 1968) and E. Ferrario, *Teorie della letteratura in Russia 1900–1934* (The Theory of Literature in Russia 1900–34) (Rome: 1977). Both of these trace connections between the Soviet avant-garde and the Slav scientific tradition, although Ferrario's date boundary halts him on the threshold of E's maturity (pp. 257–68).

26 Quotations from C. Prevignano, in *La semiotica nei paesi slavi* (Slavic

Semiotics) (Milan: 1979), pp. 23–99. Prevignano made a detailed analysis of 'the corpus of images, models and research procedures which came into existence between the 1910s and 30s, and was then taken up and elaborated by further Slav contribution to semiotics in the 60s and 70s'. Today there is general recognition of the Slav semiotic 'tradition' and in a special issue of *Strumenti critici* no. 42–3, 1980, entitled 'La cultura nella tradizione russa del XIX e XX secolo' (Culture in Russian tradition in the nineteenth and twentieth centuries), D'Arco Silvio Avalle proposes a division of the Russian history of semiotics into three main periods: the generation '1960–70', that of '1910–40', and a generation of the second half of the nineteenth century whose main representatives were the great 'philologists', Veselovsky and Potebnya. Other surveys include E. M. Meletinsky and D. M. Segal, 'Structuralisme et sémiotique en URSS' (Structuralism and Semiotics in the USSR), in *Diogène* no. 73, 1971, pp. 94–117; Yu M. Lotman and B. A. Uspenskii, 'Introduction', in *Richerche semiotiche* (Turin: 1973), pp. xi–xxvii; E. M. Meletinksy *et al.*, 'Russian Folklore and the Problems of Structural Method', ibid., pp. 401–32; and A. Shukman, 'Soviet Semiotics and Literary Criticism', in *New Literary History* vol. 9, no. 2, 1978, pp. 189–97.

27 K. Eimermacher, 'Zur Entstehungsgeschichte einer deskriptiven Semiotik in der Sowjetunion' (On the origins of descriptive semiotics in the Soviet Union), in *Zeitschrift für Semiotik* vol. IV, no. 1–2, 1982, p. 2.

28 Direct references to E and his theoretical work appear frequently in the writings of V. V. Ivanov. The most important texts are: 'Eisenstein et la linguistique structurale moderne' (E and modern structural linguistics); 'Doctor Faustus'; and the book *Ocherki po istorii semiotiki v SSSR* (Essays on the History of Semiotics in the USSR) (Moscow: 1976). Of secondary importance are 'Significato delle idee di M. M. Bachtin'; 'Growth of the Theoretical Framework of Modern Poetics', in *Current Trends in Linguistics* vol. 12, no. 2 (Paris and The Hague: 1974), pp. 835–61; and 'The Semiotic Theory of Carnival'.

29 V. V. Ivanov, 'L'approcio dinamico allo studio dell'evoluzione della lingua, del testo e della cultura' (The dynamic approach to the study of the evolution of language, mind and culture), in *Rassegna Sovietica* no. 6, 1983, p. 17.

30 J. P. Courtois, 'Sur *Montage Eisenstein*', *Ça cinéma* no. 18, 1979, p. 72.

31 D. M Segal, 'La ricercha sovietiche nel campo della semiotica degli ultimi anni' (The Soviet contribution to the field of semiotics in recent years), in *Ricerche semiotiche*, p. 452.

32 Studies by P. Montani published in parallel with the Selected Works in Italian have defined the relationship between E and semiotics, following the theses outlined by E. Garroni in *Ricognizione della semiotica* (Appreciation of Semiotics) (Rome: 1977).

33 First published in E. Bruno and E. Ghezzi, *Walt Disney* (Venice: 1985), pp. 25–58; English translation *Eisenstein on Disney* (see Introduction, note 80).

34 Ibid., p. 6.

35 Ibid., p. 23.

36 In 'The Growth of the Theoretical Framework', Ivanov links Veselovsky, E and Propp:

> Eisenstein's conception belongs to the diachronic tendency which was characteristic of the most interesting Russian humanist scholarship in the first half of this century. Veselovsky, who tried to build a vast edifice of historical poetics and who influenced Propp's morphological research, can be considered its precursor.
>
> (p. 852)

37 My essay 'Eisenstein e il progetto di *Regissura*' dwells upon the main concerns of E's thought between 1927 and 1929, and in particular the studies that lead up to *Direction*, the work of E's maturity.

38 To complete Ivanov's reference, let us recall N. Kleiman's definition of the *Grundproblem*: 'One can give a simple and brief definition of this problem as that of the correlation between the logico-rational and the sensory in art, in the creative act, in the structure of a work and in the process of its perception.'

39 Ivanov, 'Doctor Faustus', p. 462.

40 'The power of the symbol is always a living power, because it belongs to the essence of palpable human reaction.' This was E's explanation in an interview with Bruno Frei, published in *Die Weltbühne* no. 32, 1928, partly republished in H. J. Schlegel (ed.), *Schriften 3: Oktober* (Munich: 1975), p. 260.

41 In his introduction to *La natura non indifferente*, Montani clarifies the significance of the 'dual unity' between logical and sensory thought which, for E, underpinned the authentic work of art. He argues that E's idea of 'sensory thought' in its 'ethnological and positivist formulation' can lead to 'regressive confusion' and that E succumbed to this more than once.

42 G. P. Brunetta, *Letteratura e cinema* (Bologna: 1976), p. 40.

43 *Teoria generale del montaggio*; translated in *ESW 2*, pp. 11–58.

44 See the chapter 'La nascità del montaggio: Dionisio' (The birth of montage: Dionysus) in *Teoria generale del montaggio*, pp. 226–31. E synthesised the theory that underlies this reasoning as follows: 'The real *cult action* is progressively transformed into a *ritual symbol* in order to become later an *art image*.'

45 Part of Eisenstein's work on language in the 20s and 30s was bound up with Vygotsky's research on the psychology of language and Luria's on neurophysiology, as well as Marr's hypotheses on gestural language. . . . At the Moscow Neurophysiological Clinic which Eisenstein often visited, experiments were carried out on the language of aphasics and on the handling of tools which led to bold hypotheses on the relation between verbal and gestural language. (Eisenstein was equally interested in the gestural composition of words: he studied the head movements which accompany the articulation of certain prefixes).

(F. Giusti, *Strumenti critici* no. 42–3, 1980, pp. 600–1)

46 M. M. Bakhtin, 'Response to a Question from the *Novy Mir* Editorial Staff', *Novy Mir* no. 11, 1970; translated in Bakhtin, *Speech Genres and Other Late Essays* (ed. C. Emerson, Michael Holquist, trans. V. McGee) (Austin: 1986), p. 2.

11 THE ESSENTIAL BONE STRUCTURE: MIMESIS IN EISENSTEIN

1 'Nachahmung als Beherrschung', first published in *Film und Fernsehen* no. 1, 1988, pp. 34–7. The first English translation appears in the present volume (Ch. 4) and all quotations here are from that version.

2 The numerous examples of magic cannibalism cited in E's speech were taken from the following books: E. B. Tylor, *Pervobytnaya kul'tura* (Primitive Culture) (Moscow: 1939), pp. 229ff. (Eisenstein, of course, used an earlier edition); A. Lang, *Custom and Myth* (London, New York, Bombay: 1898), pp. 53–4.

3 W. Benjamin, 'Problème de sociologie du langage', in *Essais II: 1935–1940* (Paris: 1983), p. 33.

4 The Russian word *obobshchenie* or 'generalisation' means to draw out the general significance of something in its context.

5 The emphasis is E's. E. Durkheim, *Les formes élémentaires de la vie religieuse: Le système totémique en Australie* (Paris: 1912), p. 179.

6 Lang, *Custom and Myth*, p. 303.

7 F. Cushing, 'Manual Concepts', *American Anthropologist* no. 5, 1892. E referred to Cushing in his unpublished work 'The Three Whales' (Tri kita) (TsGALI, 1923/2/239) and also in the memoirs: *IP 1*, p. 484; translated in *Memories*, p. 212.

8 L. Lévy-Bruhl, *Pervobytnoe myshlenie* (Primitive Mentality) (Moscow: 1930), p. 106.

9 J. Lindsay, *A Short History of Culture* (Leningrad: 1939), p. 49.

10 'The Three Whales'.

11 Ibid.

12 'Montage 1937' (Montazh 1937), *IP 2*, p. 241.

13 Ibid., pp. 351, 342.

14 'Odd and Even' (Chët-nechët), first published in *Vostok–Zapad* (East–West) (Moscow: 1988), p. 235.

15 'The Three Whales'.

16 Ibid. The Russian word *cherta* can mean both 'line' and 'facet' or 'feature'.

17 Quoted in N. Kleiman and M. Nesteva, 'Vydayushchiisya khudozhnik-gumanist' (An Outstanding Humanist Artist), *Sovetskaya muzyka* no. 9, 1979, p. 72.

18 *The Psychology of Composition* (see Introduction, note 80), p. 54.

19 Note dated 30 September 1941, TsGALI, 1923/1/1041.

20 'The Three Whales'. Elsewhere he wrote:

> Here there seems to be a contradiction: the highest form of integral perception – the generalised image – appears *as a plastic sign* to correspond to the most primitive type. But this contradiction is only an apparent one. In essence we have in this instance *precisely* that 'supposed return to the old' that Lenin mentions in relation to the dialectic of phenomena. The fact is that generalisation is *really integral*, that is it is at the same time both a complex (unmediated) and a differentiated (mediated) representation of a phenomenon (and a notion about the phenomenon).
>
> ('Montage 1937', *IP 2*, pp. 386–7)

E's dialectic constantly led to explanations like this in order to expose in the generalisation both the higher and the lower at the same time.

21 'The Three Whales'.

22 W. Worringer, *Abstraktion und Einfühlung* (Abstraction and Empathy) (Leipzig and Weimar: 1981), p. 17 (E of course used an earlier edition). He also referred to Worringer in the unpublished 'Searches for a Father' (Poiski ottsa) (TsGALI, 1923/1/234). E's search for abstraction followed closely the whole line of abstraction in aesthetics from Riegl, Hildebrand and Wölflin to Klee and Kandinsky.

23 'The Three Whales'.

24 Ibid.

25 Lévy-Bruhl, *Pervobytnoe myshlenie*, p. 106.

26 'On the Detective Story' (O detektive), first published in *Priklyuchencheskii fil'm* (The Adventure Film) (Moscow: 1980), pp. 142–4; translated in *The Psychology of Composition*, pp. 57–84.

27 'Natasha', TsGALI, 1923/2/238.
28 'On the Detective Story', p. 144.
29 'The True Paths of Invention' (Istinnye puti izobreteniya), *IP 1*, p. 177.
30 'The History of the Close-Up' (Istoriya krupnogo plana), *IP 1*, p. 507.
31 Untitled fragment, *IP 1*, p. 509.
32 Ibid.
33 'Museums at Night' (Muzei noch'yu), *IP 1*, p. 433. *Memories*, p. 173.
34 *IP 1*, p. 441; *Memories*, p. 180.
35 E, while admitting that Swedenborg 'like all mystics has a certain knowledge', thought his principal error was too materialistic an understanding of image or, metaphorically expressed, too limited an exclusion of day vision. According to E, with mystics the 'sprouting of *sensation* becomes and develops not into consciousness (in our sense) but into a metaphysical ideogram: image understood materialistically' (TsGALI, 1923/2/233). Thus E indirectly admitted his own link with mysticism, but claimed to have overcome it through a higher level of abstraction.
36 Ibid.
37 Ibid.
38 Worringer, *Abstraktion und Einfühlung*, pp. 17–18.
39 *Direction: The Art of Mise-en-Scène* (Rezhissura: Iskusstvo mizanstseny), *IP 4*, p. 125. In 'On the Detective Story', p. 148, he stated:

> Step by step, a shift is produced in the reader towards reading phenomena in terms of the objects or representations which accompany their shape or appearance, but not their content or meaning; i.e. a reorganisation towards the so-called 'physiognomical' – directly sensuous perception.
>
> (Upchurch trans., p. 71)

40 From the 'Superobjectivity' section of 'Pathos' in *Non-Indifferent Nature* (Neravnodushnaya priroda), *IP 3*, p. 204; trans. *NIN*, p. 170.
41 Ibid.
42 'Beyond the Shot' (Za kadrom), *IP 2*, p. 285, trans. in *ESW 1*, p. 140.
43 Unpublished notes dated 17 August 1940 and entitled 'Expressive Movement' (Vyrazitel'noe dvizhenie), TsGALI, 1923/1/236.
44 'The Kangaroo' section of 'Pathos' in *Non-Indifferent Nature*: *IP 3*, pp. 225–6; *NIN*, p. 191.
45 'Montage 1937', *IP 2*, p. 354, fig. 9; *ESW 2*, p. 31, fig. 2.9.
46 Ibid., p. 389; *ESW 2*, p. 100.
47 Ibid., pp. 389–90; *ESW 2*, pp. 99–103.
48 *The Psychology of Composition*, p. 279.
49 Ibid., p. 280.
50 A. Besant and C. W. Leadbeater, *Les formes-pensées* (Thought Forms) (Paris: 1905), p. 3.
51 M. Voloshin, *Liki tvorchestva* (Images of Creativity) (Leningrad: 1988), p. 211. Voloshin also appreciated the importance of evolutionism, distinguishing three periods in the development of art: (1) the conventional symbolism of the sign; (2) strict realism; (3) generalised stylisation (ibid., p. 216). This schema corresponded in its essentials to those of Worringer and E.
52 'Beneath the hills of these valleys you can distinguish the features of swollen ribs, the long ridges reveal the backbones concealed beneath them and featureless and predatory skulls rise from the sea' (ibid., p. 316). In this context the predilection that Voloshin (like the representatives of Western European Modernism) felt for Gothic architecture, with the 'skeletal' structure of its

cathedrals, acquires special significance. See: '"Dukh gotiki" – neosushchestv-lennyi zamysel M. A. Voloshina' ('The Spirit of the Gothic': Voloshin's Unrealised Project) in *Russkaya literatura i zarubezhnoe iskusstvo* (Russian Literature and Foreign Art) (Leningrad: 1986), pp. 317–46. Cf. Mandelstam's lines: 'What is more considered than the stronghold of Notre Dame. I have studied your monstrous ribs.' O. Mandelstam, *Nôtre Dame*, in *Kamen'* (*The Stone*, 1913); *Collected Works* (Washington, DC: 1964), vol. 1, p. 24.

53 A. Bely, *Petersburg* (Leningrad: 1981), p. 239. On the other hand, bones and a skeleton have often become the key metaphor for an aesthetics that cultivates an orientation towards line, beginning with Hogarth, whom Eisenstein esteemed so highly. See Ch. 10, 'O kompozitsii so zmeevidnoi liniei' (On Composition with a Serpentine Line) in: *U. Khogart: Analiz krasoty* (W. Hogarth: The Analysis of Beauty) (Leningrad: 1987), pp. 149–50.

54 Bely, *Petersburg*, pp. 235–9. We should note the particular attention that Eisenstein paid to Bely's work.

55 'On Bones' (Na kostyakh), *IP 1*, p. 300; *Memories*, p. 72.

56 'How I Learned to Draw' (Kak ya uchilsya risovat'), *IP 1*, p. 267; partially translated in *Memories*, p. 46. Also translated by R. Taylor in Christie and Elliot, p. 58.

57 The quotation from p. 99 of Chiang Yee's book comes in 'Montage 1937', *IP 2*, p. 350; *ESW 2*, p. 28. In 'On Bones' (see n. 55 above) E refers to the book *Bruges-la-morte* by Georges Rodenbach (Paris: no date): *IP 1*, p. 296 (Marshall misses the reference, p. 69). This book was almost entirely devoted to the theme of the similarity between the living and the dead, the real and the imaginary. It is significant that Rodenbach, in analysing the mechanisms of similarity, remarks: 'The similarities are always confined to the lines and to the totality. If you delve into the details, everything is different' (*Bruges-la-morte*, p. 128). [Rodenbach's book also served as the basis for E. Bauer's film *Grezy* (Daydreams) in 1915; see Y. Tsivian *et al.*, *Silent Witnesses: Russian Films 1908–1919* (Pordenone and London: 1989), p. 256. – Ed. note]

58 'Montage 1937', *IP 2*, p. 351; *ESW 2*, p. 28.

59 'The History of the Close-Up', *IP 1*, p. 506.

60 Unpublished note dated 19 February 1937, TsGALI, 1923/2/233.

61 TsGALI, 1923/2/232 (unpublished).

62 'Foreword', *IP 1*, p. 210; *Memories*, p. 1.

63 'On Folklore' (O fol'klore), TsGALI, 1923/2/1082 (unpublished).

64 Cf. the sensation of 'being outside oneself' in Bely's *Petersburg*:

> You feel as if some kind of bandage has fallen away taking your feelings with it . . . as if you are being torn to pieces and your limbs are being pulled in opposite directions: your heart is being dragged from the front and your back from behind. . . . I felt in a quite corporeal and physiological sense that I was *outside myself*.
>
> (Bely, *Petersburg*, pp. 258–9)

65 'On Folklore'.

66 Translator's note: I am extremely grateful to Natasha Ward, who did the simultaneous translation for the original conference presentation of this paper, for her inspiration of some of the more felicitous passages in this version.

12 EISENSTEIN AND THE THEORY OF 'MODELS'; OR, HOW TO DISTRACT THE SPECTATOR'S ATTENTION

1 Most Soviet film-makers in the 1920s entered the debate about 'types' but, unlike E, did not use them in leading roles. These 'models' (*naturshchiki*) are as a rule simply extras, shown one after another in brief close-ups to achieve two effects: (1) constructing a litany by sequencing 'x' interchangeable faces which the audience interprets as 'he is very bourgeois', or 'he is very poor'; (2) accumulating many different portraits to demonstrate the lack of cohesion in a social group, notably the peasantry and sub-proletariat.

2 'Yudif'' (Judith), from which this quotation comes, was written in 1947 but only published for the first time in 1968, in *IP 5*, pp. 364–96; French translation in *Mémoires 2*, *Oeuvres* vol. 5, pp. 195–244; quotation from p. 234 of this edition.

3 At least three versions of *The Old and the New* are in circulation. I worked from the two 16mm prints in the Cinémathèque Universitaire in Paris. The first of these, titled in English and duped in New York by Glenn Photo Supply, appears to be the 1926 version, entitled *The General Line*. The second, identical to the print in the Cinémathèque Française, with French titles, is the 1929 version, retitled *The Old and the New* (in the epilogue a Ford tractor bears the date 1929). I noted five major variations:

1 The titles opening the narrative are different. *The General Line* starts with 'Not 10', 'Not 20', 'But exactly one hundred', 'One hundred million peasants', 'Uneducated', 'Illiterate', 'Backward'. *The Old and the New* starts with a quotation from Lenin: 'It is essential that our country be transformed from an agrarian country into an industrial country (Lenin)'; followed by 'Rows of tractors or giant collectives', 'A primitive land', 'Centuries behind', 'Such is the heritage left', 'BY THE OLD REGIME'.

2 The episode dealing with the co-operative has been reworked. In 1926, the platform is occupied by the district Agronomist (announced before he appears) and by a blond *Komsomol* member who reads the resolutions (which are not communicated). The Technician from the city is absent. In 1929, introduced by a title, the Technician enters before the Agronomist and the *Komsomol* remains in the background. Three titles emphasise organisation: 'The party cell', 'The local cell', 'Propose a solution'.

3 The scene at the Ministry has also been modified. In 1926, the technician expedites bureaucratic decisions by shouting: 'Remember' / 'The Leader'. His command is intercut with shots of a statue of Lenin. In 1929, the character shouts: 'W. P. I.', 'Worker', 'Inspection', 'and Peasant'. He and Marfa, in a subjective shot, see a tableau of the elderly Lenin reading *Pravda*. A left-right pan discovers an official, already in frame, in a similar pose.

4 The 1926 ending is a palimpsest of *A Woman of Paris* (USA, 1923, dir. Chaplin). The tractor driver from the city has transformed himself into a peasant. Stretched out in the hay in the back of a wagon, he passes Marfa at the wheel of a tractor and the narrative process concludes: 'The story of Marfa', 'Like all stories', 'Ends well'. The 1929 epilogue ends with the Taylorised factory. Intertitles enjoin: 'More iron', 'More steel', 'The triumphal march', 'Legions of steel', 'They advance', 'Forward to Socialism'.

5 The Gosfilmofond copy which I viewed at the Helsinki Cinémathèque is the 1929 version, but the end is truncated. The ballet of tractors is missing and the child who joins Marfa when the defective engine is repaired has gone.

4 On the distinction between semiotic and agential subjects, see M. Lagny, M.-C. Ropars and P. Sorlin, *Générique des années 30* (Paris: 1986), p. 97. The semiotic subject is the character who mediates the audience's viewpoint. He can be an agent of vision (revealing an object, whether or not anthropomorphised, in subjective shots) and/or an agent of perception (perceiving images understood by the audience as mental images attributable only to this character). The agential subject is the character who is empowered to achieve a goal and so assumes control of the narrative, directing its syntagmatic concatenation.

5 At the bottom of the letter/testament, the signature Yakov Strongin is clearly legible.

6 The two sailors, seen in profile, first in medium close-up then from waist-level, are not only wearing the same uniforms, but have similar moustaches and physiques.

7 He falls clutching his cap, a metonym for the *Potemkin*.

8 E, 'Organic Unity and *Pathos*', in *NIN*, p. 13.

9 In the original scenario he is named as 'Voinov'. He first appears in the same frame as one of the sphinxes on the University Embankment, one of the most prosperous districts of Petrograd.

10 M.-C. Ropars and P. Sorlin, *Octobre, écriture et idéologie* (Paris: 1976), p. 139.

11 Ibid., pp. 145–53.

12 Repression is first indicated, by synecdoche, when a single machine-gunner moves into the front rank.

13 M. Lagny, M.-C. Ropars and P. Sorlin, *La Révolution figurée: film, histoire, politique* (Paris: 1979), p. 203.

14 E, 'The Milk Separator and the Holy Grail', in *NIN*, pp. 45–6.

13 EISENSTEIN AND THE THEORY OF THE PHOTOGRAM

1 *Photogramme* has been extensively used in French film theory as a quasi-technical term for the individual film frame when it is considered as an element in the series of frames which comprise a shot. This contrasts with '*cadre*', referring to the composition (framing) of the image, which is the usual sense of 'frame' in English. The issues at stake in his essay – perceptual, semantic, philosophical – suggest that Albera's '*photogramme*' is best rendered by the somewhat unusual 'photogram'. [Trans.]

2 *Osnovnoi kinofenomen*, or in his German writings *Urphänomenon des Films*. 'Montage' is newly translated in *ESW 2*, pp. 11–58.

3 On the '*phi*-effect' considered in relation to early Soviet film theory, see V. Petrić, *Constructivism in Film* (Cambridge, Mass.: 1987), pp. 139–48; also, more generally, I. Montagu, *Film World* (Harmondsworth: 1964), pp. 13–30. [Trans.]

4 The text referred to here as 'Stuttgart' was commissioned from Eisenstein by El Lissitsky and Sophie Küppers, the organisers of the Soviet section in the 'Film und Photo' exhibition. It has since appeared in differing truncated versions under various titles: as 'La Dramaturgie du film' in *Bifur* no. 7, December 1930; as 'The Principles of Film Form' in both *Close Up* vol. 8, no. 3, September 1931, and *Experimental Cinema* no. 4, February 1933; as 'A Dialectical Approach to Film Form' in *Film Form*; and as 'Dramaturgie der Film-Form' in H.-J. Schlegel (ed.), *Sergej M. Eisensten: Schriften 3. Oktober*, (Munich: 1975). The full text remains unpublished and for this study I have used the typescript deposited by Jay Leyda in the Museum of Modern Art, New York. The English translation made by Ivor Montagu in Hollywood in 1930 under Eisenstein's supervision

served as the basis for publication in *Close Up* and *Experimental Cinema* – although these versions differ from the original and each other in several respects! – and quotations here are from this typescript, also deposited at MoMA. See also *ESW 1*, pp. 317–18, n. 51.

5 V. Nilsen, *Tekhnika kombinirovannoi kinos'ëmki* (The Technique of Trick Photography) (Moscow: 1933). Eisenstein's introduction is translated as 'George Méliès's Mistake' and first published in *ESW 1*, pp. 258–60 (see also p. 324, n. 26).

6 This and subsequent quotations are from the respective MoMA typescripts. See also *ESW 1*, p. 164.

7 See *ESW 1*, p. 34.

8 'Za kadrom', written as a postscript to N. Kaufman, *Yaponskoe kino* (Japanese Cinema) (Moscow: 1929). Translated by Leyda as 'The Cinematographic Principle and the Ideogram' in *Film Form*, pp. 28–40; and as 'Beyond the Shot' by Taylor in *ESW 1*, pp. 138–50; see p. 144.

9 In 'Stuttgart', we can see the term *Bildausschnitt* displacing the earlier *Stück*. In his (unpublished) 'Afterthoughts on Stuttgart' of 24 July 1929, Eisenstein wrote: 'Congratulations to the Germans for their expression *Bild-Aus-schnitt* [*Bild-Schnitt-Ausschnitt* = image-editing-framing]. This term amounts to the equivalent of the Russian *kadr*, as Nilsen explains in a passage (Ch. 2, p. 30) omitted from the English translation, *The Cinema as a Graphic Art* (London: 1936), of his *Izobrazitel'noe postroenie fil'ma* (The Graphic Construction of Film) (Moscow and Leningrad: 1936).

10 The concepts of 'ecstasy' (*ekstaz*) and 'image' (*obraz*) had been in common use by the Russian avant-garde since the first decade of the century. After Uspensky developed them from the Neoplatonist philosophy of Plotinus in his *Tertium Organum*, they reappear in many other contexts, including Aleksei Kryuchenykh's definition of Futurist poetry as *zaum* (trans-sense) rather than ordinary instrumental use of language (and Eisenstein would later speak of *zaum* in connection with certain passages of *October*). The painter and musician Mikhail Matyushin, in his translation of Gliezes's and Metzinger's *Du Cubisme* also in 1913, made use of Uspensky's notion of the 'fourth dimension', as did Kazimir Malevich and Eisenstein (the latter in his 1929 'The Fourth Dimension in Cinema', *ESW 1*, pp. 181–94). Such terms, emerging from a mystical conception of knowledge, served to proclaim the allegiances and express the aims of an avant-garde, while also perpetuating an ambiguity which is evident in Eisenstein. The goal of expanding consciousness (political or social) is often expressed in terms of the Neoplatonic expansion of vision (towards a 'total' revelation).

11 'The world, for [Bergson], is divided into two disparate portions, on the one hand life, on the other matter. . . . Life is one great force, one vast vital impulse.' B. Russell, *History of Western Philosophy* (2nd edn, London: 1961), p. 757. See also G. Deleuze, *Cinéma 1: L'image-mouvement* (Paris: 1983), especially Chs 1 and 3, on the continuing significance of Bergson for a philosophy of cinema. [Trans.]

12 'The Montage of Film Attractions', *ESW 1*, pp. 39–58.

13 See Ch. 11 above, especially pp. 178–80.

14 Stéphane Mallarmé (1842–98) defined his 'new poetic' thus in a letter of October 1864. [Trans.]

15 'We: Variant [Version] of a Manifesto', *Kino-Fot* no. 1, 1922; translation in A. Michelson (ed.) and K. O'Brien (trans.), *Kino-Eye: the Writings of Dziga Vertov* (Berkeley, Calif., London and Sydney: 1984), pp. 5–9; also *FF*, pp. 69–71.

16 F. de Saussure, *Cours de linguistique générale* (Geneva: 1915); trans. W. Baskin

as *Course in General Linguistics* (London: 1960); on the concept of 'value', see pp. 111–22.

17 'Painting should not be exclusively retinal or visual; it should have to do with the gray matter, with our urge for understanding.' Interview with Duchamp, 'Regions which are not ruled by space and time' (1956), in M. Sanouillet and E. Peterson (eds), *The Essential Writings of Marcel Duchamp* (New York: 1973), p. 136. [Trans.]

18 'Béla Forgets the Scissors', *ESW 1*, pp. 77–81.

19 On the 'October' group, see J. E. Bowlt (ed. and trans.), *Russian Art of the Avant-Garde: Theory and Criticism 1902–1934* (New York: 1976), pp. 273–9. [Trans.]

20 K. Malevich, 'I likuyut liki na ekranakh' (And Faces are Rejoicing on the screen), *Kinozhurnal ARK* no. 10, October 1925, pp. 7–9. It should be noted that there are two terms for 'face' in Russian: the religious, *lik*, for the face of Christ in icons and the secular *litso*. This opposition is similar to that between *obraz*, signifying an image distinct from its manifestations, and *izobrazhenie*, meaning representation or resemblance. Malevich's second text on cinema, 'Khudozhnik i kino' (The Artist and Cinema), appeared in *Kinozhurnal ARK* no. 2, February 1926, pp. 15–17.

The 'Wanderers' (*Peredvizhniki*), also known as the 'Itinerants', invoked by Malevich to stigmatise E and Vertov, were a group of young painters inspired by democratic ideals, although relatively conservative in aesthetic terms, who seceded from the Petersburg Academy of Art in 1863 and organised a series of touring exhibitions with the avowed aim of bringing art to the people. See *The Itinerants: Society for Circulating Art Exhibitions* (revised edn, London, Sydney and Leningrad: 1982). [Trans.]

21 On the 'Das Kapital' and 'Glass House' projects, see *EAW* pp. 35–7.

22 On the origins of the concept of *zaum* (trans-sense), see V. Shklovsky, 'O poezii i zaumnom yazyke' (On Poetry and Trans-sense Language) (1916), trans. G. Janacek and P. Mayer in *October* no. 34, Fall 1985, pp. 3–24. [*Trans.*]

The links between Fernand Léger and E deserve a study in their own right. We know that Léger's *Ballet mécanique* was classed by E among the 'children's playthings' of cinema in a 1926 text which pokes fun at almost all the pioneers of European avant-garde cinema, including Picabia, Léger and Chomette ('Béla Forgets the Scissors', *ESW 1*, p. 77). However it is also clear that Léger's film exercised a profound influence on E, notably in *The General Line* (the cream separator, filming of everyday objects, the role of intertitles and lettering). In an interview he gave to *Mon Ciné* on 27 March 1930, E recalled 'Léger's *Ballet mécanique* . . . which remains unsurpassed. . . . Despite being a painter, Léger has nevertheless understood the formal essentials of cinema.' But he never wrote anything about the film, even though Léger asked him in February 1933 to contribute to a special issue of *Cahiers d'art* devoted to the latter's work on the occasion of an exhibition in Zurich (unpublished letter, Eisenstein Cabinet, Moscow).

23 See Tsivian, Ch. 5. Is this a script or an editing plan? Tsivian has decided in favour of the former, but there remains something unexplained. Shot no. 409 refers to 'cows panicking', yet Grigori Alexandrov wrote in his memoirs: 'There remained not a single image with cows! . . . Yes, what a shame that all the painstaking labour which went into filming Alexandra Fyodorovna Romanova's personal stable resulted in nothing because of technical faults. He was bitterly disappointed!' G. Aleksandrov, *Epokha i kino* (The Epoch and Cinema) (Moscow: 1976), p. 103.

24 N. Kleiman, 'Tol'ko pyatnadsat' fotogramm' (Only Fifteen Photograms), *Iskusstvo kino* no. 3, 1976.

25   Reduced to its most fundamental procedures, any psychoanalytic reflection on the cinema might be defined in Lacanian terms as an attempt to disengage the cinema-object from the imaginary and to win it for the symbolic, in the hope of extending the latter by a new province. . . . the imaginary, opposed to the symbolic but constantly imbricated with it, designates the basic lure of the ego, the definitive imprint of the stage *before* the Oedipus complex.

(C. Metz, *Le Signifiant imaginaire* (Paris: 1977); trans. C. Britton, A. Williams, B. Brewster, A. Guzzetti as *The Imaginary Signifier: Psychoanalysis and the Cinema* (Bloomington, Ind.: 1982), pp. 3, 4)

Metz's book provides an extended and systematic account of the extensive use made of Lacan's concepts in the last twenty years to theorise the spectator's relationship to cinema. [Trans.]

26   I have analysed at length in my thesis the sequences of the flag-carrier's death during the July 1917 demonstrations and the sack of the Tsarina's bed-chamber. These offer a series of inverse symmetries – fugitive vs pursuer; armed vs unarmed; seer vs seen; male vs female; revolutionary vs reactionary – which enable them to be compared and contrasted, in terms of narrative vs discursive and metaphoric vs metonymic. However splendid the scene of 'raising the bridges', it clearly makes uses of an earlier rhetoric, the 'pathetic' of *Potemkin*, which E thought at this time outdated. F. Albera, *'Stuttgart': dramaturgie de la forme cinématographique: S. M. Eisenstein et le constructivisme russe*, doctoral thesis submitted to the Faculty of History of Art, University of Geneva, 1987; published as *Eisenstein et le constructivisme russe* (Lausanne: 1990).

27   D. Bordwell, 'Eisenstein's Epistemological Shift', *Screen* vol. 15, no. 4, Winter 1974–5, pp. 32–46.

28   Seton, p. 218. The letter is undated and, somewhat confusingly, appears in Seton's narrative amid references to later events, such as *Que Viva Mexico!* in 1932. However, the reference to a change in the format of *Close Up*, which took place in January 1931, enables it to be identified more precisely. Seton speaks of an 'article entitled "Film Form"', but this can only be an abbreviation for 'The Principles of Film Form', which appeared in September 1931 in McPherson's and Bryher's review. E noted that 'it might be presented as a page of my still (and I am afraid for ever!) "forthcoming" book!'

29   *ESW 1*, pp. 165 and 318 n. 61.

30   E came to regard Honoré Daumier (1808–79) as 'a genius, ranging alongside the greatest artists of the greatest epoch of art' (*Memories*, p. 2). Valentin Serov (1865–1911) started his career as a landscape painter, influenced by the nationalist revivalism of Mamontov's Abramtsevo colony, but soon emerged as the leading Russian portraitist of his generation. [Trans.]

31   *IP 2*, pp. 393 *et seq*.

32   V. B. Shklovsky, *Literatura i kinematograf* (Berlin: 1923); Fr. edn (Paris: 1985).

33   H. Bergson, *L'Évolution créatrice* (Paris: 1907; 1983 edn), pp. 272–3.

34   V. B. Shklovsky, *Literatura i kinematograf*, pp. 113–14; see also his *Za 60 let* (From 60 Years) (Moscow: 1985).

35   Shklovsky, 'The Semantics of Cinema', in *FF*, p. 133.

36   A. Piotrovsky, '*October* Must be Re-Edited', in *FF*, p. 216.

37   A reference to Duchamp's abandoned major work, 'The Bride Stripped Bare by her Bachelors, Even', also known as the 'Large Glass' (1912–23). [Trans.]

38   Léger's short film, *Ballet mécanique* (1924) co-directed with Dudley Murphy, was known in the USSR during the 1920s. Joseph Plateau (1801–83) was the Belgian inventor of the Phénakistoscope, which animated successive drawings

viewed in a mirror. W. G. Horner's 'Zoëtrope' was another of the many optical toys which preceded cinema. [Trans.]

39 Yu. Tynyanov, *Problema stikhotvornogo yazyka* (Leningrad: 1924); trans. M. Sosa and B. Harvey, *The Problem of Verse Language* (Ann Arbor: 1981). In this translation, *Abschnitt* is rendered as 'halt' or 'stop' in the context of Tynyanov's discussion of metre as a component of rhythm (pp. 47, 59). [Trans.]

40 Charles Dekeukeleire (1905–71), Belgian experimental and later documentary film-maker. His second film, *Impatience* (1928, 511 metres) introduces four 'characters' in its credits: 'The Mountain, The Motorcycle, The Woman, Abstract Blocks'. See K. Thompson, '(Re)Discovering Charles Dekeukeleire', *Millenium Film Journal* nos. 7/8/9, Winter–Fall 1980–1, pp. 115–29. [Trans.]

41 Paul Sharits (b. 1943), American experimental film-maker and theorist, best known for such 'flicker' films as *Ray Gun Virus* (1966) and *N:O:T:H:I:N:G* (1968). Peter Kubelka (b. 1934), Austrian experimental film-maker, who has produced a small body of extremely short perfectionist works, including *Adebar* (1957), *Arnulf Rainer* (1958–60) and *Unsere Afrikareise* (Our Trip to Africa) (1961–6). On these and other formal or 'structural' film-artists, see *Film als Film: 1910 bis heute* (Film as Film: 1910 to the present), catalogue of a touring exhibition organised by B. Hein and W. Herzogenrath (Cologne: 1978); also *Film as Film*, catalogue of an expanded version of the exhibition at the Hayward Gallery, London (London: 1979) [Trans.].

42 Werner Nekes (b. 1944), German experimental film-maker and historian of pre-cinema optical devices and early cinema. His films include *Jüm-Jüm* (1967), *Uliisses* (1980–2) and *Was geschah wirklich zwischen den Bildern?* (What Really Happened Between the Pictures, also known as Film Before Film) (1986). Nekes has elaborated a semiotics of film in which the minimum unit is the '*kine*', or relationship between two frames. See his text, 'Whatever happens between the pictures', *Afterimage* (USA) vol. 5, no. 5, November 1977.

14 THE FRAME AND MONTAGE IN EISENSTEIN'S 'LATER' AESTHETICS

1 P. Wollen, *Signs and Meaning in the Cinema* (London: 1972), p. 62.

2 N. Burch, 'Sergei M. Eisenstein', in R. Roud (ed.), *Cinema: A Critical Dictionary* (London: 1980), vol. 1, p. 323.

3 D. Bordwell, 'Eisenstein's Epistemological Shift', *Screen* vol. 15, no. 4, Winter, 1974–5, pp. 32–46.

4 On issues around this question see Stanley Mitchell, 'Marinetti and Maya-kovsky: Futurism, Fascism, Communism'; and P. Wollen, 'Some Thoughts Arising from Stanley Mitchell's Article', in *Screen Reader 1: Cinema/Ideology/Politics* (London: 1977), pp. 380–93.

5 B. Brewster, 'Editorial Note', *Screen* vol. 15, no. 4, Winter 1974–5, pp. 29–32.

6 Stanley Cavell, *The World Viewed: Reflections on the Ontology of Film* (enlarged edn, Boston, Mass. and London: 1979), pp. 207–9.

7 Ibid.

8 R. Barthes, 'Diderot, Brecht, Eisenstein', in *Image-Music-Text* (London: 1977), pp. 69–78.

9 'Dickens, Griffith and the Film Today', in *Film Form*, p. 242.

10 Barthes, 'Diderot, Brecht, Eisenstein' in *Image– Music– Text*, p. 70.

11 Ibid., pp. 72, 73.

12 *NIN*, p. 349.

13 I would like to thank Jill McGreal, A. L. Rees, Ian Christie and Richard Taylor for their critical remarks on earlier drafts of this essay.

Index

All titles are given in English (or in the form commonly used in English), with the author's name in brackets for books, and the director and year of production/release for films. Italicised references are to illustrations.